quality
RESEARCH
papers

SECOND EDITION

quality
RESEARCH
papers

For Students of Religion and Theology

Nancy Jean Vyhmeister

ZONDERVAN®

ZONDERVAN.com/
AUTHORTRACKER
follow your favorite authors

ZONDERVAN

Quality Research Papers – Second Edition
Copyright © 2001, 2008 by Nancy Jean Vyhmeister

Requests for information should be addressed to:

Zondervan, *Grand Rapids, Michigan 49530*

Library of Congress Cataloging-in-Publication Data

Vyhmeister, Nancy Jean.
    Quality research papers : for students of religion and theology / Nancy Jean
Vyhmeister. – 2nd ed.
      p. cm.
    Includes bibliographical references and index.
    ISBN 978-0-310-27440-7
    1. Religion – Research. 2. Theology – Research. I. Title.
BL41.V94 2007
200'.72 – dc22   2007006702

Interior design by Matthew Van Zomeren

Printed in the United States of America

---

10 11 12 13 14 15 16 17 18 19 20 • 23 22 21 20 19 18 17 16 15 14 13 12 11 10 9 8 7 6 5

TABLE OF CONTENTS

LIST OF ILLUSTRATIONS

Tables

Figures

INTRODUCTION

Books giving instructions for doing student research in biblical, theological, and pastoral research tend to be somewhat one-sided, often concentrating on bibliography and sources. Possibly their authors assume that their target students have already taken a course in research methods and know how to organize a paper and give it a correct format. More often than not, this is not true. This handbook tries to put several aspects of research writing—bibliography, search techniques, organization, and form—into a balanced perspective.

Born of a great need at the Seminario Adventista Latinoamericano de Teología, the original text was written in Spanish in 1980 for South American graduate students. The first English version (1989) was designed to meet the needs of students working in English as a second language at the Adventist International Institute of Advanced Studies in the Philippines. The 2001 Zondervan edition incorporated my experience teaching research and dissertation writing to graduate students at the Seventh-day Adventist Theological Seminary, at Andrews University, Berrien Springs, Michigan, through the 1990s. This updated edition takes into consideration further teaching experience at the Adventist University of Africa. It also notes important advances in Internet technology since the first edition.

The ideas and techniques in this book are not original. They have been collected from many authors, as the bibliography will attest. Over the years, these instructions have been given, with slight variations, to students in the Americas, Asia, and, more recently, in Africa. The students' reactions and concerns have, to a certain extent, helped to shape this handbook. Therefore, this book is the result of the combined efforts of many people. To all who have somehow contributed, many thanks!

Several different research formats exist. The one used in this text is based on Kate Turabian's work, followed by the University of Chicago and commonly used for theology and religion. Matters of detail may be consulted in either Turabian's book or *The Chicago Manual of Style*.[1]

---

1. Kate Turabian was dissertation secretary at the University of Chicago from 1930 to 1958; her seminal work (1937) has been continuously revised and updated; the latest edition is Kate Turabian, *A Handbook for Writers of Term Papers, Theses, and Dissertations*, 7th ed., rev. Wayne C. Booth, Gregory G. Colomb, Joseph M Williams, and the University of Chicago Press Editorial Staff (Chicago: University of Chicago Press, 2007). *The Chicago Manual of Style*, 15th ed. (Chicago: University of Chicago Press, 2003) has more details and may be useful to advanced researchers and professors of research.

Quality Research Papers has four purposes:

1. to stimulate and develop students' capacity for doing careful and fruitful research
2. to help students improve their ability to clearly express the results of their research
3. to assist theology students to meet the requirements of their educational programs
4. to allay students' fear of doing research by improving their skills and tools.

Because most people learn better when they are shown than when they are told, models are provided to show how your paper should look. In addition, many aspects of the book itself are models. The different levels of headings, the footnotes, the tables and figures, as well as the bibliographical entries show you how to do the different parts of your paper. Only four items, which enhance the graphic design of this book, do not represent what you will be doing: the lack of indentation of the first line of the first paragraph following a heading, the page-wide separator line between the text and the footnotes, full justification in the text, and the many enumerations. In your "quality research paper" you will indent all paragraphs, use a two-inch separator line (default), left justify all text, and follow the instructions for enumerations given on pages 110–111.

The first thirteen chapters present the steps and procedures of research. Chapters 14 through 18 describe specialized forms of research: exegesis, description, program development, the case study, and book reviews. Chapter 19 discusses statistics, graphs, and tables as used in research. Chapter 20 deals with theses and dissertations, while chapter 21 presents instructions for writing a Doctor of Ministry project. Together, these chapters give the basic guidelines for students in theological education who desire to achieve success in research.

May your research be fruitful, stimulating, and even enjoyable!

Nancy Jean Vyhmeister

chapter 1

WHAT IS RESEARCH?

What makes research different from other types of studying and writing? What are the specific objectives of research? What are the essential steps in doing research? What pitfalls are to be avoided? How can one tell research from other forms of communication? What are the values and benefits of student research? These are questions this chapter endeavors to answer.

Definition of Research

Research can be defined as a method of study that, through careful investigation of all evidence bearing on a definable problem, arrives at a solution. To research a topic is to collect, organize, evaluate, and present data. This process cannot take place without analysis and synthesis, for research is more than a compilation of information. The results of research must be presented in a clear and concise way so that anyone can follow the process, without having to repeat any of the steps, in order to see how you, the researcher, have arrived at your conclusions.

A four-part definition of research is given by Isaac Felipe Azofeifa: "Research is a (1) systematic search for (2) adequate information to reach (3) objective knowledge of a (4) specific topic."[1] Each element deserves individual analysis.

---

1. Isaac Felipe Azofeifa, *Guía para la investigación y desarrollo de un tema* (San José, Costa Rica: Dpto. Publicaciones de la Universidad de Costa Rica, 1975), 5, translation mine.

1. *Systematic search.* This requires effort. It does not just happen. A researcher must develop and use a clear method and a logical system. Research is not easy; it requires time, energy, thought, and effort.
2. *Adequate information.* Research does not look for someone's ideas about matters touching on the problem; it seeks precise answers to the questions being asked. The information presented must be from authoritative sources, speak to the problem, and be duly documented.
3. *Objective knowledge.* In order to reach objective knowledge, you must have prior knowledge of the topic. To this prior knowledge you will add facts, not suppositions or possibilities. Research is done with the head and not the heart. Research looks at facts, not conjectures, nor even possibilities, much less long-cherished pet ideas.
4. *Specific topic.* It is impossible to do adequate research on a large topic. The research paper is not an encyclopedia. A specific, clearly delineated problem is the only one that can be solved.

Research may be writing a ten-page paper on Nazareth in the time of Christ. Research is what the writer of an M.A. thesis does for weeks on end. Persistent research efforts—over long months—go into producing a dissertation. As used in this book, the term *research* applies to all scholarly studies at undergraduate, graduate, or postgraduate level. Some teachers may call it a *research essay*; others may label it a *term paper.* Most of what students write for classes involves research.

Research is the search for truth—for God is truth—whether it be historical, scientific, or theological. It is all God's truth, as Frank E. Gaebelein points out.[2] This makes research an appropriate activity for believers. Yet, because God is ultimate truth and human beings are limited and finite, our arrival at truth must not be considered final. We may never be able to see the whole picture. Furthermore, what is "truth" today may be changed tomorrow by a new discovery. For this reason, even a careful researcher must be humble.

Even in the area of theology we should be open to truths not seen before. In 1892, Ellen White wrote about the attitudes that should exist in those who study the Scriptures. "We have many lessons to learn, and many, many to unlearn. God and heaven alone are infallible. Those who think that they will never have to give up a cherished view ... will be disappointed."[3] Discussing the search for theological truth, White had already written: "Truth

---

2. Frank Gaebelein, *The Pattern of God's Truth* (Chicago: Moody Press, 1968), 20, 23.
3. Ellen White, "Search the Scriptures," *Review and Herald*, July 26, 1892, 1.

is eternal, and conflict with error will only make manifest its strength.... We must study the truth for ourselves. No living man should be relied upon to think for us. No matter who it is, or in what position he may be placed, we are not to look upon any man as a perfect criterion for us."[4] Thus, we research, in search of all truth, humbly using our God-given minds to accomplish the search.

The Research Process

Although the research process will be studied carefully in the following chapters, at this point a brief synthesis of this endeavor is useful. In addition, we will consider some of the hindrances to the successful completion of research.

In its simplest form, the research process involves identification, collection, evaluation, and presentation. Once you have selected a topic, you must identify the problem or issue to be tackled. The issue must be specific, often expressed as a research question, not something vague and general. After you know exactly what the problem to be solved is, you can begin collecting data. Gather information carefully from many sources. Organize your data in a way that is clear and logical to you and others. After you have gathered all the information, you will need to analyze and evaluate it: Not all sources are equally valuable; not all opinions are of the same weight. Finally, after you have gathered the evidence, you must draw conclusions regarding the solution of the problem. You will then write a research report that gives a clear view of the problem, of the information gathered, and of the solution reached.

Some of the most dangerous pitfalls for researchers are those that relate to a previous mindset. When a cherished idea is being defended, for example, it is extremely difficult to be objective, to take into account adverse evidence, to break out of a limited thinking pattern. The prejudices (meaning here "prejudged results") taken into a research project set the tone and often determine the answer to a question. People usually see what they want to see. It is impossible to do research without presuppositions. One must, then, recognize what these presuppositions are, state them in the introduction to the research, and proceed from there. For example, if you accept the Genesis 1:26 statement that human beings were made in the image of God, whatever conclusions you reach on the treatment of psychological problems in children will reflect that basic understanding.

---

4. Ellen White, "The Necessity of Dying to Self," *Review and Herald*, June 18, 1889, 1.

Other errors are those of hurriedness, inaccuracy, or carelessness. It is easy to come to premature conclusions, without having finished the research because of lack of time or bibliography. It is also easy to miss an important detail or to write down an erroneous fact. Researchers do not mean to make this kind of mistake. But these errors do happen, especially to students who are scrambling to survive the term. Research demands extreme caution and care—and much time.

Kinds of Research

Many different types of papers are written as part of theological education. Here is a list of eleven different ones.

1. *Essay*: a short paper (1–10 pages) that explores a topic without the rigor of a research paper. While the opinions of the writer may be prominent, referenced footnotes are required for all quotations, citations, and allusions.
2. *Report*: a short paper (1–10 pages) that summarizes findings on an assigned topic. All quotations must be referenced.
3. *Sermon*: a paper written as the basis for a later oral presentation. While research may be needed, it is not reported in the same way as in other papers. However, quotations should be referenced.
4. *Term paper or research paper*: a major paper (15–30 pages) that investigates a specific issue. Such a paper needs a clear introduction as well as a summary and conclusions. All quotations, citations, or allusions are referenced. (The rest of this book will dwell on this type of paper.)
5. *Book review*: a short paper (2–4 pages) that describes and briefly evaluates a book or article (see chapter 18).
6. *Project*: a paper, either for a class or a degree, that emphasizes planning and doing as much as reading and writing. Projects are common in applied theology, from undergraduate through graduate courses, but especially in the Doctor of Ministry program.
7. *Thesis*: a major paper required for the completion of a master's degree. Its length is usually around 100 pages. A written proposal must be approved before the task is undertaken. Theses may have to be defended before an examination committee (see chapter 20).
8. *Pastoral theology paper*: a major paper (20–30 pages) that applies the findings of research to a pastoral situation (see chapter 18).

9. *Case study*: a paper (20–30 pages) that presents a case, analyzes factors affecting it, interprets what happened theologically, and proposes pastoral action to resolve the situation. The case study is used in practical theology, especially in the Doctor of Ministry program (see chapter 17).

10. *D.Min. dissertation or project*: a paper that ends the Doctor of Ministry program. It tends to be practical, as is the degree (see chapter 21).

11. *Ph.D./Th.D. dissertation*: a major study, similar to a thesis, but longer and more complex, often 250–300 pages long. It must be written on an issue not previously researched (see chapter 20).

While all these papers are different and are measured and evaluated by different criteria, professors still expect to find the following general attributes in any one of them:

1. Correct English, including spelling, grammar, syntax, and paragraph construction
2. Clarity of expression
3. Logical organization
4. Appropriate introduction and summary
5. Conclusions naturally derived from evidence
6. Correct format (in most English-speaking seminaries, this format is Turabian), the format recommended in this book[5]

What Research Is Not

Perhaps giving some ideas on what research is *not* will help to clarify what it is.

Research is not simply a compilation of quotations. True, quotations are used to document and clarify findings. But research is not the result of an afternoon spent with scissors, glue, and photocopies. A good research paper shows that its author has assimilated and synthesized (digested, if you like) the material and drawn logical conclusions.

Research is not simply rewriting other people's words and ideas into a neat description. In secondary or high school, we wrote papers by summarizing what we found in the textbook and the encyclopedia. The paper we proudly handed in gave a nice description of Outer Mongolia or the migration of Canada geese. It might have qualified as research at that level; however, it

---

5. Some seminaries, especially for ancient Near Eastern, biblical, and early Christian studies, have adopted *The SBL Manual of Style* (Peabody, MA: Hendrickson, 1999).

no longer counts! At the tertiary level, students need to analyze — break ideas and facts into small parts — and then organize those ideas and facts into the appropriate thought "boxes." Only then can they write the research report or essay.

Research is not a defense or apology of my own convictions. This type of writing too often ignores unfavorable evidence and tends to look at one's position through rose-colored glasses. Research seeks truth; it does not hide — for any reason — what may disagree with esteemed ideas. If the position being maintained is tenable, research can defend it; if the position is not based on truth, it is defended in vain. We cannot allow ourselves to use unsound arguments, even for a good cause.

Likewise, research is not polemical. Its objective is to clearly present truth, not to fight others' positions, even if those may be erroneous. In good research, truth is presented in such a logical and convincing way that there is no need for harsh language.

Research is not the presentation of one's own opinions. Research demands showing facts, data, and information. Naturally, the conclusions we reach are somewhat modified by our personal opinions, but whoever reads the research report must be able to follow the logic and the evidence to see how we reached our conclusions.

Finally, especially for theology students, research is not a sermon. It is different in content, style, and language. Some research may be involved in the preparation of a sermon, but the main purpose of a sermon is to reach the heart and change people's lives. The language and the message are appropriate to this goal. Research, however, seeks to inform and convince the mind. Research vocabulary is neutral, free of superlatives and emotional language. Furthermore, a sermon becomes effective through the delivery, whereas in research writing, there is no dramatic rendition from the pulpit. What appears on paper must stand, just as it is written, without any further embellishment.

The Value of Research

No one doubts the importance of the research that made vaccinations against polio or smallpox available. Neither do most people worry about why some erudites sit at their desks and read, study, and write, day after day. But some students question the importance of doing research papers since they are not researchers and do not plan to become researchers. They should realize that going through the discipline of research is valuable beyond the information obtained in the course of preparing the paper.

Learning to do research teaches you how to recognize a problem and how to go about solving it. Evidently, even educated people will not know all the answers; they should, however, know where to find answers. Doing a research paper helps you learn how to find answers, in a library or elsewhere.

Writing a research paper can teach you far more than a teacher could. On the topic of the research paper, you become an expert, sometimes knowing more about it than the professor who assigned the paper. Besides, when you learn by doing, you learn better.

Preparing a quality research paper teaches skills of observation, analysis, synthesis, and judgment. You will learn to think differently when you think research. The ability to think critically—and that does not mean criticism, but weighing carefully all the evidences—is enhanced by learning the research process. In addition, writing a research paper helps develop character. When the going is hard and the task becomes drudgery, sticking with the work is a discipline that enhances the worth of any student.

Finally, the preparation of a research paper gives opportunity for the development of good writing skills. Learning to write well takes hours of rewriting and correcting. But being able to write clearly is a worthy achievement, which will prove useful to you as a student now and later as a professional.

Aside from these considerations, I should mention the satisfaction of a job accomplished and the joy of discovery as important outcomes of writing research papers. Most students agree that research done well is worth the time and effort it takes.

With this chapter as a basis for research, the following chapters will discuss, one by one, the steps and procedures of research. The first step is to explore the topic through reading, first of all in the library.

chapter 2

USING THE LIBRARY

Now that you know what research is (and is not), you are ready to get started on your adventure. However, you find too many questions at once: What will I write about? Where will I get information? How can I keep together all the information I find? How will I organize it into a paper that will get me a good grade? Activities described in chapters 2 through 8 may happen at the same time; the order of the chapters is arbitrary, to facilitate the organization of the book.

Whatever you do, consider the library basic to choosing a topic, finding the right sources, and gathering the information needed. True, the Internet is an important source of information—so important that it deserves a full chapter—but the library is the traditional beginning point of research. It remains the cornerstone of research, not only because there are thousands of pages of resources, but because these materials have been handpicked for you—chosen by experts to support the coursework offered at your school. The library is also the academic gateway to the Internet.

The first task is to become acquainted with your home (school, seminary, university) library and all its departments. Read the library handbook, if there is one. Study the library's website. Walk through the library, noting where different collections are housed—indexes, reference works, electronic media. Find out where the reference and circulation desks are located and what services they offer. Do not forget such basic services as restrooms and drinking fountains! Sign up for whatever library orientation programs are offered, even if they are not required. Make sure you know and understand the loan policies of the library, including those for interlibrary loans.

At the beginning of a semester, the library staff usually offers students a general library orientation. These sessions are helpful, but they may not answer all the questions. Since your main interest is theology/religion, you should meet the theological librarian or bibliographer (the person who chooses and orders books for the theology collection) and ask for an orientation to that specific area.

All library use must begin at the catalog, whether paper or electronic. It will then continue to departments such as periodicals, reference, electronic media, and the rare book rooms.

The Library Catalog

One gains access to the materials in a library through the catalog, where all the holdings (library lingo for books, journals, and other materials) are listed. While there are differences between the paper-technology card catalog and the newer electronic catalog, the search approach is similar in both.

Card Catalog

The first step in using a card catalog is to find out how it is organized. Card catalogs list materials alphabetically: by author, title, and subject headings. In "divided" card catalogs, books listed by author and title are in one section, whereas books listed by subject heading are in another. Some libraries have a "unified catalog," with one alphabetical listing, containing authors, titles, and subject headings.

Catalog cards contain all the information needed for a bibliographical entry: author, title, place of publication, date of publication, editor, illustrator, series to which the book belongs, and sometimes notes about the book. You will also find the call number, which tells you where to look for the item, and one or more subject headings at the bottom of the card.

When you know the author or title of a book you are looking for, you can start with that information. Remember, however, that the author's last name comes first. In addition, the initial article, definite or indefinite, in whatever language, does not count for alphabetization. Look under *Greek-English Lexicon*, rather than *A Greek-English Lexicon*. Yet, please remember that in the rest of the title, articles do count.

When you do not have an author or title, you must search by subject heading. Although this kind of search is the most fruitful, it can be confusing at first. Subject headings are predetermined. You cannot change them, nor can your local librarian. The trick is to find out what subject headings are used for your topic. You may ask for the classification book and study it, or you may get at your information through the "back door."

For example, suppose you want to research "church planting." Dead-end street: the Library of Congress system does not have such a subject heading. What might the heading be? You try "church work," but the subject area is too large, not specific enough. Then you remember that you just read a book on church planting by Russell Burrill. You check the author catalog, under Burrill, Russell. You find the book *Rekindling a Lost Passion: Recreating a Church Planting Movement*. At the bottom of the card you find the subject heading: "Church development, new." Now you can look under that heading and discover other sources for your research.

All subject headings for topics related to Scripture begin with "Bible." You will find the subheadings "Bible. NT" and "Bible. OT." You will then find sub-subheadings, "Bible. NT. Acts" and so on. Even in "Bible. NT. Acts" there are subdivisions: "Bible. NT. Acts 1 – 12. Commentaries" is an example. Here is something else to remember: Librarians did not expect everyone to know the books of the Bible in order, so they have arranged them alphabetically: Revelation comes before Thessalonians.

Not all books that touch on a given topic are classified under the same subject heading. If the author's approach is sociological, the classification will be different from that of a psychological or religious approach. That means that you need to think of many and diverse possibilities. Keep asking yourself: What other words could be used to describe my topic?

Call numbers on the library catalog cards tell you where to find a book. The call number is usually given in Dewey Decimal or Library of Congress numbering systems. Whichever system is used, the result is the same: a fingerprint of the book. The first line (in Dewey) or first two (in LC) give you the subject category. The second (or third) line, beginning with a letter of the alphabet, identifies the author. The third (or fourth) line gives the date of publication. Learning the cataloging system of your library will save you time.

Mastering the card catalog may take an hour or two. Nevertheless, the benefits far outweigh the effort.

Electronic Catalog

Electronic library catalogs are fast becoming the norm for academic libraries. Not only are they faster to use, they also permit transfer of information to a printer or to your own computer. Typing and computer skills make their use even more effective. (This is not the last time you will hear about the need for these skills in doing research.)

The information contained in the electronic catalog—the bibliographic information, subject headings, and call number—is the same as in the card catalog. Only the delivery system is different. What was said above about the contents of the cards stands. The way you approach electronic catalogs varies from library to library. However, once you have learned to use one, you can quickly learn another.

When you enter an electronic catalog, you find several options for searching. Usually they are keyword, author, title, subject heading, and author/title. Of these, the most fruitful is often the keyword search, especially when you are beginning your study and do not know too much about the topic.

In electronic catalogs, the second most effective search strategy uses the subject heading. What was said before about subject headings in a card catalog still holds: You can only guess at the headings used in cataloging. However, those guesses can become educated. The system provides electronic help. At the Andrews University Library website, I type "Acts"; the first option is "Bible. N.T. Acts." I click and find thirteen different items.

Once you find one book on your topic, you can search for others like it by clicking on its subject heading. You can also click on the call number to see what other books sit on the shelf near the one you have chosen. Since books are shelved by topic, this can be a useful technique, whether you click on the call number in the electronic catalog or visually inspect the neighbors of your book on the shelf.

To better understand the electronic catalogue (and other electronic searches) two concepts are basic: fields and Boolean operators.

Fields

Fields represent areas where the search engine will look. The simplest catalogs have at least author, title, keyword, and subject heading. More complex searches add other fields. For example, the Loma Linda University Library offers the possibility of searching in the following fields: keyword, exact title, journal title, author, medical subject, general subject, call number, ISSN/ISBN,[1] course reserves by course number, and course reserves by professor's name. The Library of Claremont Colleges adds call number (either Dewey or LC) and OCLC number. The catalog of the EbscoHost Research Databases has seventeen fields!

Choose fields that you are sure about (the author's name *is* spelled Smyth) or that will produce the fewest hits ("servant leadership" rather than the more general "leadership").

---

1. ISSN is the standard number assigned to each journal; ISBN is the standard number assigned to each book. Such a number is unique to one item.

Boolean Operators

Quite often these are simply called "search terms." Whatever their name, they are important. Search engines have been taught to do math with the fields: add this one, subtract the other. You will use parentheses, just as you did in algebra. The most familiar Boolean operators are these:

Cats AND dogs brings up only items that have both terms.

Cats OR dogs brings up anything that has one term or the other.

Cats AND NOT dogs brings up anything that has cats but no reference to dogs.

Cat* brings up any word that starts with cat: cats, catsup, catheter.

If I type in baptism AND (child* OR infant*) my findings will include everything about the baptism of infants and children. Some catalogs and indexes save you the trouble of typing in the operators by letting you fill in the blanks in an advanced search.

Here's an example to show you how these operators work. In October 2006, I went searching in the Andrews University Library; when I typed "planting," I got 252 entries. I soon realized that there was some agriculture there, so I limited my search to "planting AND NOT agriculture"; I still got 242 hits. I tried "church AND planting" and found 134 items containing both words. Then I wondered if by not having other forms of the verb "plant" included I might miss something, so I typed "plant* AND church" and was informed that the library owned 206 items that matched my query. The asterisk I added told the computer to look for words beginning with "plant," but that add other letters, such as "planter," "planted," or "planting." Perhaps, I wondered, authors used other words for church planting, so I tried "(plant* or start*) AND church." As a result I found 339 entries. Not all of these are going to be useful to my study. To begin my research, I would like to have 20–50 useful references to a topic.

Most electronic catalogs allow you to transfer information from their systems to your notes. At times you may print the references you find on a printer near the computer where you are working. You can also download bibliographical information to your own computer at home or your laptop at the library. You may also email yourself any number of entries. The problem with printed pages is that you still have to copy them to your note cards—and mistakes can creep in. If you have an electronic version of your bibliographical entries, you can edit it without having to retype completely. You will need to experiment with transmission of data from your library's electronic catalog to your computer to find the most efficient transfer system. Endnote™, a software package designed to manage bibliographies, can prove useful to you to download data. Research it!

Now that you are well acquainted with the catalog at your library and the location of items in the library, you are ready to explore other ways to find sources.

Other Library Resources

Indexes

Whether you use this now-preferred spelling or stick with the traditional "indices," these books or electronic media do for periodicals what the card catalog does for library books. In a printed index you can usually search by author and subject. Electronic media, such as CDs and the Internet, give more flexibility.

Print Indexes

General periodical indexes may not be very useful to theology students. Thus, my listing only notes the most important ones in religion. Many United States libraries no longer use the print indexes, but students from the two-thirds world are happy to find them!

ATLA Religion Indexes in print. These have been published under different names since 1949 and were for decades the gold standard in religion indexes. In the early days the index had three sections: subject index, author/abstract index, and book review index. As the book got fatter and fatter, the author index was dropped and the yearly book became *Religion Index One.* The book reviews went into a separate volume, *Index to Book Reviews in Religion,* and ceased publication in 2000. The subject index to multiauthor books became *Religion Index Two* and was published in print until 1995. To find materials in these books, you will need to search each volume separately. The subject headings are those of the Library of Congress. Today these indexes are usually electronic.

Three important publications index periodical articles and give abstracts (short summaries) as well. Since 1958 the *Religious and Theological Abstracts* has covered the areas indicated by its name; it abstracts a limited number of journals. *Old Testament Abstracts* and *New Testament Abstracts* cover the two areas of biblical studies. Foreign language articles are abstracted in English.

Some denominational indexes may be helpful on subjects that deal with specific religious groups. The *Catholic Periodical and Literature Index* does just what its name says: It indexes articles in Catholic journals and magazines in yearly volumes until 1997, and now in electronic form. A similar index, the *Christian Periodical Index,* notes articles in Protestant journals and magazines. The *Seventh-day Adventist Periodical Index* does the same for Adventist publications. All three were in book form for years, but are now electronic.

Advanced students will find *Elenchus of Biblica* useful. Its editors, at the Pontifical Biblical Institute in Rome, have a hard time keeping up; the index is usually two to three years behind. While *Elenchus* covers many of the same periodicals listed in the *ATLA Religion Index*, it includes additional items in biblical studies, especially in foreign languages. Doctoral students should not forget the *Internationale Zeitschriftenschau für Bibelwissenschaft und Grenzgebiete* [International Review of Biblical Studies], for it will contain additional materials (from 1951 onward).

Your topic may require you to search in indexes in other fields—such as education, psychology, or philosophy. If your library has these in printed form, go ahead and use them.

For decades, the printed indexes were indispensable to research. They were better than nothing, but one had to search year by year. Now very little is only in print form.

CD-ROM Indexes

An amazing quantity of information fits on each CD-ROM. Furthermore, powerful search engines and increasingly rapid readers make the CD-ROM a tremendous improvement, quite helpful to the research process. While each CD-ROM has its own special features, most are user-friendly and require minimum instruction from a librarian. If your library has CD-ROM indexes, you will be able to perform a more efficient search than in printed indexes. Advantages to this format are finding all materials in one source, not having to search year by year, and being able to transfer information to a printed page or disk.

Searches are made by author, title, and subject. In addition, most CD-ROMs permit search by key words, which is probably the most effective way. For example, one could search for the words "bibliography" and "gospels" to find any item that has those two words in the author, title, series, or notes. Usually libraries facilitate printing a bibliographical entry from the CD-ROM to a disk or making a hard copy on an attached printer. CD-ROMs are usually updated at least once a year.

CD-ROM resources are increasingly dedicated to full-text documents rather than periodical indexing. What were once printed indexes became available on CD-ROM, but now are going directly to the Internet.

The *ATLA Index* on CD-ROM is the electronic version of *Religion Index One, Religion Index Two, Research in Ministry,* and *Index to Book Reviews in*

Religion. This is a veritable gold mine of information, but is scheduled to be discontinued in the near future. *Religious and Theological Abstracts* is also available on CD-ROM.

Dissertation Abstracts International (DAI) may be found on CD-ROM in some libraries. It used to occupy shelves and shelves of large paper-bound books. For doctoral students, *DAI* is an indispensable tool, especially useful since doctoral dissertations must be written on a topic not studied previously. All you can see is the abstract of the dissertation, together with information on the author, advisor, and institution where it was written. To get a copy of the actual dissertation, talk to your librarian, who may consider purchasing the item or will help you borrow it from another library.

Online Indexes

As you have already seen, the progression stops here for now. What is barely available in hard copy is fairly easy to retrieve from a CD-ROM. But with the Internet, cyberspace is the limit.

Many online indexes are only available through a subscribing library. Let us hope yours is one of these! If your library subscribes, you should be able to enter these online sites using your institutional student or faculty username and password.

ATLAReligion is probably the most profitable index for religion/theology students. Once you have searched for your topic, using Boolean search techniques, however, you will still have to find the articles, unless you happen to find and choose full-text articles. *Proquest Religion* can give similar results.

Academic Search EBSCO—one of several online academic indexes, including *First Search*—searches many, many journals covering the social sciences, humanities, general science, multi-cultural studies, education, and much more. The search screen tells me to type in a word and allows me to choose one of seventeen fields, but for me the keyword is the most productive. Using Boolean operators, I can have one keyword, one subject heading word, and one author word. In October 2006, I typed "theological" and "education" as two keywords. The search turned up only seven hits; when I typed "theological education" into the subject field, I got 95.

Dissertation Abstracts provides information on dissertations written in hundreds of American universities. Search by keyword, author, advisor, institution. You can read the abstracts and initial pages before deciding whether you must have it for your own paper.

If you need to search in areas other than theology/biblical studies—for example, anything dealing with education or young people—take note of ERIC, *Educational Resource Information Center.* You may also check *Psych Info* for materials on psychology. If your paper requires medical information (such as something on HIV/AIDS), you will want to use *Medline* or *Pubmed*.

WorldCat. One of the most helpful online resources is the Online Computer Library Center (OCLC). *WorldCat* contains the catalogs of thousands of libraries. Use it to find a book you would like to borrow through interlibrary loan. Use it to ascertain the exact information for your bibliography (much easier than going to the library at 2 a.m. the night before your paper is due!).

Most of the resources listed here are licensed. Someone has to pay to use them. Let it be your library!

Reference Materials

Reference materials such as dictionaries, encyclopedias, and concordances are useful in the *initial* search for information. Later on, once the topic has been defined, these general works are less important, but can be helpful to clarify details. In addition, their bibliographies may contain valuable references. A visual check of the call numbers that yielded sources in the stacks should be made in the reference section.

Bibliographies

In times past, books such as *Index to Periodical Literature on Christ and the Gospels*, compiled under the direction of Bruce M. Metzger, were tremendously helpful to students who had no access to electronic indexes. Bibliographies figured prominently in the search strategy of advanced students. Today topical bibliographies have become less important, at least for current materials; they are, however, very important to older materials. Some bibliographies are still being prepared, often using modern technology. An example is:

The Keswick Movement: A Comprehensive Guide. Lanham, Maryland: Scarecrow, 2006.

Bibliographies may be located in the Z section (LC classification) or in the appropriate subject area. Wherever they are physically, such items are first found in the library catalog.

Periodicals

The Periodicals Department in an academic library contains vast amounts of information. But the hundreds or thousands of volumes sitting on the shelves can only share their wealth through the use of indexes—paper, CD, or online. That is, unless you want to read the heavy tomes from cover to cover. You need to explore this section to discover how your library shelves periodicals. The most common way is to shelve them alphabetically, by title. Some libraries give them call numbers, according to the subject content. Once you find what periodicals are useful to you, be sure to look at the current issues, which may not yet be indexed.

Special Departments

Archives, rare book room, heritage center, manuscript center, media center, pamphlet files—these can be sources of precious information. Usually, materials held in these special departments appear in the library catalog. If these special materials do not appear in the general catalog, they certainly will be in some kind of departmental listing. You may need to visit each department to find out what it can offer to your topic.

Interlibrary Loan

A most important library resource, this office will bring to you books and articles not in the library of your institution, citations for which you have found in printed indexes, CD ROMs, or online indexes. Of course, you must do the searching and let the person in charge of interlibrary loans know what you want and perhaps even where the material is available. Often you make your request and supply the information online.

Full-Text Materials Online through the Library

Much of what you used to have to go to the library for can now be done from the comfort of your own home. Online services go beyond simply accessing the card catalog or helping you find articles or books not held in your library. More and more online sources provide searchable, full-text materials. Use is normally limited to students and faculty.

Different libraries will provide access to different sources. My examples come from JeWeL, the electronic catalog of the James White Library (and yes, someone got a prize for thinking up that cute name), at Andrews University. I have done so because it is impossible to write in the abstract.

Current Contents. This database permits searching in subject headings and abstracts of articles in social and behavioral sciences, as well as physical, chemical, and earth sciences, beginning with 1998.

ATLAS, a full-text database of journal articles on religion.

JSTOR. This resource provides access to full-text articles from journals in different disciplines. Not usually considered a premier source for religious and biblical research, it nevertheless provided 428 hits (October 2006) when I did an advanced search for ministry AND pastors OR clergy AND NOT government.

NetLibrary (ebooks). NetLibrary provides searchable full-text books on many topics, but religion is not prominent.

Thesaurus Linguae Graecae, which covers Greek writings over a period of some fifteen centuries. The writings are fully searchable.

Librarian Terry Robertson from Andrews University reports two "exciting new resources that use the same interface: the *Digital Library of Classic Protestant Texts*, almost 1000 titles published during the 15th to 17th centuries, full text and fully searchable [in the original language], and *The Digital Library of the Catholic Reformation*, with about 300 titles."[2]

Libraries pay for most of these services. For that reason you usually need to be a student or have some kind of password to be able to use them. As distributed education becomes more common, the library of your school will probably have some way for you to access their services from many miles away.

Before you finish learning about your library, find out whether it is a member of a consortium of libraries. Then ascertain what resources are yours through the consortium. Cooperation among libraries makes more resources available.

Knowing your way around the library and being familiar with its services and resources will aid your research. In addition, your student life will be enriched by this practical knowledge. And now, on to the frontier of knowledge, the Internet.

---

2. Email communication, November 8, 2006.

chapter 3

TAMING THE INTERNET[1]

The Internet is a new and wild environment—usually better handled by an adolescent than by his or her parents. Today's students have no choice but to tame the beast, however, if they are going to find what they need: up-to-date information on a myriad of topics. The Internet has been described as follows: "A different culture, born in Defense Department research labs, nurtured in the halls of academe, exploited in college dormitories, and now attracting ordinary citizens worldwide with its milieu of opinions, trivia, and sometimes valuable information."[2]

Three aspects of the process of taming the Internet are vital. The first is to know what resources are available. The second is to figure out how to find and use them. The third is indispensable: how to evaluate Internet resources. After that you will need to record your sources for footnotes and bibliographical entries.

Online Resources

As we move into the twenty-first century, online resources are more and more abundant. They are also vital to the research process. As noted in chapter 2, academic libraries provide access to many online resources, especially indexes

---

1. My thanks to Annette Melgosa, former librarian of the Adventist International Institute of Advanced Studies in the Philippines, and to Shawna Vyhmeister, who teaches graduate research courses at the same Institute.

2. John A. Butler, *Cybersearch: Research Techniques in the Electronic Age* (New York: Penguin, 1998), 92.

and full-text journal articles, documents, and books. These are different from other Internet resources, however, as they generally refer to published works, often from refereed journals. In that sense, online access to print periodicals is no different from reading the print form.

The wild part of the Internet is freelancing—searching on your own, surfing the World Wide Web. Here you venture into an area that is neither edited for quality nor guaranteed for continued accessibility, and, as I mentioned above, is not indexed in any comprehensible way. Documents on the web may describe an institution; they may set forth someone's cherished opinion. They provide hard data along with idle thoughts. Today conversations among those who know little about a topic appear alongside the results of serious research.

"Blogging" was added to our vocabulary in 2004: it refers to "a frequent, chronological publication of personal thoughts and web links" (according to http://www.marketingterms.com/dictionary/blog/). Evidently, the web musings of an individual you are studying would be important. However, just someone's feelings about things do not make a good research source.

Billions of pages populate the Internet. Since a fifty thousand book library could have at most some fifteen million pages, the monstrous size of the Internet is evident. However, there is a major difference: A library collection is selected by experts; the Internet has grown like Topsy.

The number of resources for research in biblical studies, theology, and ministry may not be as large as the number of sources that provide information on entertainment and computers. However, the web is worth exploring. To "surf the Net" you will need to have a fast computer with plenty of RAM, a good connection to the Internet, and plenty of time.

An attempt to systematize information on cyberspace resources in religion was made by Patrick Durusau in 1996. That the second edition appeared only two years after the first shows the constant need for updating in this field, where change occurs almost daily.[3] That there have been no further editions goes along with Durusau's admission on his website (http://durusau.net) that there is no possibility of putting all the sites in one book.

Your library undoubtedly provides its users access to many databases. See, for example the long list of databases at the James White Library (http://www.andrews.edu/library/screens/databases/onlineresources.html). The full-text databases are only available to students, faculty, and staff. Click on the alphabetical list of Online Resources to see a very long list, most of which are available to the public. You can go directly to these databases, without

---

3. Patrick Durusau, *High Places in Cyberspace: A Guide to Biblical and Religious Studies, Classics, and Archaeological Resources on the Internet*, 2nd ed. (Atlanta: Scholars, 1998).

going through JeWeL. Enjoy reading the list and finding out which ones can be useful to you.

Two valuable databases can be accessed directly. (1) ERIC (eric.ed.gov) specializes in education, but also has information on the social sciences. Some of its newer documents are full text; the older ones are not. (2) WorldCat (worldcat.org) contains the electronic catalogs of thousands of libraries. You can use it to find an item you would borrow through interlibrary loan; my main use for it is to check the accuracy of footnotes and bibliography entries. You may find it useful, in the wee hours of the day your paper is due, to be able to find out whether the book you are quoting from your notes was written in 1985 or 1995 and exactly how the author's name is spelled. Another resource you may want to examine is the Christian Classics Ethereal Library (http://ccel.org). Check the alphabetical list of authors to get a feel for its richness.

Three important caveats on online resources: They do not always behave as they are supposed to; what is written about them today in this text may well be obsolete within six weeks; and finally, I take no responsibility for the time you spend surfing!

Searching the Internet

Chapter 2 gave pointers about using library-provided access to the web; there is no need to repeat the information here. However, the concept of "fields" and "Boolean operators" (or search terms) holds for other forms of Internet searching.

One of the most popular websites that students often use for getting answers to questions may be that self-written encyclopedia, the Wikipedia (http://www.wikipedia.org). The welcome page tells me this is a "free encyclopedia anyone can edit." How can quality be maintained that way? My experience, cited below, tells you why I have serious reservations about Wikipedia.

I typed the word "baptism" in the query box and found an interesting and descriptive article on baptism through the centuries and across Christian denominations. I have no idea which volunteer submitted her class paper on baptism as an authoritative source and who modified it subsequently. At the very end I found a box of resources with the title "In Defense of Infant Baptism." No resources show the opposite position. Perhaps this is somewhat one-sided?

At the bottom of the page, in "Other Areas of Wikipedia," I get the chance to ask volunteers for information. Where do they get their facts? Do they know more than I do? I also looked at "Sister Sites."

Conveniently, Wikipedia does tell you how to reference an article in the Chicago/Turabian style (http://en.wikipedia.org/wiki/Wikipedia:Citing_Wikipedia#Chicago_style). However, I do not imagine that citing an unknown "Wikipedia contributor" will impress your professor.

To summarize, Wikipedia is an amazing source of information. You can find something about almost anything. However, the information does not necessarily originate with specialists or authorities. Thus, use it to find out basic information, but do not use Wikipedia to footnote your quality research paper.

To find what you want in cyberspace, you will need to use a search engine. Some search engines are organized by keyword, and some topically. Some sites provide both approaches. Keyword searches actually take you to a database maintained by "crawlers" or "spiders" that constantly search the web to add new sites. The search engine will find your word anywhere in a web page and bring you a list of hits in seconds. The more times the word appears in a document, the closer to the top of the list it will be.

The problem is, of course, that you can get false hits, as this is a mechanical search, and the search engine will find the word you searched for whether the meaning is related to what you are studying or not. When you begin searching for a research topic, it is often easier to begin with a topical search, where you can drill down through categories until you find your area of interest. Both types of search engines work, and it is often worthwhile to compare results rather being satisfied with one engine.

My favorite search engine is Google (http://www.google.com). I can search the web for images, videos, news, maps, and more — including Google Books and Google Scholar. Take the time to play with searches in Google. Be sure to click on "more" to find more options; you may want to create an account.

Naturally, others may have their favorite search engines. Try your search on several engines to see which is best for what you want to find. I searched "discipleship" in several engines with the following results: Dogpile, 79; Lycos, 1,740,000; Gigablast, 2,817,849; Yahoo, 3,540,000; and Google, 4,980,000.

Search strategy is everything. Make your search string so unique that you do not get a lot of false hits. Remember the Boolean operators. In the advanced search option, you are practically led by the hand to a good search. Sit down at a computer with an Internet connection, go to Google, and enjoy the chase. Wrestle with it until you get a reasonable number of hits — neither 2 nor 20,000, and most of them quite closely related to your topic. Remember that most search engines put what they consider the "best" hits near the top of your results list, so there are usually diminishing returns as you work down through the list.

Evaluating Internet Sources

Since it takes only a little know-how and less money, it is fairly easy for anyone to develop a website. So, how do I know whether the information at any given website is trustworthy? While each website you visit is a potential source of information for your research, please remember that not all websites are created equal. You must evaluate by asking questions. Let's consider some of them.

1. What is the purpose of this website? Is it for entertainment? Information? Research? To keep the family together (e.g., http://vyhmeister.info)? Your common-sense answer to this question will start you on the right track.

2. Who sponsors the site? A credible organization, such as a university? A professional society? An advocacy group? Or is it a company trying to sell something? An individual interested in the topic? Obviously, the first is better than the last! You might use a less valuable website to gain access to serious information. Researching the history of deaconesses through the centuries, I found very useful materials at http://womenpriests.org—a site that advocates the ordination of Roman Catholic women to the priesthood. The site was simply a portal to historical resources.

3. When was the material written? At least, when was the site last updated? This information is not always forthcoming. You may have to search various pages. At times, the best you can do is to find the date when the site was updated. There's nothing wrong with old information; in some cases it is very good. But for evaluation, you need to know when something was written.

4. Who is the author of the piece you are reading? A professional? A student? Just somebody? I do not mean to denigrate common people, but we are talking research, serious study. Maybe there is no author named—suggesting that the piece may have come from elsewhere or that no one was willing to put a name to that piece. Even if you cannot find the author's name, make sure you know who or what organization is responsible for the site.

5. What are the author's qualifications, either academic or professional? Is this person an author in her own right? Is he an amateur? Use the Web to find more information about the person. Use Google Scholar (http://scholar.google.com) to find out what the person has written. For example, for Nancy Vyhmeister, the thirty-nine hits (August 2007) include articles and books authored, as well as citations in the

writings of others (friends and foes!), and which courses use *Quality Research Papers* as a textbook.

6. Is this material available elsewhere? On the Web? In a printed source? Use search engines to find this out.

7. What is the tone of the material? "I know it all"? "You are stupid if you do not agree with me"? "This is an observation I have made"? Does this sound like someone searching for truth or simply pushing an idea?

8. What company does this piece keep? If there are hyperlinks in the piece or on the site, what are they about? Whom does the author cite? Recognized scholars? Journals and recent books? Or, citing no one, is she the ultimate authority?

9. How do you think your professors will rate this information? Ask them. Get help to evaluate websites and web authors, especially if you are a beginner.

10. Never stop asking questions—about websites and everything else. After all, questions form the basis of good research.

Footnotes and Bibliographies for Internet Materials

Bibliographies and footnotes require precise information about where you found your information. See more on that in chapters 9 and 10. Here are some specifics and a few examples.

1. Refer to electronic sources only when items are not available elsewhere.

2. Make sure the electronic address is accurate, even to the spaces and dots.

3. If you must write the URL (Uniform Resource Locator) on two lines, divide only immediately before a dot, underline, or hyphen, or after a slash.

Things change. Ten years ago, the URL was placed in angle brackets. This rule has been dropped. We used to add the phrase "available at," followed by the URL. No longer needed! In fact, http:// is obsolete with some publishers, but not yet with academicians. Also, professors always required students to place at the end of the entry the date the document was accessed. This may or may not be required in your school. In case the access date is needed, place it in parentheses at the end of the entry (accessed November 11, 2006, or simplified to 11/08/2006. Use the form your school prefers.). Also note that *http* always appears in lower case.

Information for notes and bibliographical entries of web materials is often elusive. You will need to search carefully for author and publication data. That may mean exploring the whole site. At the end, you may not have all the information traditionally used for a bibliographic entry. Obviously, there is no page, which means you must give the exact URL for the piece you are quoting. If there is no date, use n.d.

By all means, retain copies of downloaded material (paper or electronic) until your paper or dissertation has been approved. Finally, "Love your neighbor as yourself" (Matt 22:39). Make it easy for the budding scholar who follows in your footsteps to find exactly what you found.

These examples may help your common sense: Notice that some do not have all the elements you would expect to find in a bibliography entry or footnote. Put in everything that is available.

Journal articles with complete bibliographic information may be done as regular journals, although you can note the online site. If page numbers are missing, be sure to give the URL. The order of elements in a bibliographical entry (B) and a reference note (N) are predetermined. You will spend much time on chapter 9, learning just how these should be done.

B   Herrell, Richard K. "HIV/AIDS Research and the Social Sciences." *Current Anthropology* 32 (April 1991): 199–203. http://links.jstor.org/sici?sici=0011–3204% 2819104%2 932%3A2%3C199%3AHRATSS%3E2.0.CO%3B2–8.

N   1. Richard K. Herrell, "HIV/AIDS Research and the Social Sciences," *Current Anthropology* 32 (April 1991): 199, http://links.jstor.org/sici?sici=0011– 3204%2819910 4%2932%3A2%3C199%3AHRATSS%3E2.0.CO%3B2–8.

B   Whitman, Shelly. "Women and Peace-building in the Democratic Republic of Congo: An Assessment of Their Role in the Inter-Congolese Dialogue." *African Journal on Conflict Resolution* 6 (2006): 29–48. http://www.accord.org.za/ajcr/2006–1/ AJCR_ vol6no1_pg29–48.pdf.

N   2. Shelly Whitman, "Women and Peace-building in the Democratic Republic of Congo: An Assessment of Their Role in the Inter-Congolese Dialogue," *African Journal on Conflict Resolution* 6 (2006): 31, http://www.accord.org.za/ajcr/2006–1/AJCR_ vol6no1_pg29–48.pdf.

B   Amorim, Nilton. "Academic Freedom in Theology Teaching." Paper presented to the Faith and Learning Seminar, Nairobi, Kenya, 1990. http://www.aiias.edu/ict/vol_ 05/05cc_237–255.htm.

N   3. Nilton Amorim, "Academic Freedom in Theology Teaching," paper presented to the Faith and Learning Seminar, Nairobi, Kenya, 1990, http://www.aiias.edu/ict/vol_ 05/05cc_237–255.htm.

B   "Female Genital Mutilation/Cutting: A Statistical Exploration." New York: UNICEF, 2005. http://www.unicef.org/publications/files/FGM-C _final_10_October.pdf.

N   4. "Female Genital Mutilation/Cutting: A Statistical Exploration" (New York: UNICEF, 2005), http://www.unicef.org/publications/files/FGM-C _final_10_October.pdf.

B   "Partial-birth Abortion." *Encyclopedia for You.* 2005. http://www.encyclopedia4u.com/p/partial-birth-abortion.html.

N   5. "Partial-birth Abortion," *Encyclopedia for You.* 2005, http://www.encyclopedia4u.com/p/partial-birth-abortion.html.

B   Schaff, Phillip. *Augustine's City of God and Christian Doctrine.* New York: Christian Literature Publishing, 1890. http://ccel.org/ccel/schaff/ npnf102.iv.ii.v.html.

N   6. Phillip Schaff. *Augustine's City of God and Christian Doctrine* (New York: Christian Literature Publishing, 1890), chapter 3, http://ccel.org/ccel/schaff/ npnf102.iv.ii.v.html.

B   Malins, Ian, and Diane Malins. "Disciple-making and Mentoring: Letting Your Life Impact Others." Intentional Discipleship Training Seminars, n.d. http://www.omega-discipleship.com/online/files/seminarnotes.pdf.

N   7. Ian Malins and Diane Malins. "Disciple-making and Mentoring: Letting Your Life Impact Others" (Intentional Discipleship Training Seminars, n.d.), http://www.omega-discipleship.com/online/files/seminarnotes.pdf.

B   "Free Spiritual Gifts Analysis." Elkton, MD: Church Growth Institute, n.d. http://www.churchgrowth.org/cgi-cg/gifts.cgi.

N   8. "Free Spiritual Gifts Analysis" (Elkton, MD: Church Growth Institute, n.d.), http://www.churchgrowth.org/cgi-cg/gifts.cgi.

Since you will search for books, articles, papers, and more throughout the research process — and even as you write — time spent learning how to use the library and tame the Internet is well spent. But, of course, you still need to choose a topic, so on to chapter 4.

chapter 4

CHOOSING A TOPIC

Topics come in many varieties: good and better and best, simple and complex, shallow and deep, interesting and boring, impossible and rewarding. Unless a teacher specifically demands a certain topic, students can make the most of a topic by choosing wisely. This chapter intends to help novice researchers make a good choice.

In high school, students do a "paper" on "The Amazon Rain Forest." Using an encyclopedia, a geography textbook, and two websites, they can construct a five-page description of the flora, fauna, economy, and human population of the area. For a college paper, they would need to concentrate on one of those aspects. At the graduate level, the paper would need to wrestle with an issue such as the "Global Effects of Deforestation of the Amazon Rain Forest." This is an example of how a topic goes from shallow to deep.

The same occurs in papers specific to the area of religion. A paper on "The Divinity of Christ in the New Testament" would be very general. You could make it more specific by limiting the study to "The Divinity of Christ in the Gospel of John." Even this might be too involved for anything less than a doctoral dissertation. Much better would be "Christ as the Bread from Heaven in John 6." Not only does the topic go from shallow to deep, it goes from impossible to feasible.

Important steps in choosing a topic are reading, asking questions, and narrowing the scope. These three steps feed on each other. Reading raises questions; questions take you back to reading. Even when the topic is assigned, following these steps can result in a better topic and, hence, a better paper.

Reading

A topic cannot be chosen in a vacuum. You cannot research an island in the sea of your ignorance. General knowledge of the area is basic. Knowing how to find sources (see chapters 2 and 3), you are ready to comb the library and the Internet for ideas for your topic.

Textbooks are a good place to start. Dictionaries and encyclopedias may also be helpful. They do not provide topics as such, but they can help to clarify parameters and provide basic information.

The following sources provide a starting place. The first two are good, however old, general religious encyclopedias. The third and fourth are more up to date.

Hastings, James, ed. *Encyclopaedia of Religion and Ethics*. 12 vols. and index. Edinburgh: T. & T. Clark; New York: Scribner's, 1908–1926.

The New Schaff-Herzog Encyclopedia of Religious Knowledge. 12 vols. and index. New York: Funk & Wagnalls, 1908–1912; reprint, Grand Rapids: Baker, 1955. Supplemented by *Twentieth Century Encyclopedia of Religious Knowledge*. 2 vols. Grand Rapids: Baker, 1955.

Adams, Charles, and Mircea Eliade, eds. *Encyclopedia of Religion*. 2nd ed. 16 vols. New York: Macmillan, 1995.

Jones, Lindsay, ed. *Encyclopedia of Religion*. 15 vols. 2nd ed. Detroit: Macmillan Reference USA, 2005.

These two encyclopedias give a specific slant to religious issues:

New Catholic Encyclopedia. 17 vols. New York: McGraw-Hill, 1989.

Encyclopedia Judaica. 16 vols. New York: Macmillan; Jerusalem: Encyclopedia Judaica, 1971–1972.

The following are examples of denominational encyclopedias:

The Mennonite Encyclopedia: A Comprehensive Reference Work on the Anabaptist and Mennonite Movement. 5 vols. Hillsboro, KS: Mennonite Brethren Pub. House, 1955–1959.

Seventh-day Adventist Encyclopedia. Commentary Reference Series, vols. 10–11. Hagerstown, MD: Review and Herald, 1996.

Among the many Bible dictionaries, the following could prove useful:

Bromiley, Geoffrey, ed. *International Standard Bible Encyclopedia*. Rev. ed. 4 vols. Grand Rapids: Eerdmans, 1979–1988.

Freedman, David Noel, ed. *Anchor Bible Dictionary*. 6 vols. New York: Doubleday, 1992.

For general church history, the following may be consulted:

Oxford Dictionary of the Christian Church. 3rd ed. New York: Oxford University Press, 1997.

On topics related to mission and mission history, consider:

Moreau, Scott. *Evangelical Dictionary of World Missions.* Grand Rapids: Baker, 2000.
Barrett, David B., ed. *World Christian Encyclopedia.* 2nd ed. 2 vols. New York: Oxford
     University Press, 2001.

InterVarsity Press has published a series of dictionaries on different themes, among which are the following: New Testament, Old Testament, contemporary religion, biblical theology, later New Testament, Christian ethics, Paul, Jesus and the Gospels. These could provide good information.

As you read, take notes of the information on your sources. You will want to be able to find the items again. Also make notes on what you read. See chapters 6 and 8 for specifics on taking notes. Be especially attentive to questions your reading brings up.

Asking Questions

Asking questions — of yourself, of your peers, of your professors, of the books you read — can help you determine whether you have a good topic. Questions can also help you narrow the topic and focus on an issue to research. Questions concern content and feasibility.

Questions on Content

Some important questions regarding the organization of the topic might be: What are its parts? Of what larger whole is this topic a part? You can find the parts of a topic in the subdivisions of an encyclopedia article or in the table of contents of a book. For example, the *New Schaff-Herzog Encyclopedia of Religious Knowledge* divides its article on sun worship in such a way that I can see that one part would be enough, perhaps sun worship among the Hittites.

I. Among the Hebrews	1. In General	Arabs, Nabateans
Names and Titles	2. Babylonians	5. The Hittites
General Conceptions	3. Egypt	6. India
Worship	4. Aramea, Syria, and Phenicia	7. China and Japan
Date of Introduction	Place Name	8. W. Indo-Europeans
II. In Other Lands	Personal Names	9. Primitive Peoples
	Monumental Testimony	

Another set of questions to ask regarding the history of the topic include: What has been written on this topic? Is this a controversial topic? Are lines clearly drawn between two opposing sides over this topic? What can I add to this history? For example, the discussion on Paul's intention when he informed Timothy that women should not teach (1 Tim 2:12) has a long history. Positions have been taken—on both sides. Is there something new that I can add to this history? Or will I merely be repeating what others have said and I could learn from reading?

Given the hours and hours you will spend researching and writing on this topic, ask yourself: Do I find this topic interesting? Can I get excited about it? To commit yourself to sixty hours (for a serious twenty-page paper) with a topic about which you could care less makes no sense.

The ultimate questions involve the usefulness of the topic. What good is this topic? How can I use the results of my research? Besides me, who else will benefit from my work?

Questions on Feasibility

While you might be inclined to make heroic efforts to research the topic of your choice, certain practical considerations must prevail. The following questions deal with the feasibility of a topic.

1. Do I have the necessary sources to do this research? If the topic chosen must be researched from original documents in Bombay, a student in Buenos Aires will be hard put to finish the task. If the chosen topic is a word study of the Hebrew word *niṣdaq* in Dan 8:14, the researcher must have access to Hebrew dictionaries, lexicons, and word studies already done on *niṣdaq*, as well as articles published in journals.

2. Am I qualified to do this research? A researcher who has chosen to study the word *niṣdaq* in Daniel 8 but knows no Hebrew will not be able to write a good research paper. Sometimes it is possible to acquire the skills needed to complete a research project—languages, statistical expertise, or thorough knowledge of a specific area in a discipline—but often there is not enough time to do this.

3. Do I have enough time to complete the research of this topic by the due date? This question is of prime importance to students, especially in intensive courses. If one needs to send halfway around the world to get information to write the paper, it may be impossible to finish by the end of the semester. Some students choose topics that require interviewing someone who lives at a distance. Interesting as that research might be, one must count the cost—in time or money—before embarking on the project.

4. Does this research demand finances I do not have? The cost of mailing questionnaires or traveling to complete research can become heavy. The expense of typing a paper (or worse, having it typed)

must also be considered. Today computer and Internet expenses must be factored in to the total cost. Of course, it is not possible to escape all financial burdens, but one must take finances into consideration before settling on a topic.

In synthesis, one does well to ask Jesus' question recorded in Luke 14:28: "For which of you, desiring to build a tower, does not first sit down and count the cost, whether he has enough to complete it?"

Narrowing the Topic

Congratulations for having chosen a good topic! Now comes the narrowing, the task of making the topic even more specific.

The questions asked about feasibility point to limitations: reasons why something cannot be done properly or done at all, limits placed on the research by circumstances. Once a topic is chosen, limitations no longer count. Now we speak of delimitations—self-imposed limits that make the topic better, clearer, and more manageable.

Delimiting a study is indispensable because in doing good research, the researcher is responsible for turning up and examining every single piece of information on the chosen topic. It is as if one were putting a fence around a certain piece of land and agreeing to turn up every stone and investigate every plant enclosed in that fence. If the piece of ground is too large, the task cannot be completed. It is better to fence a small piece of ground and examine every pebble and blade of grass on it—not forgetting the small insects that might be hiding under the surface. In doing research one must become a specialist in the chosen area.

One delimitation could be that of a time period. A research project studying the chronology of the kings of Judah would take several years to complete. It would be wiser to study the chronology of the reign of Josiah. Considering the chronological problems involved, it might even be better to study only the date of the death of Josiah. Because you set forth this time delimitation, no one will ask why you did not include other kings.

Another delimitation could have to do with sources you will use. Your topic could be an examination of the "kingdom of God" concept in the works of G. E. Ladd. Unless you are writing a dissertation, you will want to delimit the sources to one work by Ladd. In a paper comparing the divorce passages in Matthew 19 and Mark 10, you could appropriately delimit yourself to the biblical passages and commentaries on those passages. Thus you would protect yourself from accusations of not having taken into account the latest Christian book on divorce.

A paper could be delimited to include only certain aspects of a topic. For example, in writing a paper on the theology of worship you might choose to exclude the issue of whether or not contemporary music is appropriate for worship. The topic would not have room for that discussion. You could, for example, state that "the study is limited to the nine texts containing the same Hebrew verb form," or that "the research confines itself to a study of the general body of Rastafarians, ignoring the splinter groups," or that "only those members whose names are on the local church books are taken into account in this study."

You will often see the phrase, "this topic is beyond the scope of" this paper/thesis/dissertation. That simply means that the author has chosen certain parameters that eliminate some aspects of the topic. Of course, too many delimitations would suggest that your topic is too narrow. Choose your delimitations with care. Make sure they make as much sense to your readers, of whom your advisor is the first, as they do to you.

Selecting a Thesis or Dissertation Topic

Most of what has been said about selecting a research topic is as valid for a thesis as for an undergraduate term paper. However, a master's thesis is expected to cover more ground. The fenced-in area is larger and the student is expected to more carefully examine the soil turned over by the researcher's spade. Normally, it cannot be simply a survey, no matter how well organized and presented, of what others have already written.

The selection of a topic for a thesis must be made in close communication with the advisor or committee. Naturally, the final choice is the student's, and the preliminary reading is his or her responsibility. Before seeing the professor about a topic, complete the initial preresearch and write down ideas on two or three possibilities. If you write out problem and purpose statements before seeing your advisor, the professor can give you more helpful advice. More information on theses will be found in chapter 20.

Just as the thesis is more complex than the term paper, the doctoral dissertation is deeper and broader than the thesis. The dissertation in theology or religion may have a practical or theoretical orientation, depending on the degree pursued. A doctoral dissertation is expected to break new ground, to provide something original. Dissertations are discussed in chapters 20 and 21.

Once a viable topic has been chosen and approved, the research plan can be implemented. The development of the research plan is the topic of chapter 5.

chapter 5

PLANNING RESEARCH

Writing a research paper takes time. Some scholars find that for every finished, double-space typewritten page, with its appropriate footnotes, they need at least two hours; most need three hours. On that basis, a twenty-page paper would take some forty to sixty hours to complete—from choosing the topic to handing the paper in. A dissertation may take as much as five hours for every page of the final version. If the professor requires rewriting, even more time must be allotted. Of the total time, about two-thirds is research time; one-third is writing time.

Planning takes time but is well worth the effort. The first step in planning is to define the problem to be addressed and state the purpose of the research. Then comes the methodology—the roadmap for the process. These elements go into the proposal, along with other items, such as a tentative outline and a preliminary bibliography. Some professors request a proposal even for a term paper; others want a proposal only for a thesis or dissertation. Even if the proposal is not required, the time spent in preparing it is amply repaid because the proposal brings the whole project into focus and saves time in the long run. A proposal is always required for a thesis or dissertation.

Chapter 5 explains the first three steps: problem, purpose, and methodology. Having accomplished these steps, you will be able to write the proposal and outline the contents of your paper. These activities are also explained.

Basic Steps

Step 1: Define the Problem

Once you have a research topic in hand, you must define the problem. The problem should point to a gap in knowledge, an unclear situation, an unresolved question, a lack of information, an unknown, a specific question to be investigated and answered, or a problem to be researched and solved. It is important to state the problem because this statement guides the research. It also helps the professor give appropriate guidance. Those who do not like the term *problem* because of its negative connotations could just as easily think of the problem as an issue or even a research question.

Whether a problem is simple or more complicated, it must be clearly stated. Exactly what is wrong and needs fixing? In most cases, the problem is expressed in a full sentence, as in these examples: There is disagreement regarding the exact date of the death of Josiah. Or, there is only scattered information on the beginning of the Methodist mission in the Solomon Islands. Or, lay members are frequently uninformed concerning their function in the church. Or, women in some churches in Zambia are not permitted to preach.

Often the problem, especially for a short paper, can be expressed in a question to which a direct answer may be given. For example, What is the relation between tithing and the receiving of God's blessings? Or, Which kind of Christian mission has won the most converts among the Muslims of Mindanao? Regarding the transmission of religious heritage in the Jewish faith, the problem could be expressed: What is the role of the Jewish family in the transmission of the religious heritage from one generation to the next?

A student, writing on the history of the Guadalajara Sanitarium in Mexico, the first Adventist medical institution outside the United States, stated his problem in the following terms: "In 1897 Seventh-day Adventist leaders declared that this sanitarium was the 'most important and the most promising enterprise of the sort to have been undertaken in modern times.'[1] However, by 1907 it had been closed. Why did the Guadalajara Sanitarium fail?" (The footnote reads: [1]J. H. Kellogg, "An Appeal for Mexico," *Review and Herald*, 29 June 1897, 408.)

A dissertation proposal lists the following problem: "Few terms in the Old Testament have caused as many differing opinions and misunderstandings, which have been so disturbing and controversial as to lead scholars to fierce polemic, as the Hebrew word *sheol*. In spite of valuable contributions by many scholars, there is no consensus in regard to the nature, function, and purpose of the term."

Another problem, elaborated for the dissertation proposal seminar, contains some background elements, which make the problem clearer:

> Evangelicals have assumed that while methods of evangelism may be changed, the evangelical salvation formula is the essential message of the gospel and therefore must remain the same. Thus when a spiritual seeker asks, "What must I do to be saved?" an evangelical Christian is likely to respond with terminology and concepts that have remained relatively unchanged for decades. Evangelistic presentations may now be accompanied by multimedia pyrotechnics and contemporary Christian music, but when a seeker wants to know how to cross over from death to life, the message is likely the same one the seeker's parents heard years before. This traditional way of describing the way of salvation, however, no longer elicits the positive response it once did. It seems to fail to communicate to the postmodern mind with clarity and impact.

Only half in jest, it has been said that a research problem that can be written on the back of one's business card is the most apt to be solved. If the question is clear, the answer will also be clear. Time spent on clarifying the statement of the problem is never wasted.

Step 2: Determine the Purpose

At this point you must determine what to do with the problem. Are you going to analyze? Compare? Reconstruct? Synthesize? Design a program? Any of these may be a valid option, depending on the problem and what you want to accomplish.

The purpose follows on the heels of the problem. It tells the reader (and the professor) what you are going to do about the problem. If the problem is that there is no information, the purpose will be to find that information. If the problem states that there seems to be disagreement between two of Jesus' sayings on peace, the purpose could be to try to bring harmony or understand the difference. Here are some examples of purposes: to reconstruct the events of a given historical period, to compare two theories, to organize certain information, to determine the relation between two events, to synthesize, to discover, or to formulate.

The purpose for the dissertation on the evangelical presentation of the gospel was described as follows: "The purpose of this dissertation is to critique the typical evangelical response to the question, 'What do I need to do to be saved?'"

The purpose of the *sheol* dissertation was straightforward: "To examine the sixty-six occurrences of the Hebrew word *sheol* in the Old Testament in order to discover the nature, function, and purpose of this term."

Suppose the problem is that the Christian church is not growing in the Czech Republic as it did in the first years after the fall of the Communist regime. The purpose might be to describe the growth patterns of the church or even to consider the factors affecting church growth. It might be to compare the growth of the church in the Czech Republic with the growth of the church in another post-Communist country. In a recent dissertation, a student proposed "to explore the contextual and institutional factors of the current Czech situation in order to develop a strategy rooted in Czech culture for revitalization of local congregations."

After completing this step, two things are settled: What the issue is and what is being done about it. The next question is how to go about solving the problem.

Step 3: Design a Methodology

Why the "method" of solving a problem is called "methodology" is not quite certain. In any case, "methodology" is the way you go about achieving the purpose already stated. This is the process you will follow. You must ask: "How am I going to do this?" In a class paper, you need only convince the professor. In a thesis or dissertation, the advisor and/or committee need to be convinced that the route chosen will lead to a successful solution of the problem.

In theological, biblical, or ministerial research, methodology is not so clearly set out as in social science research. In fact, scholars on that side of the campus may look at the "method" used in seminary research and find only "madness." Various methods are used in seminary research. Note the difference between the method to uncover the meaning and function of *sheol* and the method to develop a premarital seminar as part of a D.Min. dissertation. Yet, any good research must have a clear and logical method—a way to get from here to there.

If your research is to be done in the library, decide where you are going to start and where you will go next. Will you trace the history first? Or will you do the exegesis of your text first? You will also need to tell your professor how you plan to use your sources. Will they be outlined? Compared? Analyzed? If the research is other than bibliographical, the methodology of the survey or experiment to be used must be even more clearly spelled out. The instrument you plan to use to gather data also needs to be described and/or prepared. All steps of the research must be clearly enunciated. In some cases, the section on methodology may become an entire chapter of the paper.

Some examples should help to clarify the idea. The method of the dissertation on the presentation of the gospel can be summarized as follows:

The study will begin by surveying crucial terms and central concepts in the typical gospel presentation. Two basic questions will then be asked: Does the evangelical response employ sound communicational principles? Does the evangelical response present a balanced New Testament teaching on how one can be saved? To answer the first question, the principles of receptor-based communications will be studied. The second question will be answered on the basis of an analysis of New Testament responses to the question "What must I do to be saved?" The last step is to summarize the results of my study and suggest biblical modifications to the traditional evangelical salvation formula that may communicate with more clarity and impact in North America at the turn of the millennium.

A church growth study of an inner-city church could have the following methodology: (1) review current literature on inner-city church growth, including theory and practical examples; (2) analyze the community in which the church functions; (3) study the church, its growth history, its activities, its climate, and its membership; and (4) design, implement, and evaluate a suggested church growth strategy for this church, based on the three previous points.

Before writing the methodology in beautiful prose, simply list the different steps. What will you do first? Second? Third? Make sure the steps are completely logical for the problem as presented and the purpose as intended. Consultation with your professor or advisor is indispensable. Additional reading may also help clarify the steps you must take.

The Proposal

As noted above, the preparation of a project or paper proposal, even when not required by the professor, is a valuable exercise. Not only does the proposal provide a clear guide for the research process, it also becomes the basis for the introduction to the paper.

The proposal described here is appropriate for a class or term paper. A thesis proposal will, of necessity, be more complex and extensive. Proposals for theses and dissertations are described in chapters 20 and 21.

Generally speaking, the research proposal needs to include the following items. (In this outline, items that have been described in the first part of this chapter are merely enumerated.)

1. *The background for the problem.* This section may also show the scope or extension of the problem. It will help the reader understand the problem.
2. *Statement of the problem.*

3. *Purpose of the research.*

4. *Significance of the research* (also called "importance"). Although a student paper may not have far-reaching consequences, any well-prepared research paper should be useful to someone. In this section of the proposal the following questions should be answered: Who will benefit from having this problem solved? How will they benefit? How important is it to answer this question? What is the value of this research to a given discipline? Why is doing this research important? No rule prohibits the writer from being one of the beneficiaries. One value or objective of a research on Christian work for people with physical disabilities might be its "use by the writer as a basis for ministry among the handicapped."

5. *Definition of terms.* An author should clearly indicate the precise meaning of terms that might not be common to the readers or might have more than one meaning. A writer might define "young adults" as "persons of either gender between the ages of 20 and 25." Thus the reader is informed of the exact meaning of the term in this paper. It is important for everyone — writer, professor, and readers — to be sure of precise meanings. When a paper is to be read by those not familiar with denominational or local terms, it is imperative for these to be clearly defined. A precise definition of theological terms characteristic of one's own tradition may be needed for noninitiated readers. Not all papers have definitions of terms.

6. *Limitations of the study.* Here the researcher honestly states the limits imposed by shortness of time, lack of library facilities, or language limitation. However, too many of these limitations may suggest that a wrong topic has been chosen or poor research is under way. These are especially useful in the rough draft of the proposal because they show your honesty and foresight. Often they are left out of the final draft.

7. *Delimitations of the study.* Not to be confused with "limitations" (see above), delimitations are parameters chosen by the researcher. "While the problem of elders who do not know how to preach proper sermons is common in the whole of Tanzania, this paper will only study the issue in the Arusha Central Church."

8. *Methodology.* The researcher must clearly show what steps are to be followed to complete the research.

9. *Tentative outline.* Give title chapters, with their main sections and subsections.

10. *Working bibliography.* This is a list of sources already consulted and found useful to the topic. This list will grow as the research pro-

gresses. The tentative bibliography helps the professor gauge the student's familiarity with the topic.

Another item may or may not enter into the proposal of a bibliographical research, but is usually present in other kinds of research: the hypothesis. A hypothesis is the researcher's tentative solution to the problem, an indication of the expected result of the study. Sometimes called a "thesis," it is the proposed solution to the problem. If a hypothesis is clearly going to direct the research, it must be stated.

For example, in a study of the history of the early change from Sabbath to Sunday observance, the hypothesis could be the following: "Second-century Christians replaced Sabbath observance with Sunday observance because they did not wish to look like Jews." The research would then present all the information to substantiate that position—without neglecting evidences to the contrary. The hypothesis could be supported or not supported by the evidence accumulated. The danger in blindly following one's hypothesis is that one might fail to see adverse evidence in the pursuit of a solution one has already decided on. If the hypothesis keeps the research on track but does not dominate it, it can be useful. See chapter 7, "Research Thinking."

Sometimes a section on the need for the study is appropriate; it may be used as background material to the statement of the problem. However, a researcher may choose to write about the need as a separate item. Need may also be put together with the significance.

A proposal for a class paper can be written in one or two pages. A thesis proposal will be much longer and will reflect a great deal of study and research already completed. Some graduates have indicated that of the total time spent on the thesis or dissertation, one-fourth had gone into the proposal. For a thesis or dissertation, the professor (or committee) usually asks for a review of literature or equivalent evidence that the student has already read amply on the topic. On thesis and dissertation proposals, see chapters 20 and 21.

Tentative Outline

Some professors ask for a tentative outline early in the research process. Even if they do not, you should prepare one before proceeding with the research. Naturally, as you read, new information may change details or even sections of the outline, but the foundation will usually remain the same. When you have finished the researching and are about to write, you will produce a final outline.

The outline is the backbone of the paper. It provides the basic organization for the research report. It is also the basis for the table of contents. Each chapter must be so well outlined that student and professor can clearly follow the development of the topic. Outlines can be written using complete sentences or only phrases. The model given is of the second kind. Parallelism in form is important. Each item that subdivides at all must have at least two parts. All subdivisions of a topic must clearly relate to the heading of which they are a part.

The following outlines, from the proposal of a D.Min. project on the Bhakti way of philosophical Hinduism, show the researcher already had a good knowledge of the topic. The first outline is done in the traditional form, using a sequence of Roman numerals, capital letters, Arabic numerals, and lower-case letters. The second outline uses Arabic numerals and the decimal system, in a style employed in many areas of the world. Both forms are correct and acceptable since they give a detailed outline of the study. Either model should be followed precisely, including all items, such as indentations, sequence of letters and numbers, and alignment of periods. Do not mix the two systems.

    I. Introduction
   II. Bhakti Yoga
      A. Definition of Bhakti
      B. Ninefold Bhakti
         1. Passive Bhakti
            a. Sravanam
            b. Kirtanam
            c. Smarmam
         2. Active Bhakti
            a. Padasevanam
            b. Archanam
            c. Vandanam
         3. Relational Bhakti
            a. Dasyam
            b. Sakhyam
            c. Atmanivedanam
      C. Madura Bhakti
         1. Symbolic Nature
         2. Allegorical Interpretation
  III. Barriers to Bhakti
      A. Women

B. Wealth
C. Wrong Company
D. Wrong Emotions
    1. Lust
    2. Anger
    3. Greed
    4. Attachment
IV. Summary, Conclusions, and Reflections

The second form is as follows:

1 Introduction
2 Bhakti Yoga
2.1 Definition of Bhakti
2.2 Ninefold Bhakti
2.2.1 Passive Bhakti
2.2.1.1 Sravanam
2.2.1.2 Kirtanam
2.2.1.3 Smarmam
2.2.2 Active Bhakti
2.2.2.1 Padasevanam
2.2.2.2 Archanam
2.2.2.3 Vandanam
2.2.3 Relational Bhakti
2.2.3.1 Dasyam
2.2.3.2 Sakhyam
2.2.3.3 Atmanivedanam
2.3 Madura Bhakti
2.3.1 Symbolic Nature
2.3.2 Allegorical Interpretation
3 Barriers to Bhakti
3.1 Women
3.2 Wealth
3.3 Wrong Company
3.4 Wrong Emotions
3.4.1 Lust
3.4.2 Anger
3.4.3 Greed
3.4.4 Attachment
4 Summary, Conclusions, and Reflections

Although the formulation of a research plan—including the writing of a proposal and the preparation of an outline—follows on the heels of choosing a viable topic, this activity takes place at the same time as the initial bibliographic search. Given the importance of correctly recording the findings of the bibliographic search, chapter 6 addresses the issue of keeping record of the books, articles, and other sources that form the bibliography.

PREPARING BIBLIOGRAPHIES

The search for bibliography begins at the same time as the selection and narrowing of a research topic. In research, the word "bibliography" has two different meanings. It can be the sum of sources used for a research project, or it can be the list of items consulted, which generally appears at the end of the paper. Chapters 2 and 3 considered the finding of sources. This chapter deals with the process of keeping track of these sources during the research process and presenting them in final form in a bibliography.

Bibliographic Records

The traditional way of keeping track of the bibliography for a paper was to make "bib cards." Today most bibliographic records are kept electronically. Both ways work; both must be done carefully, making sure no errors creep in.

"Bib Cards"

Bibliography cards, usually called "bib cards," but also "source cards," can be made on three-by-five-inch (or four-by-six-inch) note cards, purchased at a bookstore. However, slips of paper cut to approximately that size work just as well—one-fourth of a typing page is also a good size. In fact, notes may be taken on paper that has already been used on one side. As long as the slips of paper are cut to the same size and are not too thin, any paper will work. Keep your "bib cards" together with rubber bands or elastics.

Start making bibliography cards at the beginning of your preliminary search. Doing this saves time later when you wish to find a certain book, but

but cannot quite remember what the title was and therefore cannot find it. Bib cards need to show all relevant information needed to find the item again—without returning to the library catalog—or to make up the bibliography for the paper without having to see the book again.

Each bibliography card must have the following information, if pertinent to the source: author(s), title, number of volumes, editor, translator, edition, place of publication, publisher, date of publication, and the exact location of the book (call number and library). In addition, you should record information about the book or article, about the part of the topic it deals with, specific pages to look at, references found in it, and other matters of interest.

If the bibliographic cards are carefully made—that is, if they contain all the information and are totally legible—they will not need to be recopied before the final typing. They will be referred to throughout the research process and then will form the basis for the final bibliography. All you will need to do is alphabetize the cards and type the bibliography.

The sample bibliography cards, which look something like the author card in the card catalog, contain all the information you will need. Note the location of each item. Note also the punctuation; this is the same that will be used in the final bibliography. The author (or editor) is first, followed by a period or full stop. Then comes the title of the book, underlined (italics in final bibliography) and followed by a period. Next is the place of publication, followed by a colon and the name of the publisher. After this, a comma precedes the date of publication, which is followed by a period or full stop.

You will find information for a bibliographic entry on the title page of a book and on its verso. Missing information can be obtained from the library

```
REF
BS
1830
A3
    Charlesworth, James H., ed. The Old Testament
        Pseudepigrapha. Vol. 1, Apocalyptic Literature
        and Testaments. Garden City, NY. Doubleday,
        1983.

    Pp. 707-719: Apocalypse of Adam, 1st to 4th cent.
    From Nag Hammadi, in Sahidic Coptic.
    Prophecy of the flood, chap. 3.
    Chap. 7 alludes to virgin birth.
    Bibl., 710.
```

```
P

    Collins, John J. "Daniel and His Social World."
       Interpretation 39 (April 1985): 131-143.

    Collins sets Daniel's life in the Maccabbean
    period and considers chaps 1-6 as legendary (135).
    See reference to Collins's other works on Daniel.
    Basic idea: the book of Daniel reflects the Sitz
    im Leben of the author, in the time of Antiochus
    Epiphanes
```

catalog. In order to save time later, these cards must be made correctly from the beginning.

If your library system allows you to print bibliographical records as you do your search, you may want to use these printouts as the bibliographical record of your search. Simply cut the page into strips, one for each source, and put them in alphabetical order. These strips may be somewhat unwieldy, but they contain all the bibliographical data, free from possible copy errors. You can write additional information on the back of each strip. This system is a cross between the old-fashioned "bib cards" and electronic bibliographies.

And now, let us consider a "better way": the electronic record.

Electronic Record

The starting place for developing an electronic record of the bibliographic search is an electronic catalog of some sort: a library catalog, the ATLA Index, a WorldCat search. The process is as follows:

1. Find an item that you want for your bibliography.
2. Following the protocol of your electronic source, save it to a list.
3. Following the protocol, download the list to removable storage (such as a thumb drive, memory card, or CD), or email the information to yourself.
4. Retrieve the list and clean up the format so that the entries look like items on a bibliography.
5. Alphabetize the list, as if you were preparing the bibliography. (Use the sort feature of your word processing program.)

6. Add notes to your items, being careful not to insert a hard return between the bibliographical entry and the added note. (You will delete these notes when you prepare your final bibliography.)
7. If you wish, print this list (and cut it up by individual items, if you like) and use it for your search in the library.

When I begin to write, I will keep the bibliography as a second document on my word processor. When I need to do a footnote, I will switch to that document and cut and paste the information into the paper, making the changes needed to transform the information from bibliography to footnote style.

My colleague Terry Robertson, Seminary Librarian at Andrews University, has written a much better description of two electronic tools than I could:

> A useful computer tool you may wish to consider is a bibliographic utility. Two excellent examples are *EndNote*™ and *RefWorks*™. Both allow you to manage a bibliography, interact with your final paper by inserting footnotes accurately according to the selected style, and format the bibliography perfectly. These tools take all the guesswork out of formatting footnotes. For example, you have a well-written paragraph with a footnote, but during the editing process, realize that it would fit better four pages earlier. Just move it, with any adjustments to the format made automatically. It is also possible to download records into the utility directly from online databases such as the library catalog or ATLA.
>
> *EndNote* is installed on your computer. It allows customization of format and sorting features. The Reference Notes field also has incredible capacity. *RefWorks* is a web-based program you access via the internet whenever you need it. *RefWorks* may be preferred when you will be working on the paper at multiple sites—at home, at work, on a library computer, or at your friend's home. It is also an excellent tool for collaborative work, where several persons are using the same bibliography. The downside is that access is by subscription fee, and when the subscription fee time is up, you lose access. Many campuses provide free access to *RefWorks*.[1]

Note Bene™ is a third option. This word processor, on your computer, manages bibliography and automatically inserts citations in proper form. It can also manage notes. Its added module, *Archive Pro*, captures bibliographical data from online databases. For Greek and Hebrew fonts, add the Lingua module.

Whatever way you keep record of your bibliography, be meticulous. Do not allow yourself any mistakes!

---

1. Terry Robertson, email communication, November 20, 2006. In an email communication on October 8 2007, Robertson suggested a free alternative to Endnote: Zotero. Go to www.zotero.org for a free download and the instructions to use it.

Format of Bibliographic Entries

As is customary in theological education, the format used is that of Kate Turabian and the *Chicago Manual of Style*. The most common types of materials used in theological studies are given here; additional forms are given in chapter 10, where footnotes and bibliographical entries are compared.

In bibliographical entries for all kinds of materials, periods or full stops follow each segment: author, title, series, publication data. Accents and diacritical marks from foreign languages must be included.

Books

Several items must be considered: author, title, edition, and publication data. In addition, there are special rules for multivolume works and series.

Author

Normally, the order of the author or editor statement is surname, comma, given names (or name and initial), period or full stop. Honorific or academic titles are not used.

When a book has more than one author, all names are given. However, only the first is inverted (surname first). Subsequent authors appear with given name first and surname last. Commas separate the names. Names of all the authors of an item must appear in the bibliography. Fortunately, books that have many authors usually have a principal author or editor. Only that one needs listing.

Hunter, George H., III. *Church for the Unchurched.* Nashville: Abingdon, 1996.
Anderson, Gerald H., Robert T. Coote, Norman A. Horner, and James M. Phillips. *Mission Legacies: Biographical Studies of Leaders of the Modern Missionary Movement.* Maryknoll, NY: Orbis, 1994.

Editor in Place of Author

McGavran, Donald, ed. *The Conciliar-Evangelical Debate: The Crucial Documents, 1964–1976.* South Pasadena, CA: William Carey, 1977.

Corporate Author

When the item has been prepared by a committee or a corporate entity, that name is used in place of an author's name:

United Nations. *Yearbook of the United Nations.* New York: Department of Public Information, United Nations, 1992.

No Author Given

If no author or editor is given, the bibliographical entry begins with the title of the book:

Encyclopedia Britannica. 15th ed. 32 vols. Chicago: Encyclopaedia Britannica, 2002.

Title

The title comes one space after the period (full stop) following the author's name. The title of a book, pamphlet, or journal must appear in italics or be underlined. If there is a subtitle, it appears after a colon and is also in italics or underlined. Titles in English have first and last and all important words capitalized. Titles in German have capital letters on the first word and on all the nouns. French, Spanish, and Latin titles have capitals only on the first word. Titles of books in non-Latin scripts may be transliterated; a translation into English should appear in parentheses, not italicized but capitalized in sentence style immediately following the title.

Schweitzer, Albert. *Das Abendmahlsproblem auf Grund der wissenschaftlichen Forschung des 19. Jahrhunderts und der historischen Berichte.* Tübingen: J. C. B. Mohr (Paul Siebeck), 1929.

Stam, Juan B. *Apocalipsis y profecía: Las señales de los tiempos y el tercer milenio.* Buenos Aires : Kairós, 1998.

Tak, Myung-hwan. *Hankuk ui Shinheung Jonggyo* (New religions in Korea). Seoul: Song Chong Sa, 1972.

Edition

If the item is of any edition other than the first, this must be indicated. Printings do not count, for a book is only changed when a new edition is made. Give the number of the edition or the exact wording (such as Amer. ed.). Note the period and one space between title and edition. A period comes after the edition, before the place of publication.

Ferguson, Everett. *Backgrounds of Early Christianity.* 2nd ed. Grand Rapids: Eerdmans, 1993.

Multivolume Works

If the source is made up of several volumes, this information is given after the title and the edition. For bibliographical entries of multivolume works with individual titles, see examples in chapter 10.

Balz, Horst, and Gerhard Schneider, eds. *Exegetical Dictionary of the New Testament.* 3 vols. Grand Rapids: Eerdmans, 1990–1993.

Series

The series to which a book belongs follows the title and is not italicized. The series statement ends with a period. A volume within the series is recorded as it appears on the title page. If the volume of the series has a number, use it. You may include or omit the comma, but do so consistently.

Overholt, Thomas W. *Prophecy in Cross-cultural Perspective*. SBL Sources for Biblical Study, 17. Atlanta: Scholars Press, 1986.

Facts of Publication

Place of publication

If the city where the item was published is well known, give the name of the city alone: New York, Manila, Hong Kong. If the town is obscure, give also the state or the country. If two or more places are given, use only the first. Abbreviations may be used, but always consistently. For the states in the United States, use consistently *only* one option: (a) postal codes, (b) abbreviations, (c) full names. In this book we use postal codes; however, not all schools accept postal codes. If there is no place of publication, either in the book or in the library catalog, use N.p. for "no place" (capitalized following the period).

Healdsburg College. *Eleventh Annual Calendar*. N.p.: Healdsburg College, 1894.

Publisher

The publisher is separated from the place of publication by a colon and one space. Certain parts of the publisher's name, such as "limited" and "incorporated," are always omitted. An abbreviated form may be used if done so consistently (as in this book): Zondervan instead of Zondervan Publishing House. However, university publishers cannot be abbreviated: Chicago University Press. If no publisher information is found, either in the book or in the library catalog, use n.p. for "no publisher."

Avondale School for Christian Workers. *Twelfth Annual Announcement*. Cooranbong, Australia: n.p., 1908.

Date of publication

The date of publication is separated from the publisher by a comma and one space. If there is no date, either in the book or in any catalog, use n.d. for "no date." The date given should be that of the edition, not of the printing. For reprint editions, give as much information as you have, in the following form.

Magil, Joseph. *The Englishman's Hebrew-English Old Testament: Genesis–2 Samuel*. New York: Hebrew Publishing, 1905; reprint, Grand Rapids: Zondervan, 1974.

If a multivolume source has different dates of publication, the beginning and end dates are given in a full bibliographical entry. If the work has not been completed, give only the beginning date: 1964–.

Charlesworth, James H., ed. *The Old Testament Pseudepigrapha*. 2 vols. Garden City, NY: Doubleday, 1983–1985.

When the material used is only a part of the multivolume set, this may be indicated as follows:

Robertson, A. T. *Word Pictures in the New Testament*. 6 vols. Nashville: Broadman, 1930–1933. 6:137–180.

Note the "en dash" between inclusive numbers, whether pages or dates. The "en dash" is longer than a hyphen. Create it in Word by clicking on Insert, then on Symbols, then on Special Characters, then on En Dash, then on Insert. I have made myself a shortcut: Ctrl + –, which works nicely: 34–35. In Word-Perfect, you want to insert (ctrl + W) symbol 4,33, to do the same.

Magazines and Journals

Magazines are usually general in nature, addressed to a lay population. Examples are *Moody Monthly, National Geographic, Time, Christianity Today*, and *Adventist Review*. The bibliographical entry below shows the correct form for magazine articles. Even if the magazine has volumes, they are not included. If the date includes a number, it is appropriate to use the Library style (also European): 9 November 2006. Otherwise, the form for this date would be November 9, 2006, as used consistently in this book. Months may be abbreviated. Notice the extra comma after the date. For safety's sake, write the page numbers in full: 200–231. Whichever form you use, do so consistently.

Bass, Dorothy. "Receiving the Day the Lord Has Made." *Christianity Today*, March 6, 2000, 63–67.
Monroe, Sylvester. "Does the Rev. Jesse Jackson Still Matter?" *Ebony*, November 2006, 170–180.

Journals are academic and generally focused on one discipline. *Missiology, Journal of Biblical Literature, Theology Today*, and *Review of Religious Studies* are considered journals. For journals, the bibliographical entry must include the volume number.

Costas, Orlando E. "The Mission of Ministry." *Missiology* 14 (1986): 463–471.

The year of the journal is added in parentheses to make finding the item easier. If paging is continuous throughout the volume, the year is enough. If each issue starts with page 1, a month or season must be included: 15 (Spring 1991): 35.

Note the space between the colon and the page(s) in a journal reference. When no month or season is given, the number of the issue follows the volume:

Merling, David. "The Search for Noah's Ark." *College and University Dialogue* 11, no. 3 (1999): 5–8.

Additional Materials

The entry for a chapter written by one author in a book edited by another is tricky. Note the *total* number of pages *before* the facts of publication. According to Turabian, this kind of entry should read as follows:

Larson, Donald N. "The Viable Missionary: Learner, Trader, Story Teller." In *Perspectives on the World Christian Movement: A Reader*, ed. Ralph D. Winter and Steven C. Hawthorne, 444–451. Pasadena, CA: William Carey Library, 1992.

Signed articles in specialized dictionaries or encyclopedias also deserve special attention:

Jepsen, Alfred, "אָמַן." *Theological Dictionary of the Old Testament*. Edited by G. Johannes Botterweck and Helmer Ringren. Translated by John T. Willis. Grand Rapids: Eerdmans, 1974–. 1:292–323.

Given the use of dissertations as research sources, an example should be included:

Gane, Roy Edwin. "Ritual Dynamic Structure: Systems Theory and Ritual Syntax Applied to Selected Ancient Israelite, Babylonian, and Hittite Festival Days." Ph. D. dissertation. University of California, Berkeley, 1992.

Examples given in this section correspond to normal entries. More examples, especially of problem bibliographical entries, are found in chapter 10.

Final Bibliography

As you put together the final bibliography of your paper, you will carefully follow the rules of form. You will also have to decide how you will organize your bibliography. Sometimes you will be asked to prepare an annotated bibliography. Instructions regarding these three topics occupy our attention now.

Form

The order of each entry is the same: author (or editor), title, number of volumes, edition, series, place of publication, publisher, date of publication. The punctuation is also standard; you have seen it in the instructions just given.

Because the typing of bibliographies demands total precision in matters of spacing, as well as punctuation and contents, be very careful. Word processing software will not place the spaces in their correct location when full justification is used; therefore, use left justification when entering a bibliography.

The bibliography always begins on a separate page. It is the last section in the paper or thesis. Set up the page with the following margins: left, 1.5 in; top, bottom, and right, 1 in. each. The title (in caps) is centered two inches from the upper edge of the paper (on the thirteenth line). Each bibliographical entry is single spaced; a blank line is left between entries. The first line (beginning with the author's surname) reaches the left margin; thereafter, the lines are indented, usually one tab space or one-half inch. Use the regular tab set of your word processor.

If there are two or more items by exactly the same author (not one as author and another as editor), the author's name is only written the first time. Thereafter it is replaced by a line, which may be an 8-space underline or a 3-em dash, either one followed by a period. (In Word, create a 3-em dash line by inserting 3 em dashes in a row: Insert, Symbol, Special characters, em dash. You may also create a shortcut.) In any case, follow the style guide at your school.

The works of each author may be arranged alphabetically by title or chronologically by publication date. While your readers will prefer the alphabetical listing, your professor may insist on the chronological approach.

Dybdahl, Jon. *Exodus: God Creates a People.* Abundant Life Amplifier. Boise, ID: Pacific Press, 1994.

_____. *Old Testament Grace.* Boise, ID: Pacific Press, 1990.

A sample typed bibliography is presented in chapter 13. The bibliography of this textbook may also be used as a model.

Organization

The simplest and most effective way to organize a bibliography is to put all entries in alphabetical order, by author. Well-made bibliography cards are simply alphabetized and typed. If you kept an electronic list, your bibliography only needs checking for details.

For some types of research, however, or to please certain professors, bibliographies may be divided into parts. Common divisions of a bibliography are books and journals; published and unpublished materials; primary and secondary sources. When dividing bibliographical entries by category, consult the preferences of the professor or thesis committee. However, remember that a reader may become frustrated at not finding sources listed under the heading where he or she thinks they should appear and having to check six different lists of sources. The alphabetical approach is the most user friendly.

Annotated Bibliography

An annotated bibliography contains the usual bibliographical information. In addition, it gives a brief description or summary of the book. At early stages of the research, professors may require an annotated bibliography to ascertain that you have read, or at least scanned, the items listed. The annotation should be between three and twelve lines, usually single spaced. Two examples show format and content.

Rouse, Ruth, and Stephen C. Neill, eds. *A History of the Ecumenical Movement.* 2nd ed. with rev. bibliography. 2 vols. Philadelphia: Westminster, 1967–1970.

> A survey of ecumenical trends from the Reformation to 1968, this authoritative work contains essays by many scholars in the field. Each volume includes an extensive classified bibliography, an analytical subject index, and an author index. Vol. 1 covers 1517–1948; vol. 2 covers 1948–1968. Vol. 2 was edited by Harold Fey.

Spencer, Donald H. *Hymn and Scripture Selection Guide.* Valley Forge, PA: Judson, 1977.

> Section 1 lists 380 hymns arranged by title. Under each hymn, brief phrases identify its subject; selected relevant Scripture passages are listed. Section 2 is a listing of Scripture passages in canonical order. Under each passage, the numbers of the more appropriate hymns are listed. This is useful for selecting hymns to go with a sermon on a particular text.

This chapter has given pointers for keeping records of the developing bibliography. It has also described the organization and formatting of the final bibliography. Chapter 7 takes us from form to philosophy—how we think when we do research.

RESEARCH THINKING

Research has a special way of thinking attached to it. Or perhaps it would be better to say that research is built on a particular way of thinking. This includes a specific mindset, certain thinking processes, and the asking of many questions.

Research Mindset

Researchers start their work from the premise that knowledge is attainable and that finding truth is possible. The quest may be long and difficult, but results are assured. Without this optimistic mindset, little research would take place. The research mindset is characterized by objectivity, focus, clearly set-forth presuppositions, logical organization, and intellectual honesty. In a more biblical frame, it is adorned by humility.

Objectivity

A much-touted component of the scientific method of research is "total" objectivity: Researchers should be able to detach themselves from their preferences and convictions, and dispassionately consider the evidence. Today we realize that total objectivity is a myth. It is not possible to put aside all cherished ideas—even in research. Furthermore, we recognize that some aspects of life on planet Earth are not subject to disinterested appraisal and total objectivity. Just as a baby is perfect to his or her mother, a researcher's "brain child" cannot be improved on.

While one might have to admit that total objectivity is not probable, a researcher's goal is to be as objective as possible. This means that one must be sure that the presuppositions are reasonable and place preferences and prejudices in abeyance. One must consider all the evidence—pro and con. When defending our own ideas, we find it easy to weight the evidence in their favor. Objectivity demands that we look also at the other side of the coin. Once I asked a student why he had not included a certain author in his paper. The answer was quick: "Oh, but he does not agree with me, so I could not use him." His objectivity score was very low, below passing.

Objectivity requires me to consider negative evidence, to analyze ideas that are foreign or different, to look at arguments that might upset my position. Being objective requires courage and humility; it demands putting pet ideas on hold while examining all the evidence; it insists on developing wisdom to consider every facet of a topic.

Focus

With Paul a researcher must say, "One thing I do" (Phil 3:13), and focus on the problem and its solution. Research thinking must fly straight as an arrow, without deviating from the goal. For that reason you cannot begin researching until you have determined your problem and purpose—what needs fixing and how you are going to do it.

Some cultures (and languages) enjoy a way of thinking that repeats ideas and information. Take, for instance, the stories of the Hebrew Bible. In Genesis 24, the phrase "Drink, and I will also draw for your camels" appears three times: when Abraham's servant prayed (v. 14), when Rebekah said the words (v. 19), and when Eliezer told her family about it (v. 44). Repetition is natural and normal. However, in research there is no space for saying the same thing twice. "Say it well, say it once" is good advice.

Another way of thinking allows for digressions, going off on tangents. You may find fascinating information, but if it does not further your argumentation, you will have to leave it aside. Keep focused on your goal! As Deut 5:32 admonishes, "You shall not turn aside to the right hand or to the left."

Clear Presuppositions

A presupposition is a basic understanding that undergirds one's thinking on a given topic. Sometimes presuppositions are called "assumptions"; they are what we take for granted. Such a presupposition appears in Heb 11:6, "Whoever would draw near to God must believe that he exists." Attempting to approach God without believing in God's existence makes no sense.

Presuppositions are the givens, the things we do not need to explain—at least not to ourselves. My understanding—of life, of what I read, of what I judge—depends to a great extent on my presuppositions. If I believe in a recent creation, this basic understanding colors everything I read about theistic evolution. If I am convinced of the depraved nature of human beings, Rogerian counseling, with its emphasis on the neutral or good nature of human beings, makes me nervous. In both cases, the opposite is equally true.

At times authors do not state their presuppositions. They may, however, give hints through their choice of sources, their way of organizing information, or their commendation of ideas or authors. If authors do not state the presuppositions, the reader spends unnecessary energy wondering: "Does she or doesn't she?" "Is he or isn't he?"

In the area of religious studies and theological education, presuppositions are usually strong, often considered matters of life and death, vitally important to who I am and what I say. To sweep presuppositions under the rug and pretend they do not exist is unwise as well as impossible. Nevertheless, it may be difficult even to admit having presuppositions.

An important task in research thinking is to ask the question: "Which of my presuppositions affect the way I think and write?" Simple presuppositions deal with assuming that readers are familiar with the topic. For example, I assume that my reader can understand the Greek words I put into my paper. At a somewhat deeper level, I accept Paul as a historical figure, an apostle, and writer of several canonical New Testament books; I assume my readers do likewise. Even more influential on my research outcome would be the acceptance of Romans as an inspired and authoritative book. These convictions will set the tone for my analysis of Paul's death-and-resurrection motif in Romans 6. To let my readers know what my basic assumptions are is not merely courteous, it ensures that they will understand what I say.

To understand someone, we need to know "where she is coming from," to use a popular phrase. To know what my writing truly means, my reader must know where I am coming from and what my presuppositions are. Thus it becomes my duty to explain to my reader the presuppositions that underlie my research. Before doing that, I will first have to bring my presuppositions into the open, list them, and decide which ones I must describe for my readers. My statement of presuppositions must be written in a way that explains my writing without making the reader feel that I consider her a heretic or a fool if she does not share my presuppositions.

To summarize, presuppositions are neither bad nor good—they simply are. And readers have a right to know which ones are guiding an author's research and writing. It is frustrating for me as a reader to wade through pages and pages wondering where the author stands on the topic he or she is writing about.

Organization

When my mother spied my messy room, she would remind me of Pope's assertion: "Order is Heaven's first law."[1] Whether order is the first or second law matters not; beyond doubt in research thinking, order and organization come near the top of the list.

Organized thinking puts similar ideas and concepts together: Everything has its own place. For example, a paper describing a target unreached people would describe various characteristics of these people: socio-cultural, religious, politico-economic. You would not expect to find their history or the plans laid by mission societies to reach them under these categories. Neither would you expect to find a description of their diet under the heading "Religion."

Organized thinking also places ideas, phrases, and words in a logical order, allowing the reader and hearer to immediately guess the criteria used to organize them. In other words, the order makes sense. For example, the organization could go from small to large, from deep to shallow, from important to inconsequential, from old to new—or any number of logical sequences. In history, for example, we expect to proceed chronologically.

Think of the organization of a zoo. Elephants and lions do not share the same enclosure. Song birds and birds of prey are not in the same cage. Cats and rabbits don't do well in the same space. There is good reason for the "organization" of livestock!

Yes, order should prevail in my research thinking and writing—not only in my messy room. Samuel Smiles was right to urge: "A place for everything and everything in its place."[2]

Intellectual Honesty

Honesty and dishonesty are defined in different ways by different peoples. Intellectual honesty and dishonesty are also differently defined in different cultures. In some cultures, to repeat the words of the masters only shows how much one respects their wisdom. Borrowing from their writings is the only way to write. Quotation marks or footnotes add nothing to that reverence.

In other cultures, the flow and beauty of the words is far more important than my admission that so-and-so wrote them; besides, that author would be

---

1. Alexander Pope, *Essay on Man*, ep. 4, 1.49.

2. Samuel Smiles quotations are widely available in print and online resources. This one occurs in *Thrift* (1875).

delighted to have me use her words and ideas! If a sick baby keeps me up all night just before a difficult examination, my friend is happy to allow me to share his learning. As an act of compassion, he may even place his paper deliberately so that I can see and copy what he has written. Cheating is a nonissue.

Without evaluating the honesty of the practices just described, we Westerners underline that none of these fit in our research culture. Here I must recognize that whoever wrote before me opened the way. Her work made mine easier. Therefore, I owe her a debt of gratitude. I must acknowledge this debt by inserting a reference to her work. In a similar vein, the writer who said what he did in words so much better than mine (compelling me to use them) produced those words; they are his work, his art. I have no business taking what is not mine and using it as if it were mine. Consequently, I must put these wonderful words in quotation marks, recognizing the author's unique claim to that phrase.

Obviously, this concept of research honesty precludes my putting my name to a paper taken from the Internet, whether I paid for it or not. It entirely forbids using my name as the author of a paper when the piece is actually an article in an obscure journal. It is equally dishonest for me to quote an author in such a way as to distort her meaning. The epitome of such dishonest usage would be to say that a reviewer found a book "magnificent," not quoting the whole sentence, which reads: "The study is a magnificent exercise in futility." All these usages fall under condemnation in the commandments: "Thou shalt not steal" and "Thou shalt not bear false witness."

Intellectual honesty at times may require me to admit that I do not know something, or even that someone else has a better answer than mine. An admission of this kind is not dishonorable. In fact, it will be applauded as honesty.

Most schools have a "Plagiarism Policy" that states just how seriously the institution takes using another person's materials as one's own. Punishment may range from a zero on the paper, to a failing grade in the class, to dismissal from school.

While the outcomes of intellectual dishonesty may be fearful—after all, those who love and make lies are left outside the pearly gates (Rev 22:15)—the results of following an honesty-is-the-best-policy attitude bring their own reward. Doing right for right's sake is always right. It is always best. See chapter 9 on footnotes for specific instructions on being honest in your papers. Do a Google search of the word "plagiarism" to see how some colleges and universities handle the issue.

Humility

Humility is a basic Christian virtue. Christ presented himself as "humble" (Matt 11:29) and indicated that those who humbled themselves would be exalted (23:12). Paul and Peter appealed for humility in the dealings of one Christian with another (Phil 2:3; 1 Pet 3:8; 5:5). James tied research and humility together by stating that "humility ... comes from wisdom" (Jas 3:13).

When a book or an article exudes arrogance — the know-it-all, better-than-everyone-else attitude — readers soon lose interest. A wiser path is to write in a way that is humble, tentative, willing to learn. This kind of writing makes room for dialogue, for reaching solutions.

Above all, conclusions should be stated in language that shows humility — willingness to learn, to accept other possibilities. After all, few researchers, especially students, are willing to lay down their lives for the results of their research.

Thinking Processes

According to Bloom's taxonomy of the cognitive domain of learning, knowing and thinking take place at different levels.[3] Knowledge is the simplest. Thinking about knowledge is more complex; for example, analysis and synthesis, evaluation and application, require more complex thinking skills. The process of making deductions and inferences is also important to research thinking.

Analysis and Synthesis

Both processes are indispensable to good research. Analysis can be exemplified by a small boy taking an alarm clock apart to find out what makes it tick. Synthesis is putting parts of three clocks together to make one functioning alarm piece.

Analysis is examining the evidence piece by piece. Analysis requires description and classification of each aspect of a topic, each piece of a history. Analysis demands considering what each piece is, what it does, and how it fits the other pieces. Before deciding how to teach a history class, the new professor carefully analyzes the syllabi of his predecessor and of two colleagues who teach the same course in other universities. He looks at all the parts, all the details, and sees what each part is and how it fits with the rest.

Synthesis, by contrast, begins with two or more ideas or systems. After studying how each one works, you put parts of the old together to form a new one. Our new history professor takes pieces and parts of the three syllabi, adds his own ideas, and creates a new syllabus for his course. While it may be built

---

3. See Benjamin S. Bloom, *Taxonomy of Educational Objectives* (Boston: Allyn & Bacon, 1984).

on previous work, his course syllabus is a new creation, a wise combination of several sources, a synthesis.

Analysis and synthesis are mental activities. They may appear in writing, but they first take place in the researcher's mind. In a paper, analysis usually appears in the body of the paper, while synthesis is more evident in the development of a model or a program, or in the conclusions at the end of the paper.

Application and Evaluation

Application and evaluation are at the deepest level of Bloom's taxonomy. These are not lightweight activities.

Application refers to using information. One applies rules of Greek orthography to write Greek correctly. One applies exegetical principles to derive a coherent meaning from the text. One applies church growth procedures to a church in order to add new members. Application of information requires thought and insight. It answers questions such as these: So what? How can this be used? What can I do with this information? Knowing without applying could make for useless knowledge.

Evaluation does not use information to do something, it uses information to decide whether something is of value. Evaluation requires setting up criteria by which to measure. One must not only answer the question, How good is this? but also, How do I know this is good?

Research must constantly evaluate. Is this quotation good? Appropriate? Is there a better one? Does this idea fit well here? Are these the best words to use? Does this author's work deserve further attention? Finally, researchers should be able to evaluate their own work: Have I done a commendable job? Where could I do better?

Inductive and Deductive Reasoning

Both inductive and deductive reasoning are used in research; both may be needed in the same paper. Yet, if I use faulty procedures, both can yield invalid results.

Induction has been defined as the process by which people discover and prove general propositions. Starting from the particulars, we formulate conclusions, laws, and principles. Inductive reasoning is at the heart of the scientific method. Inductive reasoning undergirds surveys, polls, and advertising.

We are acquainted with "inductive" Bible study. We might carefully study the Sermon on the Mount (Matt 5–7) and then state the principles of the kingdom that Jesus taught in that sermon. In a similar vein, I could taste apples from a hundred different trees, noticing the color, the texture, the flavor of the fruit. From my research I could induce that apples are a sweet-tasting fruit, with whitish flesh and seeds in the center.

As useful as inductive reasoning is for research, it has evident pitfalls. One of the most serious is using limited observations. If I only taste red apples, I could conclude that all apples are red. Recently I saw a poll of students' favorite drinks on a certain campus. I was interested until I found that the report was based on the preference of fifty-five students on a campus of more than three thousand students. Furthermore, there was no information on how these students were chosen. Were they buddies of the researcher? Were they all women? What were their ages? Did they really represent the whole student body? How could I be sure that a certain cola drink was truly the favorite?

Inductions will be more accurate the more thorough the study of the phenomena. To find out what Paul says about church elders, I need to study all the passages in his writings and in Acts that even touch on what elders should be and do. I need to analyze and compare them, especially where I see discrepancies. Only then will I be able to induce and synthesize what Paul thinks about elders.

Another important issue is the way I state my conclusions. Apples are sweet. Always? Could I have missed a variety that is sour? Perhaps, then, I need to state that apples are generally sweet. I leave room for further conclusions, technically called *inductions*, derived from studying particulars.

While inductive reasoning goes from the particulars to the principle, deductive reasoning starts from the general, the universal. *Merriam Webster's Collegiate Dictionary* defines deduction as "the deriving of a conclusion by reasoning; *specifically*: inference in which the conclusion about particulars follows necessarily from general or universal premises"; and "a conclusion reached by logical deduction."

In philosophy and theology deductive reasoning is more common than in scientific research. After all, we work from grand and everlasting principles. For example, God is love. Because God is love, we deduce that everything God does is loving. So we look at God's activities to understand what it means for God to be love. It is easy to see that this manner of thinking can lead to circular reasoning.

Asking Questions

Doubt is considered by some as basic to research. Others call the same principle *criticism*. Neither term sounds good to godly ears. However, asking questions is acceptable. Research asks hard questions, questions about the source of information as well as about the content and meaning of that source. See chapter 8, "Research Reading," for further suggestions on asking questions.

My father-in-law read his Bible and the *Reader's Digest*. Whatever he read, in either source, was true. For many, what is printed is to be believed. Research thinking demands that I question the source of information. I am especially interested in the author and publisher. Questions about the author include: Who wrote this? Is he an expert in his field? Is she a recognized scholar? Who funded this research? Questions about the publication in which the material appears are also important: Is what I am reading published in a reputable journal? Is the book from a creditable publisher? Just as important, does this publisher have an "angle"?

As I read critically, I need to query the content. What exactly is the author saying? Is it the same thing throughout the piece I am reading? Is the author consistent with himself throughout the piece? How does this compare with other items she has written? I will also ask what presuppositions undergird the argument, what research techniques the author is using. The answers to these questions will help me discern meaning.

I will also ask what the writer wants me to know and believe after reading this piece. Is she trying to inform me or convince me? What is her intention? Obviously, if I sense that there is an attempt to coerce my thinking, I will rebel.

In my freshman English class I read an article about the importance of an open mind. The author posited that the mind is something like a can. If it is closed, nothing comes in or goes out. If it is open on one end, ideas come in and go out. If the lid is used as a strainer, ideas coming in or out can be evaluated, straining out the bad, leaving in the good. Finally, a can that is open at both ends is of absolutely no use, for ideas flow in and out with no evaluation. Research thinking demands a mind like the can with a strainer lid.

At first, the research mindset may feel uncomfortable. As you read, think, and write, you will become more and more comfortable in this way of thinking. Your professors will notice the improvement in your writing. Learning to do research thinking is worth the effort.

So, with your mind in research gear, you can go on to reading and taking notes. These topics are discussed in chapter 8.

chapter 8

RESEARCH READING

Reading for a research paper takes time, thought, and skill. Research reading requires the implementation of advice given in chapter 7. To get the most benefit from this major part of the research activity, you will have to constantly evaluate or weigh what you are reading. You will also need to make notes of what you read. This chapter gives suggestions for reading, evaluating, and taking notes.

Reading

Reading is one of the most profitable of all intellectual activities. In reading, ideas and facts go from one brain to another through the printed page. However, not all books have the same effect on the reader. Francis Bacon, English philosopher and writer of the sixteenth century, said that some books should be tasted, others swallowed; only a few might be chewed and digested.[1] Some books are light reading and can be finished in one evening. Most of those needed for research are heavy and must be chewed and digested. Research reading—beyond the early exploratory reading—takes time and thought. The search for information and concepts demands concentration, determination, and time—much time.

Research reading demands the understanding of (1) words—look up in the dictionary ones you do not know; (2) phrases and sentences;

---

1. Francis Bacon, "Of Studies," in *Harvard Classics*, ed. Charles W. Eliot (New York: Colliers, 1909), 3:128.

(3) paragraphs—try summarizing the contents of each paragraph in one sentence; (4) the chapter—summarize each in a maximum of three sentences; and (5) the book—summarize it in one paragraph. Making these summaries, mentally or on paper, fixes the content in your mind.

Research reading begins with finding information about the author, possibly on the back cover or the dust jacket of the book. It continues with the title page and its verso, where there is information regarding the publisher and date of publication. After carefully examining the table of contents, you should examine the introduction, where you find information about the author's purpose, the recognized limitations of the work, and the audience for whom it is intended. Next, read—or at least browse—the concluding chapter, in which the author summarizes and draws conclusions. Only after all this work are you prepared to read the body of the book. By then, you may have decided to put the book aside as not useful to the study.

Here are some suggestions for successful reading:

1. Read in an appropriate place. You will need good light and ventilation. You need a place to write or type, for you will be taking notes. Find a quiet place without distractions. Be prepared with pencils, cards, and other materials—not least of which may be your computer—so you do not need to interrupt your study.

2. Read when you are most apt to be awake and alert. Some people do best in the morning; others at night. Find your own best time and use it well.

3. Alternate periods of study with moments of relaxation and physical exercise. Although some people can sit for hours, most tend to lose their power of concentration after an hour or so. Some scholars say they like to study hard for about fifty minutes, then get up for a drink and five minutes of exercise before returning to their desks. If you cannot sit still that long, build up your resistance by five minutes at a time. Start by forcing yourself to sit and concentrate for fifteen minutes. Eventually you will be able to endure an hour. To work efficiently, keep your body in top condition with proper rest, diet, and exercise.

4. Take notes of what you read. The intellectual exercise of putting information on paper or into your computer helps your brain absorb the materials you read. Only if you assimilate your reading can you organize, analyze, and synthesize it.

5. Do not wait until you feel like reading or studying. Make yourself a schedule and stick to it. Do not let yourself be distracted by other matters, interesting as they may be.

Evaluating Sources

You could read for years—in books, journals, or online—for there is much written on almost every topic. However, not all written materials are of the same value, even if they deal with the subject you are researching. Here are fourteen questions, the answers to which can help you weigh what you read.

1. Who is the author? Information about the author may be found on the back cover, on the dust jacket, or in the preface. You will find the author's qualifications and a list of other books she has written. Some libraries keep the dust jackets and other materials in a special author file; ask the librarian. If you cannot find information about an author, ask your professor, who knows most of the important people in his or her area. To find information about authors the following sources are helpful: *Who's Who in Religion*, which gives brief biographical data about living scholars, and the fourth volume of *Directory of American Scholars*, which lists scholars in the areas of religion and philosophy. Check the ATLA Index and WorldCat for items this person has written. Go online and consult Google Scholar. These sources will show you the author's areas of expertise, and what journals and publishers carry his or her work.

2. Who is the publisher? Not all publishers are equally serious. Some specialize in learned books; others publish popular works. Whether the book was published by a Protestant or Catholic publisher makes a difference, if you are interested in a certain approach to your topic. If a book was published by the author or has no imprint at all, it is appropriate to question whether a publisher was unwilling to take the manuscript. Or would the author have chosen to self-publish because the financial remuneration was better? Serious publishing companies are careful to have their imprint only on quality books. Ask the librarian or a professor about publishers.

3. If the source in question is an article, is the journal in which it appeared recognized as a specialized and serious journal? An article about an archaeological finding in *Time* is not worthy of as much confidence as one on the same finding in *Biblica* (from the Pontifical Biblical Institute in Rome) or *Biblical Archaeologist* (from the American Schools of Oriental Research). Somewhere between the two extremes would be an article in *Biblical Archaeology Review*, which admits its purpose is the popularization of biblical archaeology. Popular magazines, such as *Reader's Digest*, *Newsweek*, *Christian Woman*, or even the *National Geographic* are not usually good research sources—unless your

research is unique. You need to take the time to become acquainted with the specialized journals in your field.

4. What is the date of publication? If you are looking for a source that includes the latest research on a Hebrew-language problem, the date needs to be recent. A 1907 book may be useful to know what authors wrote then, but it will only be of value to the history of your problem. On the other hand, if the research concerns the history of Presbyterians in Korea, a book written in Korea in 1907 about Presbyterian mission activity would be valuable. The date that counts is that of the copyright or edition, not that of a printing, when no substantive changes are made to the book.

5. What is the author's purpose? Generally the introduction to a serious book will give the author's basic philosophy, the purpose for writing the book, the audience to which it is directed, and maybe even a hint on the conclusions reached. You can safely judge a serious book on the basis of its introduction (written by the author, not to be confused with a foreword or preface written by someone else). After reading the introduction to some books you may decide to drop them from the list of potential sources.

6. Is the style of writing popular or serious? This question is answered by reading a little here and there. If the answer is "popular," the source may not be valuable for serious study. That does not mean that research writing is all dry. It does mean that books written for entertainment may sacrifice content to readability. Items written with quoted conversations, colorful language, or abundant contractions are suspect.

7. Is there a bibliography? How extensive is it? Are there footnotes? Are they complete? The presence of these items indicates the writer has done a serious piece of work. Notes and bibliography show that the author took the time to look at other people's work and was honest enough to note what was borrowed.

8. Are there tables? Graphs? Maps? Not all sources need these items, but a book that contains well-made graphs and tables, together with the source and date for the information presented in them, usually can be considered a serious work. A map can say something about the book: If it is sloppily made, or a copy from a lesser atlas, it may indicate carelessness. On the other hand, pictures in a book—unless the topic is archaeology or something of that sort—do not enhance the research value of a source.

9. Is the table of contents detailed? Is there an index? Much information may be obtained by reading the table of contents. A very sketchy

one may suggest lack of precision and care for detail — unforgivable flaws in research. In modern English-language books, the index is often a mark of a good research source. The same cannot be said for other languages. Certainly, an index facilitates research and is to be considered a plus.

10. In the footnotes and bibliography, are the works recent and the authors specialists in their fields? Sometimes a fairly recent work quotes rather old sources. This would indicate that the research was done some time ago and the author did not take the trouble to update the material. If authors quoted or consulted are not specialists, it is fair to wonder if the writer knew who the specialists in the field were.

11. What is the tone of the writing? Is it sober and objective? Or is it emotional? How are adjectives and adverbs used? Are epithets applied to people? Some authors are not able to convince their readers by the information they give or by their logic, so they use emotional phrases that appeal more to the heart than the mind. When the language is strong, the content may be weak. If an author needs to tear down an opponent in order to build up his or her work, there is a problem. The best research sources are clearly written, in an objective style.

12. Is the style of writing clear and easy to read? Is the phrasing concise? Is the vocabulary as simple as the topic will permit? There is no virtue in using long sentences and unnecessarily difficult words; in fact, such writing may suggest the author is hiding ignorance behind fancy language. Good research writing is simple and straightforward.

13. Has this source been translated from another language? How many editions has it had? An item translated from another language has been considered important enough to receive wider dissemination. A book that has been reedited has evidently been deemed significant. Thus, a positive answer to both questions suggests a good research source. One additional suggestion: In choosing between the original and the translation — if you can read both — choose the original.

14. Is this a primary source? A primary source on Vatican Council II would be the documents put out by the council. A secondary source would be a book that comments or interprets those documents. In the secondary source the author can interject his or her ideas and thus color the reader's understanding of the original. Likewise, what the Latter-day Saints say about themselves is a primary document;

what someone else says about them is secondary and is liable to bias or distortion. Using primary sources minimizes the danger of mis-interpretation.

Asking these questions is literary criticism. It is not finding fault with authors, but deciding which works are most trustworthy and appropriate for your research. Mistakes in judging can happen, but experience sharpens your skills and makes the process easier. These queries are similar to those answered in a book review. Although the critical review of books or articles is not usually considered research, such work demands critical thinking and good writing. Critical reviews of books and journal articles are dealt with in chapter 18.

Taking Good Notes

The making of bibliographic notes has already been discussed in chapter 6. Notes considered here are those we take to remember what we read. These notes must be complete and painstakingly detailed. Time spent taking proper notes is time saved in the total process. There is no way to do good research without taking good notes, either manually or on a computer.

A Method for Manual Notetaking

Notes for research can be taken in a notebook or on large sheets of paper. However, the most effective method uses note cards or slips of paper. These slips or cards are easy to organize; they can be arranged and rearranged to suit changes in outline or approach. Cards may be added or deleted without affecting the total scheme. Finally, when put in order, they almost write the paper by themselves.

Note Cards

All the cards should be of the same size, usually 3 by 5 or 4 by 6 inches. Typing paper cut in four equal parts may also be used. Some researchers prefer a larger card, but the small one is a reminder of a basic rule of note-taking: only one item on a card. Since bibliography cards are used at the same time as note cards, it is helpful to use a different type or color of paper, or slips of a slightly different size so the two kinds are not confused.

Filing System

Before beginning to read and take notes, prepare one card—a little larger, stiffer, and of a different color than the note cards—for each of the sections of the paper, as envisioned in the tentative outline. These index cards are labeled to serve as dividers for a simple filing system. Rubber bands or elastics may be used to keep each packet of notes together, or a small box may be used as a file cabinet. As you read you will certainly add and modify headings.

As you do your reading, take notes as needed. At the end of your reading session, put your notes in the appropriate section of your file. This system is simple, yet effective.

Parts of the Note Card

Each note card has three indispensable parts: (1) heading, (2) text, and (3) source. Notes may be written in ink or pencil; the first looks messy when corrections are made, but the second tends to dim with time and use. Some library research rooms only allow the use of pencils; in that case, pencil will have to do.

Heading

The headings on the cards correspond to sections of the paper. A paper on the history of Nestorianism in China would include a section on Rabban Sauma. Thus, one heading would be RABBAN SAUMA. There would also be several subheadings under the main heading: biographical data, relation with Rabban Mark, travels in Europe, return to Mongolia, and so on. Sub-subheadings may also be used. As you review your cards, especially if you change your outline, you may need to revise your headings. For starters, however, give the information a place where it can belong.

Headings on the note cards may be written in a different color; however, changing pens every few minutes may be a nuisance. Whatever the color, write clearly. The heading must always be located in the same place on the note card. The upper right corner is quite handy.

Text

The text of a note card may be a direct quotation, a summary of what has been read, or the researcher's reaction to the reading.

Direct quotations. A quotation card must say exactly what the source said. No spelling or punctuation differences are allowed. Even if there is an evident error, it must be copied. But immediately following the error, place the bracketed word [sic], which is the Latin for "thus" and means that, right or wrong, this was what appeared in the source. If you omit anything the author wrote, use ellipsis marks. For an omission within a sentence, three double-spaced dots (...) are used. If the omission includes a break between sentences, four dots are used (....). If the quoted sentences or phrases are from two different paragraphs, ellipsis marks are not permitted; you must record two quotations. If a quotation comes from two pages (80, 81), mark the page break // on your note, so that if you use only part of the quotation, you can tell whether it is from page 80 or 81. Put quotation marks around all quoted material.

Summaries. It is not always necessary to copy an author's actual words. A summary or synthesis may be sufficient. However, when you do this, be careful not to change the sense or thrust of the author's thought. Make sure that summary cards tell you they are summaries, not quotations.

Comments. I can easily forget my reactions to a certain reading. Thus I need to jot down my comments and impressions. These may be notes on the reading, ideas about possible sources, or suggested modifications to any part of the paper. They may be doubts or questions, sometimes only tangentially related to the topic. However, I need to write them down and give them a heading—possibly that of the item that triggered them—so that later I can retrieve my brilliant ideas. A date on the comment card can help me reconstruct my intellectual pilgrimage. I initial these cards to identify them as comments or queries.

Source

Each note card must record the source from which the material was quoted or summarized. The page(s) and the author's last name are usually enough, except when you are using two books by the same author or items whose authors have the same last name. In the first case, an abbreviated form of the title must be used: Bruce, *Acts*, 24. In the second case, an initial with the surname is enough: L. Smith, 78.

Computer Notetaking

Those of us who are computer addicts cannot write any other way. Taking notes on the computer not only saves time but ensures accuracy and readability. Whether I take a laptop to the library or bring the books to my desk, I can easily take notes on the computer. The problem is sorting the cards. Let me share instructions for a hybrid system that works well for a visual person like me.

1. Make your page margins as small as the printer will allow; then subdivide your page (either letter or A4 size) into 4 or 6 pages. Number your subpages in small font (bottom center).
2. Take notes as described in the manual system. Be sure to put in appropriate headings and subheadings. Do not forget to write down the source. If you have a two-page note, be sure to indicate the number of the first page on the second one so you can put them together (something like "follows 35").

3. Use two files simultaneously—one for bib cards, one for content notes. Make an alphabetical listing of bib entries on one; take notes on the other file. Save often.

4. Print out your note cards, cut the pages up, and sort as you would manually. You will be able to see what you are doing and arrange and rearrange your piles.

5. When you input your paper into the computer, using your piles of notes, have three files open. One has the bibliography (from which you will take the sources for your footnotes); another holds the notes; the third, the developing paper. When you come to a quotation, simply paste it in place from the note file, without retyping it. Cut and paste bibliographical information from the bib file (remembering, of course, to change bibliography form into footnote form).

This up-to-date technological information comes from Terry Robertson, Seminary Librarian, at Andrews University. It is much clearer than what I could write:

> A couple of electronic tools that can be used to emulate the traditional card system for managing notes include database software such as *Microsoft Access*, or a spreadsheet such as *Excel*. With these tools, you will be able to efficiently sort the entries, search the entries for keywords, and copy and paste entries into the paper. If the original source is in electronic form, then it is even possible to copy and paste text into the database.
>
> *Microsoft Access* has a couple of advantages. The memo field can contain more material and there is less risk of loss of data should the computer suddenly quit. Sorting is also less prone to error than with *Excel*.
>
> However, *Excel* is more readily available, is generally easier to set up and use, and has an auto-fill feature that is nice. It is important to remember to save work often; before sorting, be sure to have a backup copy. For short projects, *Excel* is more than adequate, though for longer projects such as a dissertation, *Access* is more stable, less prone to accidental corruption, and has significant advantages in terms of space for content and sorting options.[2]

Useful Advice

The most useful note card is the short one, which contains only one idea, one reference, or one precise piece of information. It is written only on one side of the card or slip. The note system just described—whether manual or computerized—is efficient precisely because any card or slip may be moved without disturbing the whole. When there is only one idea on a card, moving it is simple. If two ideas are copied on one card, organization may later

---

2. Terry Robertson, email message, November 20, 2006.

demand they be separated—which will require recopying. Obviously, when only one idea is written on each card, there will be many cards, but the ease of organization makes up for having to deal with many cards. Model note cards are shown beginning on the next page.

When to quote and when to summarize? When dealing with ideas, you can summarize, but always take care not to distort the meaning or emphasis of the original. When an author expresses an idea with lucidity or in picturesque words, better than any other way to express that idea, you probably should quote. In any case, when in doubt, copy the actual quotation. Later you can decide whether to quote or to summarize. You will be happy to have the full information when you are writing your paper late the night before it is due.

The system of taking notes described in this chapter may be new to some students—and even to some professors guiding research. However, there is little doubt that it works well. The first attempt may take some time, but the ease and precision gained should make the time spent worthwhile. By using this system conscientiously, you will avoid returning to the source once you have done your reading.

Finish all your reading on a given topic (or section of your topic) and sort your notes before sitting down to write. This will give you a full picture of your topic. It will also allow you to write seamless prose, blending different authors into their correct position in your writing.

In sum, here are ten specific tips for better notetaking:

1. Use cards or slips of paper of uniform size; do this manually or on the computer. Make heading cards for each section of the paper and keep slips organized, in a box or using rubber bands.
2. Write clearly (or type) on one side only.
3. Put only one idea, one thought, one piece of information on each card to facilitate the organization of the paper.
4. Make short notes (remember number 3), but if you do need a second card, clearly indicate that it is a second card of a set.
5. Put a heading and a subheading (and even a sub-subheading) on each card.
6. Indicate clearly (yet in abbreviated form) the source of information.
7. Indicate clearly whether you have quoted or summarized. Be consistent in your system.
8. Summarize as often as possible; only quote when the author's words are impossible to improve on.
9. When quoting, copy material exactly as it appears. Use ellipsis marks for omission. Use [sic] to show the error is copied from the original.

10. Make your notes so clear and understandable that anyone else could take over your incomplete work.

This chapter has discussed reading, evaluating sources, and taking the notes. These notes will be the building blocks of the paper. They will also supply the information you need for preparing footnotes, which are presented in chapter 9.

Sample Note Cards

These samples illustrate what has been explained. Use your own creativity— always within an organized system—to produce useful note cards for your paper.

```
Codices—Earliest Christian—Egypt

    The existence of Christian codices in Egypt
"was historically plausible if not downright
necessary." There are no historical or technical
arguments against their existence.

    Tiede, 7
```

R. Sauma—Report on Mongols

Asked by the cardinals in Rome about his religion, Sauma said: "Know ye, O our Fathers, that many of our Fathers have gone into the countries of the Mongols, and Turks, and Chinese and have taught them the Gospel, and at the present time there are many Mongols who are Christians. For many of the sons of the Mongol kings and queens have been baptized and confess Christ. And they have established churches in their military campus and they pay honour to the Christians, and there are many among them who are believers."

Budge, 174.

chapter 9

FOOTNOTES: WHY, WHEN, AND HOW

Student researchers are often in doubt concerning whether or not they should footnote a given item. Once they have decided they should, they wonder how to do it. This chapter seeks to elucidate both aspects of the problematic footnote. A comparison of footnotes and bibliographical entries appears in chapter 10.

One should really speak of *notes*, for this term includes content and reference notes, whether they are located at the bottom of the page (footnotes) or at the end of a chapter (endnotes). Endnotes are considered appropriate for short papers and are always numbered consecutively through the chapter or paper. Footnotes are normally required in theses and dissertations; they can be numbered consecutively through the chapter (as in this book) or page by page.

Why Footnotes?

At times, writers employ footnotes to impress the reader by using foreign languages and difficult words. Some footnotes seem to convey false modesty: "I don't want to parade my learning, but I've read a lot of books." Some seem to be trying to sell: "See my book on this topic." Others suggest the writer had a piece of information that did not fit in anywhere and put it in the footnote in order to get it in somehow. At times footnotes are used to show snobbery: "In an interview with the author, the celebrated artist XX said." A "see above" note may suggest the reader has a very poor memory or is not intelligent enough to look for herself. And finally, "there is the flattery footnote: 'The reader will naturally recall. . . .' (And if the reader does remember, he is pleased; if he does not, he is happy the author thought he might.)"[1] These uses are not appropriate for research and should be avoided.

There are, however, legitimate uses for footnotes. Reference notes (collectively called documentation; designated as footnotes if placed at the bottom of a page, or as endnotes at the end of a chapter or paper) are provided to show where information was obtained. They serve a triple purpose: (1) to indicate that there is authority behind statements made, in order to strengthen the researcher's assertions; (2) to help the scholar who is looking for information on the topic to easily find the material referred to; (3) to honestly admit intellectual indebtedness to another author.

Content notes provide information that could disrupt or unnecessarily complicate the text. The content footnote may point out a contrast or discrepancy, give further explanations, or indicate sources for further study. These notes are more usual in theses and dissertations than in short research papers. You may also find them in research articles. They are also more varied in style than reference notes. Since many readers do not read footnotes, the text should make sense without the content footnotes. Obviously, if a content note quotes or cites, it must give a source.

When to Footnote

Content notes are used at the discretion of the writer — any time the addition of a note would enrich or enhance the elaboration of ideas. Reference notes are used whenever materials from another author are cited or quoted.

A reference note is used to indicate the source of a quotation — whether it be three words or three lines. It is also used to show the source of an idea, even though that idea may be expressed in the researcher's own words. Failure to use quotation marks for quoted materials or give due credit to a source by using a reference note is considered a major flaw in research. Plagiarism, as such illegitimate copying is called, is considered a dishonest use of another's property — intellectual thievery. Therefore, a writer must give references for all quoted or cited words or ideas, and remember to use quotation marks for every borrowed phrase or sentence.

No footnotes are needed when the ideas and words in the paper are yours or are common knowledge. But if you present a paper with no footnotes, your

---

1. Taken from Carter V. Good, *Essentials of Educational Research* (New York: Appleton Century-Crofts, 1966), 401.

reader would surmise that you did everything by yourself, that you are not indebted to anyone. Such a paper would contain only your opinions or be superficial, consisting exclusively of general knowledge; it would not qualify as research. Of course, facts that everyone knows—such as A.D. 79 for the eruption of Mount Vesuvius—need no footnote. For an idea or a piece of information to qualify as common knowledge, it must appear in several places. But if eighteen authors say one thing and two say something different, you will want to note the dissenters in a footnote.

How to Footnote

Footnotes come in two main kinds: content notes and reference notes. At times the two elements are combined, producing a content note with its references.

Content Footnotes

The purpose of content footnotes is to provide additional information to the reader. This added information is interesting, shows you have read and researched extensively, but is not indispensable to understanding the paper. In any case, you must give the source for these words of wisdom.

Doctoral dissertations often have extensive content notes—almost as many pages of notes as of text. Given the varieties of structure and form of content notes, what is asked of them is that they be clear, logical, and as short as possible. Usually these notes are only read by the professor and a few specialists. Make sure the basic material you want read is in the text.

To make the reading of content notes easier, put the reference in correct format *after* the information. For example:

1. J. I. Packer identifies different explanations of what Christ's death achieved. The first focuses on the subjective effect of the cross on humans while the second focuses on the "satisfaction" for human sins ("What Did the Cross Achieve?" *Tyndale Bulletin* 25 [1974]: 19–25).

Notice that the reference appears in parentheses at the end of the comment, and the parentheses in the reference become square brackets. If this were the second reference to Packer's work, the reference would follow the short form: ("What Did the Cross Achieve?" 19–25). Packer is not named again because the note is short. If there were any possibility of confusion, put his name in again. Remember that the reference follows the comments.

Another example:

2. On this topic, see also Joel Musvosvi's affirmation that "John's use of the OT is not haphazard or coincidental" ("The Issue of Genre and Apocalyptic Prophecy," *Asia Adventist Seminary Studies* 5 [2002]: 55–56).

A few schools may require a different format, which uses a period following the comment and allows the reference to remain exactly as required of a reference note.

1. J. I. Packer identifies different explanations of what Christ's death achieved. The first focuses on the subjective effect of the cross on humans while the second focuses on the "satisfaction" for human sins. "What Did the Cross Achieve?" *Tyndale Bulletin* 25 (1974): 19–25.

In either case, use the same format throughout the paper. Changing from one to another will confuse the reader and infuriate the dissertation secretary.

Reference Notes

Since the purpose of a reference note is to permit a reader to find the original source, you must provide sufficient information to make locating it easy. Using a uniform format helps the reader and impresses your professor.

In the text, the footnote appears only as a superscript Arabic number at the end of the quotation, citation, or allusion. This number refers the reader to the footnote below the text (notice this location!), at the bottom of the page. Traditionally, the number in the text and the one in the footnote were superscript. Today, the new style is that of this book: the number at the beginning of the footnote is full size and followed by a period and one space. To make your footnotes look like the ones in this book—the right way according to Turabian and *The Chicago Manual of Style*—you will need to modify your word processing defaults. Open Office and WordPerfect™ require little expertise to make the changes. For Microsoft Word™ you will need to create a macro.[2] If I could do it, I am sure you can!

In reference notes, abbreviations are commonly used. Be sure to use them consistently. In current usage, the abbreviation for page or pages is omitted. In indicating pages, 2–4 means pages 2 through 4, including page 3; using 2, 4 means only pages 2 and 4. The publication data are in parentheses, and the only full stop is the final one.

---

2. Instructions to make the number in a footnote full size rather than superscript, and followed by a period and a space are available at http://word.mvps.org/FAQs/MacrosVBA/UnSuperscptFnotes.htm.

Full Reference Notes

The following are examples of full reference notes, given the first time an item is mentioned. They are the basic models: a book, a journal article, a magazine article, a chapter in a multi-author book, a thesis, and a signed dictionary article. Use the bibliographical entry as the basis for your footnote (chapter 6). Chapter 10 shows the relation between bibliography and footnote formats.

Book

Author's name in normal order, book title in italics with first and last and all important words capitalized, publication data in parentheses, page (or pages) used at the end of the note. For a city that may not be well known, you must give the state or the country. The state may be written in full (Massachusetts), abbreviated (Mass.), or identified by postal code (MA). Another choice shows in my use of Hendrickson for Hendrickson Publishers. If I use a short form for one publisher, I must use the short form of all other publishers: Zondervan, Orbis, Baker.

As you would expect, there are exceptions to the rule. The names of university presses cannot be shortened: University of Chicago Press, Andrews University Press. In addition, if clarity demands, use the full name of the publisher. Using Moody Press distinguishes between the publisher and Moody Bible College; using InterVarsity Press distinguishes between the publisher and Intervarsity Christian Fellowship.

3. Gordon D. Fee, *Gospel and Spirit: Issues in New Testament Hermeneutics* (Peabody, MA: Hendrickson, 1991), 14–16.

Journal article

Title of article in quotation marks (in English, commas usually go *within* the quotation marks!), title of journal in italics, no comma before or after volume number, date of issue in parentheses, colon, one space, page number. If paging is continuous in each volume (as in the first example), the year is enough. If paging is not continuous, month or season should be given, as in the second example.

4. Stephen Thompson, "The End of Satan," *Andrews University Seminary Studies* 37 (1999): 257–261.

5. Keith A. Russell, "Resurrection," *Living Pulpit* 14 (April–June 2005): 1–40.

Magazine article

Do not give volume number; the date is enough. The date may be expressed in traditional American style, as here, or in library or European style: 24 April 2000. Use one style or the other, but do so consistently.

6. Loren Wilkinson, "Saving Celtic Christianity," *Christianity Today,* April 24, 2000, 80.

Chapter in a multiauthor book

Note the "in," showing that the material to which you refer is a *part* of a book. Note also the editor *after* the title of the book. Here "ed." means "edited by"; it is not pluralized. Since this is a note, you can use "and others" or "*et al.*" for the three other editors. In the bibliography, you need to give all the names.

7. Dana L. Robert, "Adoniram Judson Gordon, 1836–1895," in *Mission Legacies: Biographical Studies of Leaders of the Modern Missionary Movement*, ed. Gerald Anderson and others (Maryknoll, NY: Orbis, 1994), 23.

Dissertation

A dissertation is not considered a published book; its title is presented in quotation marks. The specific degree, the university, and date are in parentheses. If the institution is not well known, its location is given.

8. Trust Ndlovu, "The Church as an Agent of Reconciliation in the Thought of Desmond Tutu" (Ph.D. dissertation, Andrews University, Berrien Springs, MI, 1999), 57.

Signed dictionary article

Start with the author of the article. Then give the name of the article in quotation marks, followed by the dictionary or encyclopedia (in italics), the editors, publication data in parentheses, and exact location of the quotation (here, volume 1, page 165). In this example, I have used the Hebrew letters; you may also transliterate (see appendix B). By placing the abbreviation for the title in parentheses, I can use it for a later reference to the same book.

9. Sverre Aalen, "אוּר,"*Theological Dictionary of the Old Testament* (*TDOT*), ed. G. Johannes Botterweck and Helmer Ringren (Grand Rapids: Eerdmans, 1974), 1:165.

A footnote (or endnote) differs from a bibliographical entry in three main ways: (1) The author's name is in normal order, (2) publication data appear in parentheses, and (3) there is usually only one period in the entire note (at the end).

Second or Later References

If reference is made to the same source more than once, consecutively, the references immediately following use "ibid." (for the Latin *ibidem*, "in the same place"). If the same page is quoted, ibid. is enough. If a different page is used, the note will read: Ibid., 3. Here the word is capped at the beginning of a note; otherwise it is in lowercase. Use Ibid. only after a note that reports one source. Also, your reader will thank you for using an abbreviated reference rather than "Ibid." as the first note of a new page.

If reference is made to the same source more than once, but not consecutively, the second time the author's surname is given, together with an abbreviated version of the title and the page number. However, if there are two authors by the same surname, distinction must be made by using at least an initial. When citing a source that will be used repeatedly—especially if the title is long—give the abbreviation in parentheses after the title the first time the work is cited. Thereafter, use only the abbreviation.

10. Laird R. Harris, Gleason L. Archer, and Bruce K. Waltke, *Theological Wordbook of the Old Testament* (*TWOT*), 2 vols. (Chicago: Moody Press, 1980), 1:103.
11. *TWOT*, 1:157.

If two or more items by one author appear following each other in the same note, the second time, the author's name may be replaced by the word "idem" (not italicized), Latin for "the same." For example:

12. Turabian, *A Manual*, 46; idem, *Student's Guide*, 68.

When using a typewriter (heaven forbid!), two or more short footnotes may be typed on the same line, with a minimum of six spaces between them. A note beginning on a line with two entries may not continue on a second line. This is for typing only; word-processing programs do not allow this. Automatic footnoting is well worth this limitation.

The following sequence of footnotes illustrates:

13. Richard N. Soulen, *Handbook of Biblical Criticism* (Atlanta: John Knox, 1976), 24.
14. Ibid.
15. William D. Mounce, *Basics of Biblical Greek: Grammar*, 2nd ed. (Grand Rapids: Zondervan, 2003), 201.
16. Soulen, *Handbook*, 28.
17. William D. Mounce, *The Morphology of Biblical Greek* (Grand Rapids: Zondervan, 1994), 302.
18. Walter C. Kaiser Jr., "What Commentaries Can (and Can't) Do," *Christianity Today*, October 2, 1981, 26.
19. Mounce, *Basics*, 52.
20. Otto Kaiser, "David und Jonathan: Tradition, Redaktion und Geschichte in I Sam 16–20: Ein Versuch," *Ephemerides theologicae lovanienses* 66 (1990): 291.
21. W. Kaiser, "What Commentaries," 24.
22. Ibid., 27.

Bible References

In a research paper on a nonbiblical topic, biblical references will probably appear as footnotes or endnotes. However, in papers dealing with ministry, biblical studies, or theology, Bible references are commonly placed in parentheses directly in the text. In English it has been accepted practice that no version is indicated when one uses the King James Version (KJV). Any version other than the KJV must be indicated. This is usually done in a footnote the first time the Bible is used (see next examples).

23. Unless otherwise indicated, all Bible references in this paper are to the New American Standard Bible (NASB) (La Habra, CA: The Lockman Foundation, 1973).

24. All Greek references are from *The Greek New Testament*, 4th ed. rev. ed. (Stuttgart: United Bible Societies, 1993).

Although you could use several versions in one paper, this practice is frowned on. When you write a serious research paper, choose one version of the Bible and use it continuously throughout. Jumping from one version to another, choosing the wording that suits your purposes, suggests that you are trying to make the Bible say what you want it to say.

In modern academic usage the abbreviations of the books of the Bible are not followed by periods. The list of appropriate abbreviations is given below.[3]

Gen	1 Kgs	Prov	Amos	Matt	Phil	1 Pet
Exod	2 Kgs	Eccl	Obad	Mark	Col	2 Pet
Lev	1 Chr	Song	Jonah	Luke	1 Thess	1 John
Num	2 Chr	Isa	Mic	John	2 Thess	2 John
Deut	Ezra	Jer	Nah	Acts	1 Tim	3 John
Josh	Neh	Lam	Hab	Rom	2 Tim	Jude
Judg	Esth	Ezek	Zeph	1 Cor	Titus	Rev
Ruth	Job	Dan	Hag	2 Cor	Phlm	
1 Sam	Ps	Hos	Zech	Gal	Heb	
2 Sam	(Pss)	Joel	Mal	Eph	Jas	

Appropriate abbreviations for the Apocrypha are as follows:

Tob	Add Dan	3 Macc
Jdt	Pr Azar	4 Macc
Add Esth	Song of Three	1 Esd
Wis	Sus	2 Esd
Sir	Bel	Pr Man
Bar	1 Macc	
Ep Jer	2 Macc	

3. This list was taken from *The SBL Handbook of Style* , 8.3.2. Except for the absence of periods, the abbreviations are identical to *The Chicago Manual of Style* (15th ed.), 15.51–53. Turabian (7th ed.) uses a shorter form (24.6.1–3). Be sure to follow the rules of your school.

This chapter has given the rationale for the use of reference notes and the basic guidelines for their format. Chapter 10 presents examples of reference notes (footnotes) and bibliographical entries for different—and difficult—types of materials.

Additional American Citation Styles

APA

APA stands for American Psychological Association. Its citation style calls for in-text notes and a reference list. If your school uses the in-text citation method advocated by the American Psychological Association, see appendix A.

SBL

The Society of Biblical Literature has developed a style for use in its own publications. Some schools use this style for papers in biblical studies and archaeology. If your school uses the SBL style, please refer to *The SBL Handbook of Style* (Peabody, MA: Hendrickson, 1999). You will find a "Student Supplement," dated 2004, online at http://sbl-site.org/assets/pdfs/SBLHS_SS92804_Revised_ed.pdf (accessed May 5, 2008).

Turabian In-Text Citations

Turabian offers an alternative to the footnote style advocated in this book. It uses in-text citations, but does not work the same as APA. This style is not common in American educational institutions. However, if your school uses it, you will find it clearly explained in chapters 18 and 19 of Turabian's seventh edition (2007).

chapter 10

REFERENCE NOTES AND BIBLIOGRAPHICAL ENTRIES COMPARED

Reference notes and bibliographical entries are similar, yet different. This chapter compares the two. The format of the entries presented here—including spaces, indentation, and punctuation—is proper Turabian academic paper style and should be carefully followed. Underlining is now passé; use italics instead. In any case, do not mix the two: either one or the other. If you use the APA style, see appendix A.

In preparing notes and bibliographical entries that do not seem to fit into any category, follow the rules as closely as possible, using common sense to make modifications as needed. References should make it easy for a reader to locate any source. Refer to chapters 6 and 9 for more details on bibliography and note format. For further information, consult Turabian, *The Chicago Manual of Style*, and *The SBL Handbook of Style*.[1]

The examples use the following abbreviations:

N (for Note) shows the format of a full reference note.
B (for Bibliography) gives the format for a common, uncomplicated
    bibliographical entry.

---

1. Kate L. Turabian, *A Manual for Writers of Term Papers, Theses, and Dissertations*, 7th ed., rev. Wayne C. Booth, Gregory G. Colomb, Joseph M Williams, and the University of Chicago Press Editorial Staff (Chicago: University of Chicago Press, 2007). Turabian agrees with *The Chicago Manual of Style*, 15th ed. (Chicago: University of Chicago Press, 2003). For ancient Near Eastern, biblical, and early Christian studies, you will find additional information in *The SBL Handbook of Style*, ed. Patrick H. Alexander and others (Peabody, MA: Hendrickson, 2007). The main difference between SBL and Turabian styles is that SBL puts editors, translators, and series within the parentheses around the publication data (*SBL Handbook of Style*, 48–51).

BP (for Bibliography Partial) indicates the format to use when only a part of the source has been consulted.

BA (for Bibliography All) indicates the format to use for the whole source (in contrast with BP).

Published Materials

Published materials include books (specialized and general), pamphlets, and periodicals (journals and magazines). Facts of publication must be given in full form in the first reference. For the format of second references, see chapter 9.

Abbreviations can be used for often-repeated titles or series. If there are only a few, give the abbreviation the first time the item is mentioned. If you use many abbreviations, put a list of them in the paper or thesis, usually between the introduction and first chapter (see appendix C for a list of accepted abbreviations). Abbreviations may be used in the notes, but not in the bibliography. When the abbreviations stand for a book or journal, they should be italicized.

General Books

Under this heading, several issues are addressed. First, and most abundant, are those related to authorship. Next come examples of how to handle multivolume works. Finally, you will find entries showing how to deal with series, reprints, and secondary sources.

Authorship

One author

N   1. Lewis Drummond, *Miss Bertha: Woman of Revival* (Nashville: Broadman & Holman, 1996), 151.

B   Drummond, Lewis. *Miss Bertha: Woman of Revival*. Nashville: Broadman & Holman, 1996.

Two or three authors

N   2. Bruce Malina and Jerome H. Neyrey, *Portraits of Paul: An Archaeology of Ancient Personality* (Louisville, KY: John Knox, 1996), 134.

B   Malina, Bruce, and Jerome H. Neyrey. *Portraits of Paul: An Archaeology of Ancient Personality*. Louisville, KY: John Knox, 1996.

More than three authors

N 3. Willem A. VanGemeren and others, *The Law, the Gospel, and the Modern Christian* (Grand Rapids: Zondervan, 1993), 78.

B VanGemeren, Willem A., Greg L. Bahnsen, Walter C. Kaiser Jr., Wayne G. Strickland, and Douglas Moo. *The Law, the Gospel, and the Modern Christian.* Grand Rapids: Zondervan, 1993.

Corporate author

N 4. Southern Baptist Convention, *Annual of the Southern Baptist Convention* (Nashville: Southern Baptist Convention, 1975), 25.

B Southern Baptist Convention. *Annual of the Southern Baptist Convention.* Nashville: Southern Baptist Convention, 1975.

No author, edition other than first, with translator

N 5. *Bhagavad-Gita as It Is,* abr. ed., trans. A. C. Bhaktivedanta Swami Prabhupada (New York: Bhaktivedanta Book Trust, 1972), 74.

B *Bhagavad-Gita as It Is.* Abridged edition. Translated by A. C. Bhaktivedanta Swami Prabhupada. New York: Bhaktivedanta Book Trust, 1972.

Editor instead of author; joint publication

N 6. James C. VanderKam and William Adler, eds., *The Jewish Apocalyptic Heritage in Early Christianity* (Assen, Netherlands: Van Gorcum; Minneapolis: Fortress, 1996), 35.

B VanderKam, James C., and William Adler, eds. *The Jewish Apocalyptic Heritage in Early Christianity.* Assen, Netherlands: Van Gorcum; Minneapolis: Fortress, 1996.

Component part by one author in a work edited by another

N 7. Richard M. Davidson, "Headship, Submission, and Equality in Scripture," in *Women in Ministry: Biblical and Historical Perspectives*, ed. Nancy Vyhmeister (Berrien Springs, MI: Andrews University Press, 1998), 266.

B Davidson, Richard M. "Headship, Submission, and Equality in Scripture." In *Women in Ministry: Biblical and Historical Perspectives,* ed. Nancy Vyhmeister, 259–295. Berrien Springs, MI: Andrews University Press, 1998.

Multivolume Works

Here are examples of several different types—from simple to complex:

N 8. Justo González, *A History of Christian Thought*, 3 vols. (Nashville: Abingdon, 1970–1975), 1:176.

B González, Justo. *A History of Christian Thought.* 3 vols. Nashville: Abingdon, 1970–1975.

Multivolume work — one author, different titles

N   9. Kenneth Scott Latourette, *A History of the Expansion of Christianity*, vol. 3, *Three Centuries of Advance* (Grand Rapids: Zondervan, 1970), 17.

BA Latourette, Kenneth Scott. *A History of the Expansion of Christianity*. 7 vols. Grand Rapids: Zondervan, 1970.

BP Latourette, Kenneth Scott. A *History of the Expansion of Christianity*. Vol. 3, *Three Centuries of Advance*. Grand Rapids: Zondervan, 1970.

Multivolume work — several authors

N   10. Bruce W. Winter, gen. ed., *The Book of Acts in Its First Century Setting*, 6 vols. (Carlisle, UK: Paternoster, 1994), vol. 3, *The Book of Acts and Paul in Roman Custody*, by Brian Rapske, 38.

B   Winter, Bruce W., gen. ed. *The Book of Acts in Its First Century Setting*. 6 vols. Carlisle, UK: Paternoster, 1994. Vol. 3, *The Book of Acts and Paul in Roman Custody*, by Brian Rapske.

If for some reason the author of the book you are citing or quoting is more important than the multivolume source, you may use the following format:

N   10. Brian Rapske, *The Book of Acts and Paul in Roman Custody*, vol. 3, *The Book of Acts in Its First Century Setting*, ed. Bruce W. Winter (Carlisle, UK: Paternoster, 1994), 38.

B   Rapske, Brian. *The Book of Acts and Paul in Roman Custody*. Vol. 3, *The Book of Acts in Its First Century Setting*, ed. Bruce W. Winter. Carlisle, UK: Paternoster, 1994.

Part of a Series

N   11. Wayne C. Booth, Gregory G. Colomb, and Joseph M. Williams, *The Craft of Research*, Chicago Guides to Writing, Editing, and Publishing (Chicago: University of Chicago Press, 1995), 155.

B   Booth, Wayne C., Gregory G. Colomb, and Joseph M. Williams. *The Craft of Research*. Chicago Guides to Writing, Editing, and Publishing. Chicago: University of Chicago Press, 1995.

Reprint

N   12. John L. Nevius, *Demon Possession* (New York: Fleming H. Revell, 1894; reprint, Grand Rapids: Kregel, 1968), 274, 275.

B   Nevius, John L. *Demon Possession*. New York: Fleming H. Revell, 1894; reprint, Grand Rapids: Kregel, 1968.

N   13. H. R. Reynolds, "Introduction to the Gospel of St. John," in *The Pulpit Commentary*, ed. H. O. M. Spense and Joseph S. Excell (Grand Rapids: Eerdmans, reprint 1977), 17:v.

B   Reynolds, H. R. "Introduction to the Gospel of St. John." In *The Pulpit Commentary*, ed. H. O. M. Spense and Joseph S. Excell, 17:iv-clxi. Grand Rapids: Eerdmans, reprint 1977.

Secondary Source

The lack of punctuation between author and title is a tradition of the fathers! Some use a comma or a period.

N   14. Pontius the Deacon *The Life and Passion of Cyprian, Bishop and Martyr* 1.3, quoted in Roger E. Olson, *The Story of Christian Theology* (Downers Grove, IL: Inter-Varsity Press, 1999), 116.

B   Pontius the Deacon *The Life and Passion of Cyprian, Bishop and Martyr* 1.3. Quoted in Roger E. Olson, *The Story of Christian Theology*, 116. Downers Grove, IL: InterVarsity Press, 1999.

Periodicals

Magazines

N   15. Michael D. Lemonick and Andrea Dorfman, "The Amazing Vikings," *Time*, May 8, 2000, 70.

B   Lemonick, Michael D., and Andrea Dorfman. "The Amazing Vikings." *Time*, May 8, 2000, 69–74.

Journals

N   16. David Shank, "Mission Relations with Independent Churches in Africa," *Missiology* 13 (1985): 27.

B   Shank, David. "Mission Relations with Independent Churches in Africa." *Missiology* 13 (1985): 23–44.

If the pagination of a periodical is successive throughout the different issues of the volume (as in *Missiology*), use only the year. If pagination begins with each issue, use a month or season. When no month or season is given for a journal that begins each issue with page 1, give the number of the issue with the volume: *Newsletter* 4, no. 1 (1980): 9. Use Arabic numerals for volume numbers.

Specialized Books

Classical Authors and Church Fathers

Generally it is enough to give the author, title, book, and section of a work of one of the classical authors or of a church father. Whatever the edition, these works, somewhat like the Bible, are always divided the same way. However, it is a courtesy to the reader to give the place where you found the work. In footnoting, Chicago style omits the comma between author and title of the work; SBL style uses it. Your advisor may have an opinion; follow it!

N   17. Irenaeus *Against Heresies* 2.2.3.

or

17. Irenaeus *Against Heresies* 2.2.3, *ANF* 1:421.

BP   Irenaeus *Against Heresies. The Ante-Nicene Fathers.* Grand Rapids: Eerdmans, n.d. 1:315–567.

BA   Roberts, Alexander, and James Donaldson, eds. *The Ante-Nicene Fathers.* 10 vols. Grand Rapids: Eerdmans, n.d.

N   18. John Chrysostom *The Priesthood* 3.17, Migne, *Patrologia Graeca*, vol. 48, col. 656.

BP   Chrysostom, John. *The Priesthood. Patrologia Graeca.* Edited by Jean Paul Migne. Paris: Apud Garnier Fratres, 1862. Vol. 48, cols. 623–692.

BA   Migne, Jean Paul, ed. *Patrologia Graeca.* 162 vols. Paris: Apud Garnier Fratres, 1857–1886.

N   19. Josephus *Jewish War* 2.14.5.

B   Josephus, Flavius. *The Works of Josephus.* Edited by William Whiston. 4 vols. New York: Oakley, Mason & Co., 1869.

Rabbinical Works

The Mishnah, which is the basic authority of rabbinic *halakah*, is divided into sixty-three tractates, which in turn are divided into *perakim* and *mishnayyoth*. This division is analogous to that of the Bible into books, chapters, and verses. Refer to the Mishnah by name of tractate, number of *perek*, and number of *mishnah*, thus:

N   20. Mishnah *Sanhedrin* 10:3.

B   *The Mishnah.* Translated by Herbert Danby. London: Oxford University Press, 1933.

The Talmud is an expansion of the Mishnah and is arranged as a commentary on the Mishnah. Therefore, it is divided into the same sixty-three tractates. But references to the Babylonian Talmud are customarily made in terms of the folio number and the side (a or b) of the folio in the most ancient Hebrew version. Because this system is unique to the Babylonian Talmud and different from that used in the identification of the parts of the Mishnah or the Jerusalem Talmud, many times the word Talmud is omitted in the reference. Thus, *Sanhedrin* 10:3 is a clear reference to the Mishnah, while *Sanhedrin* 97a is a reference to the Babylonian Talmud.

N   21. B. T. *Sanhedrin* 97a.

or

21. B. Talmud *Sanhedrin* 97a.

B   *The Babylonian Talmud.* Edited by I. Epstein. London: Soncino, 1935.

The Jerusalem Talmud is referred to by the same system used for the Mishnah. Care must be taken to add the letter "J" to distinguish from the Mishnah.

N   22. J. *Berakoth* 3:5.

or

          22. J. T. *Berakoth* 3:5.

SBL style mandates an *m.* for Mishnah, a *b.* for the Babylonian Talmud, and a *y.* for the Jerusalem Talmud—all in italics. If you are doing a specialized paper in this area, your advisor will have "traditions" for you to follow; be sure to check.

Bible Commentaries and Concordances

References to commentaries can be complicated. Some have one author for the whole commentary; others have one author for each book in a series, which may or may not have numbered volumes. Some have several authors for each book. Yet others have no known authors, only an editor. These variations show in the references.

Commentaries — author given

N   23. John B. Polhill, *Acts*, New American Commentary (Nashville: Broadman, 1992), 175.

B   Polhill, John B. *Acts*. New American Commentary. Nashville: Broadman, 1992.

N   ·   24. Edward R. Campbell, *Ruth*, Anchor Bible 7 (Garden City, NY: Doubleday, 1975), 27.

B   Campbell, Edward R. *Ruth*. Anchor Bible 7. Garden City, NY: Doubleday, 1975.

N   25. F. Delitzsch, *Biblical Commentary on the Book of Job*, 2 vols., Biblical Commentary on the Old Testament (Grand Rapids: Eerdmans, 1949), 2:115.

B   Delitzsch, F. *Biblical Commentary on the Book of Job*. 2 vols. Biblical Commentary on the Old Testament. Grand Rapids: Eerdmans, 1949.

N   26. Fred B. Craddock, "The Letter to the Hebrews: Introduction, Commentary, and Reflections," *New Interpreter's Bible*, 12 vols. (Nashville: Abingdon, 1998), 12:75.

B   Craddock, Fred B. "The Letter to the Hebrews: Introduction, Commentary, and Reflections." *New Interpreter's Bible*. 12 vols. Nashville: Abingdon, 1998. 12:3–173.

N   27. G. Ernest Wright, "Exegesis of the Book of Deuteronomy," *Interpreter's Bible* (New York: Abingdon, 1954), 2:331.

BP Wright, G. Ernest. "Exegesis of the Book of Deuteronomy." *Interpreter's Bible*. New York: Abingdon, 1954. 2:331–540.

BA Buttrick, G. A., ed. *Interpreter's Bible*. 12 vols. New York: Abingdon, 1951–1957.

Commentaries — no author given

N   28. Edward Hastings, ed., *The Speaker's Bible*, 18 vols. (Grand Rapids: Baker, 1971), 17:159.

To point out the exact phrase commented on, the following entry may be used:

N   29. "The Blood of Christ" [Heb 9:13 – 14], *The Speaker's Bible*, ed. Edward Hastings (Grand Rapids: Baker, 1971), 17:159.

BP "The Blood of Christ" [Heb 9:13 – 14]. *The Speaker's Bible*. Edited by Edward Hastings. Grand Rapids: Baker, 1971. 17:159.

BA Hastings, Edward, ed. *The Speaker's Bible*. 18 vols. Grand Rapids: Baker, 1971.

Concordances

N   30. Robert Young, *Analytical Concordance to the Bible*, 22nd Amer. ed. (Grand Rapids: Eerdmans, n.d.), s.v. "soul."

B   Young, Robert. *Analytical Concordance to the Bible*. 22nd American ed. Grand Rapids: Eerdmans, n.d. S.v. "soul."

Dictionaries and Encyclopedias

Dictionaries and encyclopedias come in many stripes. Some deal with modern languages: Webster's and Larousse, for example. Some deal with themes: *Theological Dictionary of the New Testament* and *The Anchor Bible Dictionary*. Most of the first category have unsigned articles, while most of the second have signed articles. These variations must be taken into account in notes and bibliographies.

Dictionaries and encyclopedias with unsigned articles

Reference to a modern-language dictionary appears in a footnote but not normally in the bibliography. While publication data are not considered important, the number of the edition or the year of edition is important.

N   31. *Merriam Webster College Dictionary*, 10th ed., s.v. "sin."

On well-known dictionaries and encyclopedias, omit the place and publisher in the note and omit the whole entry from the bibliography.

N   32. *Columbia Encyclopedia*, 4th ed., s.v. "war."

Specialized dictionaries and encyclopedias with unsigned articles do not need the place or publisher in the note, but they do need an edition or date. Note the format for the date rather than edition. This type of source goes in the bibliography, with complete publication data.

N   33. *Nelson's New Illustrated Bible Dictionary* (1995), s.v. "angel."

BP   *Nelson's New Illustrated Bible Dictionary*. Revised edition. Edited by Ronald F. Young-
        blood. Nashville: Nelson, 1995. S.v. "angel."

BA   *Nelson's New Illustrated Bible Dictionary*. Revised edition. Edited by Ronald F. Young-
        blood. Nashville: Nelson, 1995.

N   34. *Seventh-day Adventist Encyclopedia* (1996), s.v. "Kingsway College."

BP   *Seventh-day Adventist Encyclopedia*. Revised edition. 2 vols. Hagerstown, MD: Review
        and Herald, 1996. S.v. "Kingsway College."

BA   *Seventh-day Adventist Encyclopedia*. Revised edition. 2 vols. Hagerstown, MD: Review
        and Herald, 1996.

Dictionaries and encyclopedias with signed articles

Full information must be given for this kind of source, both in the note and
the bibliography. The only exception is the use of abbreviations when the
item appears in a list of abbreviations at the beginning of the paper. The first
example presupposes the existence of such a list.

N   35. Hayim Lapin, "Rabbi," *ABD*, 5:601.

    or

N   35. Hayim Lapin, "Rabbi," *Anchor Bible Dictionary*, 6 vols., ed. David Noel Freedman (New York: Doubleday, 1992), 5:601.

BP   Lapin, Hayim. "Rabbi." *Anchor Bible Dictionary*. 6 vols. Edited by David Noel Freed-
        man. New York: Doubleday, 1992. 5:600–602.

BA   Freedman, David Noel, ed. *Anchor Bible Dictionary*. 6 vols. New York: Doubleday, 1992.

The Greek or Hebrew word may be transliterated and italicized, or typed
in the original script. Handwritten script is not acceptable. An acceptable
transliteration scheme is given in appendix B.

N   36. Rudolf Bultmann, "*Aidōs*," *Theological Dictionary of the New Testament* (Grand
Rapids: Eerdmans, 1964–1976), 1:169.

BP   Bultmann, Rudolf. "*Aidōs*." *Theological Dictionary of the New Testament*. Grand Rapids:
        Eerdmans, 1964–1976. 1:169–171.

BA   Kittel, Gerhard, and Gerhard Friedrich, eds. *Theological Dictionary of the New Testament*.
        10 vols. Translated by Geoffrey Bromiley. Grand Rapids: Eerdmans, 1964–1976.

N   37. Aaron Demsky, "Education: In the Biblical Period," *EJ*, 6:384.

    or

N   37. Aaron Demsky, "Education: In the Biblical Period," *Encyclopaedia Judaica*
(Jerusalem: Encyclopaedia Judaica, 1971–1972), 6:384.

BP   Demsky, Aaron. "Education: In the Biblical Period." *Encyclopaedia Judaica*. Jerusalem:
        Encyclopaedia Judaica, 1971–1972. 6:382–398.

BA   *Encyclopaedia Judaica*. 16 vols. Jerusalem: Encyclopaedia Judaica, 1971–1972.

Collected Works of Individual Authors

A great deal of variation is observed in references to collected works of well-known authors. When in doubt, use common sense. Be consistent in whatever you do.

N   38. Karl Barth, *Church Dogmatics*, III/3 (Edinburgh: T. & T. Clark, 1960), 82.

BP   Barth, Karl. *Church Dogmatics*. III/3. Edinburgh: T. & T. Clark, 1960.

N   39. Martin Luther, *Sermon on the Sum of Christian Life*, *Luther's Works* (*LW*), Amer. ed. (Saint Louis: Concordia, 1955–1976), 51:260.

BP   Luther, Martin. *Sermon on the Sum of Christian Life*. *Luther's Works*. American edition. Saint Louis: Concordia, 1955–1976. 51:259–287.

BA   Luther, Martin. *Luther's Works*. American edition. 55 vols. Saint Louis: Concordia, 1955–1976.

A second reference could read:

N   40. Luther, *On the Sum of Christian Life*, *LW*, 51:259.

Book Reviews

N   41. Carol Meyers, review of *The Archaeology of Israel: Constructing the Past, Interpreting the Present*, ed. Asher Silberman and David Small, *Journal of Biblical Literature* 118 (1999): 530–531.

B   Meyers, Carol. Review of *The Archaeology of Israel: Constructing the Past, Interpreting the Present*, ed. Asher Silberman and David Small. *Journal of Biblical Literature* 118 (1999): 530–531.

Unpublished Materials

The search for information should not be limited to published materials. Theses and dissertations, interviews and voice recordings, as well as manuscripts—all of these academic or nonacademic unpublished materials can contribute worthwhile data to a research project.

Academic Sources

Theses and dissertations are the most commonly cited unpublished academic papers. Other miscellaneous academic papers may also be used.

Theses and Dissertations

N   42. Phuichun Richard Choi, "Abraham Our Father: Paul's Voice in the Covenantal Debate of the Second Temple Period" (Ph.D. dissertation, Fuller Theological Seminary, School of Theology, 1997), 189.

B   Choi, Phuichun Richard. "Abraham Our Father: Paul's Voice in the Covenantal Debate
       of the Second Temple Period." Ph.D. dissertation, Fuller Theological Seminary,
       School of Theology, 1997.

N   43. Hotma Silitonga, "Christological Implications of Leviticus 16:11–23: A Study
from an Indonesian Perspective" (M.Th. thesis, Adventist International Institute of
Advanced Studies, Silang, Cavite, Philippines, October 1988), 35.

B   Silitonga, Hotma. "Christological Implications of Leviticus 16:11–23: A Study from
       an Indonesian Perspective." M.Th. thesis, Adventist International Institute of
       Advanced Studies, Silang, Cavite, Philippines, October 1988.

Miscellaneous Academic Papers
Class papers

N   44. Teresa Reeve, "The 'Just Man' in the Writings of Philo," a paper presented for
THEO 611 Philo Seminar, University of Notre Dame, December 1997, 13.

B   Reeve, Teresa. "The 'Just Man' in the Writings of Philo." A paper presented for THEO
       611 Philo Seminar, University of Notre Dame, December 1997.

N   45. Wann Marbud Fanwar, "He Who Created the Heavens and the Earth: Contributions of Isaiah to Rev 14:7c," seminar paper for GSEM 920 Religious Studies Seminar,
Andrews University, Berrien Springs, MI, May 1999, 19.

B   Fanwar, Wann Marbud. "He Who Created the Heavens and the Earth: Contributions
       of Isaiah to Rev 14:7c." Seminar paper for GSEM 920 Religious Studies Seminar,
       Andrews University, Berrien Springs, MI, May 1999.

Syllabi

N   46. Nancy Vyhmeister, Course outline for GSEM 854 Ph.D. Proposal Seminar,
Theological Seminary, Andrews University, Berrien Springs, MI, 1999, 7.

B   Vyhmeister, Nancy. Course outline for GSEM 854 Ph.D. Proposal Seminar, Theological
       Seminary, Andrews University, Berrien Springs, MI, 1999.

Class notes

In referencing class notes, you may wish to emphasize the class (first example)
or the illustrious professor (second example).

N   47. Class notes, Program in Language Acquisition Techniques, Missionary Internship, Farmington, MI, September 1980.

B   Class notes. Program in Language Acquisition Techniques. Missionary Internship,
       Farmington, MI, September 1980.

N   48. Brembong Owusu-Antwi, lecture notes for OTST 632 Biblical Archaeology,
Adventist University of Africa, Solusi Extension Campus, January 2006.

B   Owusu-Antwi, Brempong. Lecture notes for OTST 632 Biblical Archaeology, Adventist
       University of Africa, Solusi Extension Campus, January 2006.

Miscellaneous Unpublished Sources

Footnotes and bibliographical entries for miscellaneous unpublished materials can be difficult. To make them useful, clarity and consistency are vital. A good dose of common sense is also essential. Examples for reports, speeches, manuscripts, letters, and interviews are provided.

Reports

N   49. Seventh-day Adventist Theological Seminary, Far East, "Financial Statement of Graduate Apartments," August 31, 1985, 4.

B   Seventh-day Adventist Theological Seminary, Far East. "Financial Statement of Graduate Apartments." August 31, 1985.

N   50. Association of Theological Institutions in Eastern Africa, "1978/79 Bachelor of Divinity Degree Syllabus," 3.

B   Association of Theological Institutions in Eastern Africa. "1978/79 Bachelor of Divinity Degree Syllabus."

Speeches and Presentations

N   51. C. Mervyn Maxwell, "Which Sacrifice, Lord?" Seminary Chapel sermon, Andrews University, Berrien Springs, MI, October 20, 1976, 10, typewritten.

B   Maxwell, C. Mervyn. "Which Sacrifice, Lord?" Seminary Chapel sermon. Andrews University, Berrien Springs, MI, October 20, 1976. Typewritten.

N   52. Jon Paulien, "The Lion/Lamb King: Reading Revelation from Popular Culture," a paper presented at the annual meeting of the Society of Biblical Literature, November 24, 1996, New Orleans.

B   Paulien, Jon. "The Lion/Lamb King: Reading Revelation from Popular Culture." A paper presented at the annual meeting of the Society of Biblical Literature, November 24, 1996, New Orleans.

Manuscripts

References to manuscripts must permit readers to know exactly what the item is and where it is found. The name of the collection and its location must be clear.

N   53. Peter L. Benoit, 1875 diary, Archives, University of Notre Dame.

B   Benoit, Peter L. 1875 diary. Photocopy of typewritten transcript of Canon Benoit's diary of a trip to America, January 6 to June 8, 1875, including descriptions of Josephite missions among freed slaves. Archives, University of Notre Dame.

N   54. Ellen G. White, Manuscript 154, 1902, Ellen G. White Research Center, Silang, Cavite, Philippines (hereafter abbreviated EGWRC).

B   White, Ellen G. Manuscript 154, 1902. Ellen G. White Research Center, Silang, Cavite, Philippines.

Letters

A letter addressed to the author of the paper is assumed to be in the author's files. If the letter referred to is addressed to someone else, information should be given regarding its location. Quotations from letters should be as easy to verify as those from published sources.

N   55. Bryan Ball, editor of *The Essential Jesus*, to Nancy Vyhmeister, March 13, 2000.

B   Ball, Bryan, editor of *The Essential Jesus*, to Nancy Vyhmeister, March 13, 2000.

N   56. Ellen G. White to Dr. Patience Bourdeau, June 8, 1905, Letter 177, 1905, Ellen White Research Center, Newbold College, Bracknell, England.

B   White, Ellen G., to Dr. Patience Bourdeau, June 8, 1905. Letter 177, 1905. Ellen White Research Center, Newbold College, Bracknell, England.

Interviews

N   57. Choo Lak Yeow, Executive Director of the Association for Theological Education in Southeast Asia, interview by author, Singapore, July 15, 1985.

B   Yeow, Choo Lak, Executive Director of Association for Theological Education in Southeast Asia. Interview by author. Singapore, July 15, 1985.

Electronic Media

See referencing the Internet in chapter 3. Here we consider CD-ROMs, videos, and sound recordings.

CD-ROM

N   58. Ellen G. White, *Education*, Complete Published Ellen G. White Writings [CD ROM] (Silver Spring, MD: Ellen G. White Estate, 1999).

B   White, Ellen G. *Education*. Complete Published Ellen G. White Writings [CD ROM]. Silver Spring, MD: Ellen G. White Estate, 1999.

Video and Sound Recordings

Some information for this type of source may be lacking. Use whatever you can find. Follow the same organization as for other materials.

N   59. *Hudson Taylor*, 85 min, Ken Anderson Films, 1989, videocassette.

B   *Hudson Taylor*. 85 min. Ken Anderson Films, 1989. Videocassette.

N   60. Luis Landriscina, "Judío en el Vaticano," in *Mano a mano con el país*, vol. 5, Phillips 64232, 1985, sound cassette.

B   Landriscina, Luis. "Judío en el Vaticano." In *Mano a mano con el país*, vol. 5. Phillips 64232, 1985. Sound cassette.

Now that you have a clearer understanding of footnote and bibliographic entry forms, you may confidently prepare these in accurate and acceptable form. Chapter 11 turns from the minute, detailed work described above to a study of the overall organization of the paper.

chapter 11

ORGANIZING THE PAPER

Organizational decisions take place from the moment you choose a topic until that last change just before you hand the paper in. You will deal with macro-organization as well as micro-organization. This chapter speaks to both issues. The larger picture deals with the organization of the parts of the paper, especially the body of the report. Micro-organization deals with smaller items, including the visible organization of headings and enumerations.

Parts of the Paper

A well-written research paper should have five main parts: the preliminary pages, the introduction, the body, the summary and conclusions, and the bibliography. If needed, appendixes may be added.

The principal parts of the paper—introduction, body, and conclusion—must harmonize. That is, they must integrate into one whole. The introduction sets the stage, preparing the reader to understand the purpose, nature, and direction of the research. The main body of the text gives a clear report of the findings. The conclusion summarizes and evaluates the results of the investigation. The bibliography documents what has been presented.

To achieve the overall harmony of the paper, take your proposal very seriously. Then begin writing with the first content chapter (chapter 1 in a paper, chapter 2 in a dissertation), leaving the introduction for later. Write all the rest of the body, chapter after chapter. Then summarize and draw conclusions. After all that, you will be ready to smooth the proposal into an introduction. Then prepare the bibliography and appendixes before going to the preliminary pages, which include the table of contents.

Preliminary Pages

In a class paper at the graduate level, the preliminary pages include the title page, the table of contents, and, if needed, lists of figures, tables, or illustrations. A thesis may include a dedication and/or acknowledgment. In a short class paper, the preliminary pages are not numbered; the introduction is page 1. In a thesis or dissertation, the preliminary pages are numbered from the title page (no number typed here!) with lowercase roman numerals, at the bottom center of the page.

Title Page

The title page includes the name of the institution where the paper is being presented, the title of the paper, the name of the class or program for which the paper is written, the name of the writer, and the date. The professor's name is not included. A thesis or dissertation also requires an approval sheet (see chapter 20). A model title page appears in chapter 13.

Table of Contents

The table of contents lists everything that comes after it, starting with lists of abbreviations and illustrations and continuing through the bibliography. Chapter titles, as well as headings and subheadings to the third level, are listed. An example of the format of a table of contents is given in chapter 13. Use Arabic numbers for your chapters to avoid the difficulty of aligning periods after Roman numerals of varied lengths.

List of Illustrations

If two or more tables, figures, or illustrations are used, these should be listed. The format to follow is shown in the list of illustrations for this book. If there are only a few of each, the list of tables and figures may be on the same page, as part of a list of illustrations.

List of Abbreviations

To avoid writing out the titles of books and journals you use repeatedly, you may insert a list of abbreviations just before the introduction and then use only the abbreviations. Some schools require that the abbreviated sources be spelled out the first time they are used, even if they are in a list; others consider that the list takes the place of the first reference. Make sure you know what your school requires.

Include in this list only items used in the paper or dissertation. This list does not take the place of a bibliography. Abbreviations of titles of books and journals should be italicized. Other abbreviations, such as PW for Pauly-Wissowa, *Real Encyclopädie der classischen Altertumswissenschaft*, are not italicized. A list of acceptable abbreviations in correct format appears in appendix C.[1]

Introduction

A carefully written proposal is the basis for a clear and effective introduction, which should contain the same parts suggested for the proposal (see chapter 5). The introduction is a reader's guide to the paper. It tells the reader what the problem studied (and solved) was and how the researcher went about finding the answers, and it may even suggest the solution to the problem.

Whereas the proposal may simply list the items included (statement of the problem, purpose of the research, significance of the research, definition of terms, limitations and delimitations, procedure, and an outline), the introduction polishes the writing and smoothes the transition from one section to the next. It often adds a paragraph or more on the background of the problem. Additionally, the future tense of the proposal becomes past tense, since the research has now been completed.

The length of the introduction varies. An introduction to a class paper may be only one page long. An introduction to a thesis may contain twenty or more pages. What is important is that all parts are included and the paper is correctly introduced.

Page one of the introduction is the first page of the paper. In class papers the title, INTRODUCTION, is given chapter standing (on the 13th line or 2 inches from the top edge of the page), but not a chapter number. In a thesis or dissertation, the introduction usually is chapter 1. A model introduction for short papers appears in chapter 13.

Main Body of the Paper

In this part of the paper you report the findings of the research. The body is naturally the longest part of the paper. It is divided into chapters (or major sections, in a short paper), each with its own divisions and subdivisions. Since the organization of the main body of the paper is so important, this topic will be covered in a separate section (see below).

---

1. For a much longer list of abbreviations, especially in biblical and Near Eastern studies, see *SBL Handbook of Style* (Peabody, MA: Hendrickson, 1999), 89–121. The ultimate list of abbreviations is available in *Theologisches Realencyklopädie Abkurzungsverzeichnis*, 2nd ed. (Berlin: De Gruyter, 1993).

Summary and Conclusions

As the title indicates, this part of the paper summarizes the findings and draws conclusions. No new evidence is brought in. The presentation of data has been done in the main body. The summary should be brief—only as long as needed to bring the issue into focus. The conclusions are then drawn from the summary. Remember that many paper/dissertation readers never look at more than the introduction and summary/conclusions. Everything you want readers to know about your research must be in those two places.

Take the time needed to craft your concluding section with care. The conclusion or conclusions must fit the problem or research question declared in the introduction of the paper. It makes no sense to ask one question and answer another. Conclusions presented may be firm or tentative. Sometimes the research only "suggests" a solution to a problem. At times the research may turn up areas that need to be investigated and could be a topic for further study. It is proper to note such items in the conclusions.

The status of the summary and conclusions must match that of the introduction. If the introduction was given a chapter number, the summary and conclusions must be considered a chapter. If the introduction was not a chapter, the summary and conclusion will not be a chapter either.

Appendixes

A paper may have one or more appendixes. These are added sections that contain materials not indispensable for reading and understanding the paper, but useful for gaining deeper insight or for validating and documenting what has been stated. Use lower case letters (appendix) to refer to them in the text of the paper. Appendixes may include raw numerical data, statistical information, photocopied materials, or whatever else the researcher needs to present. Appendixes are much more common in dissertations than in papers. When there are several appendixes, as in this book, each has a title and is listed in the table of contents.

Bibliography

The bibliography documents and gives weight to the research. It tells the reader how serious the study was. It also leads readers to sources for further study on the topic. Instructions on preparing bibliographies appeared in chapter 6. Model bibliographies are those at the end of this book and in chapter 13.

A general overview of the organization of the paper may suffice. But organizing the body of a paper demands special attention. The next section deals with this specifically.

Organizing the Body of the Paper

There are no firm and exact rules about the way the body of a paper should be organized. Whatever system you choose must be clear and logical—to you and to your advisor, as well as to your readers. Ask your advisor and your peers for a critique of your suggested outline. Be able to defend your organization: Why does it make sense for you to start where you do and follow the thought path you do? Reread the section on "Organization" in chapter 7.

Each chapter must be a self-contained unit. That is, everything on one topic should be in the same chapter. Everything in one section should be related to the same matter; no extraneous material should be allowed. The same topic should not be discussed in several sections. Naturally, there may be references from one section to another, but good organization demands dividing the topic into independent units, tied to each other in some logical manner, but not repeating the same information.

The outline approved by the professor or advisor when the proposal was presented was a good starting point; it served as the skeleton for your paper in its initial stages. However, after reading and studying, you may feel the need for changing that outline. Remember, though, to talk to your advisor before you write on the basis of a new outline.

Two sample outlines were given in chapter 5. One important rule of outlining is that a section that is subdivided must have at least two subsections. You cannot cut an apple into one piece! Likewise, you cannot have a section A (or 1 or a) without a corresponding section B (or 2 or b). Another rule is to make subsections parallel to each other, in form and, to some extent, in content.

Since there is no one accepted method of organizing a paper, this section presents a sampling of possibilities. Again, consultation with the advising professor is indispensable.

Historical topics lend themselves to a chronological method. What happened first is narrated first. The biography of Hudson Taylor, missionary to China, can be divided into sections: childhood, youth, early mission, death of wife, founding of the China Inland Mission, and so on.

The spatial (geographical) method might be used in reporting the research on an ancient city. The New Testament city of Ephesus could be described part by part: the port, the theater, the library, the Temple of Diana, the marketplace, and so forth.

A comparative method could be used in comparing the Buddhist and Hindu beliefs concerning death. First, each would have to be described fully; then they could be compared.

For some studies a cause-to-effect method is appropriate. A study of the rapid growth of Christianity in Korea could use this method. The different factors leading to this phenomenon would be studied, one by one. Then, the effect (the growth of the Christian church) would be delineated.

Some topics do well with an unfolding method. Here one idea needs to be clearly explained so that it can lead to another. For example, an understanding of the ceremonies of the Israelite tabernacle would need to be established before progressing to an analysis of the way the author of Hebrews deals with these ceremonies.

A practical theology project or thesis normally has a theoretical basis and a practical application. That means the work is organized into two main parts. The theoretical foundation may be divided into biblical, theological, and sociological parts. The practical part may well be chronological—what happened first, what next. D.Min. projects often use this form; see chapter 21.

The starting point for research need not be the same in every case. One may begin from the specifics and arrive at general conclusions—inductive reasoning. Or one may begin with general facts and arrive at specific conclusions—deductive reasoning. What is important is that the research process is so designed and executed as to make sense to the readers and to the professor.

Someone has suggested that writing a research report is like building a temple. One must lay the foundation, then erect each of the pillars. Finally, the roof is placed on the structure. As happens with all parables, this one, too, falls short. However, it does illustrate the need for balance and careful building so that a clear and convincing result may be achieved. It also suggests that each research paper is a unique construction and, to some extent, a work of art.

Specific guidelines for the organization of literary and bibliographic research are scarce. More is said about descriptive and program-development research in chapters 15 and 16. Specific schemes for organizing biblical-theological-pastoral research must be designed by the student, preferably in collaboration with the professor or committee for whom the paper or thesis is written.

Practical Helps for Organizing the Paper

The final organization of the topic takes place once all the research is finished. The task is difficult and important. This section gives practical suggestions for dividing up the topic and arranging its sections, and for planning the visible organization of the written report.

Organizing the Note Cards

When you use note cards, you have an advantage, as long as each note card or slip has its heading and subheading. The notes can easily be separated into piles. Use a table—or the floor—and separate the slips by headings and sub-headings and sub-subheadings, if there are any. Then look through each pile, reading the notes as you do so. Organize each pile into a logical sequence. If there are notes that do not belong, take them out; put them where they do belong or discard them. Do not be surprised if the tentative outline no longer seems to fit. Once all the cards are distributed, a better outline may suggest itself.

When all the small piles are organized within themselves and put in a logical sequence with the other small piles that belong with them in a larger topic, the order and organization of each section or chapter of the paper is easily seen. Put an elastic or rubber band around each section to keep it separate and organized (if yours is a long paper, try using a shoe box). Then confirm your decision regarding the sequence of chapters.

Now, read the note cards in sequence, trying to feel (or see or hear) how these bits of information fall into place. If you are not satisfied with the way the cards fit together, you may start your sorting over again. It may take three sortings to organize the cards—and your paper. But the time will be well spent, for you will write with greater ease and speed for having gone through this process.

When you use a computer program, such as Access™ or Excel™, you will need to sort them on the computer. The work is done quickly, but you will not see more than a few notes at a time.

Visible Organization in the Written Report

Using different levels of headings and enumerations helps to visibly organize the contents of a paper. How to do so is discussed in the following paragraphs.

Headings
Throughout this book different kinds or levels of headings have been used. These headings show how a topic is divided and subdivided and what belongs with what. The headings and subheadings represent the different parts of the outline. Once more, a heading must have two subheadings, or not be divided at all.

A first-level heading indicates a main division of the chapter. In this chapter, **"Practical Helps for Organizing the Paper"** is a first-level heading. It is centered and bolded.

The second-level heading indicates a subdivision of that main division. In this chapter "Visible Organization in the Written Report" is a second-level heading. It is centered but not bolded. Its "twin" is "Organizing the Note Cards." The graphic presentation shows it is a part of **"Practical Helps for Organizing the Paper."**

The third-level heading indicates a part of the second-level subdivision. In this chapter **"Headings"** and **"Enumerations"** are third-level headings. These headings are placed flush with the left margin and bolded. In the three kinds of headings already listed the first, last, and principal words are capitalized.

The fourth-level heading indicates a division of a third-level heading. It is flush with the left margin, using the same font as second level but not bolded. Only the first word is capitalized. "Within the paragraph" is an example of fourth-level heading in this chapter.

The fifth-level heading, the smallest organizational subdivision in a paper, shows that what follows is a part of a fourth-level heading. This heading is reserved for a small segment of the paper, often only a paragraph. A fifth-level heading is part of the paragraph; it is indented (like the paragraph), bolded, and followed by a period or full stop. Only its first word is capitalized. Below, **"With short sentences"** and **"With longer sentences"** are examples.

If the organization of a paper does not need so many levels of headings, you may choose to use only three — for example, those that are bolded. However, you cannot use one scheme (complete sequence) in one chapter and the incomplete scheme (bold only) in another chapter. Consistency is indispensable.

Following the outline scheme (see chapter 5), the chapter title corresponds to the Roman numeral; the first-level heading, to the capital letter; the second-level heading, to the Arabic numeral; the third-level heading to the lowercase letter. However, the letters and numbers that you use in an outline do not appear in headings or table of contents of a paper or dissertation.

Enumerations

Enumerations help to visibly organize materials in the written report. They can be used within a paragraph and within a sentence. Instructions follow.

Within the paragraph

Enumerations within a paragraph can be done in two ways. In both cases, periods after numbers must be aligned.

With short sentences. If most of the sentences are shorter than one line, place the numbers at the left margin. When one does run over, start the second line under the first letter of text in the first line. Final periods are needed only for complete sentences. For example:

1. The linguistic context must be accounted for.
2. The historical context must be considered.
3. The purpose of the author must be noted.

With longer sentences. The second style is used when the sentences in the listing are long or each number has more than one sentence. In this case the number is indented, as are the paragraphs, and followed by a period. The following lines reach the left margin. Dots after numbers are aligned. For example:

1. The Arabic number is typed after the same indentation as the paragraph and followed by a period or full stop. Skip one space and begin the text..

2. Double spacing is used as in the rest of the paper.

3. A period or full stop follows each item. There may be several sentences after each number.

4. If double-digit numbers are used, the indentation must be modified so that all the periods are aligned.

Within the sentence

An enumeration within a sentence may use letters or numbers, set in parentheses. Numbers usually represent a larger division; letters, a smaller one. The items are set off by commas unless they have punctuation within them, in which case they are set off by semicolons. For example:

He gave three reasons for his resignation: (1) age, (2) gradually failing eyesight, and (3) desire to live under less pressure.

His failing eyesight is due to: (a) age, now 65 years; (b) a congenital, worsening disease; (c) stress, caused by the responsibilities of the job.

This chapter has explained the general organization of the paper and given suggestions, both theoretical and practical, for organizing the material in the research report. Chapter 12 gives instruction on good research writing.

Chapter 12

WRITING THE PAPER

Your research is now complete. You have consulted all relevant sources. Your note cards, organized according to the final outline, are ready to be transformed into a written report. The time to write has come. You have already put in about two-thirds of the total time needed to complete the paper; writing and rewriting will take another third. For many, this last third is the hardest part of all. If you do not write the report, however, your well-done research will pass unnoticed. Therefore, you need to write a clear, concise, readable report.

This chapter describes research English, makes suggestions on how to write coherent and interesting paragraphs, and instructs on the use of transitional and introductory phrases. It also outlines the stages of the writing process and lists helps for the novice writer.

Research English

English research writing uses simple, concise, and clear language. Other words to describe it are impersonal, objective, formal, dignified, factual, and unbiased. One author has said: "Research writing is exact writing, featuring well-planned sentences with proper subordination of minor elements and at the same time employing concrete, specific words."[1]

Impersonal language minimizes the importance of "me" and "I." Generally speaking, the first person singular does not appear in research writing.

---

1. James D. Lester, *Writing Research Papers: A Complete Guide*, 2nd ed. (Glenview, IL: Scott Foresman, 1976), 57.

For example, instead of saying in the introduction, "I decided to limit this paper ...," write, "The natural limits of the topic determined the shape of the paper." A modern trend does allow for the use of the first person singular, especially in the introduction and conclusion; even then, the emphasis must not be on the writer but on the research topic.

Some writers refer to themselves as "the writer" or "the researcher" to avoid use of the first person pronoun. Others use the first person plural, "we." Neither of these devices is desirable. While the passive voice ("this paper was written in order to probe ... ") can be employed to avoid the first-person pronoun, its use makes sentences heavy. While minimizing yourself, avoid the impersonal passive as much as you can. As often as possible, use the active voice. Keep your writing alive! Write naturally, directly. Be sure to consult the preferences of your school and advisor on the matter of impersonal language.

A paper or thesis is not the place to use fancy words, metaphors, and similes. You should shun imaginative phrases and comparisons as well as superlatives (best, finest, largest). Idiomatic expressions are out of place. Exclamation marks do not fit.

Research language is modest and tentative. Instead of definite and dogmatic words such as "never," "all," or "none," use "some," "somewhat," or "often." Even when you have evidence for what you write, do not overstate your case.

A well-written research paper will not contain as many adverbs and adjectives as nouns and verbs. Adverbs such as "marvelously" do not fit. Unfortunately, in research language no one is going to be "an outstanding success." On the other hand, research language should not be boring. Instead of a general noun such as "man," use a more specific one: "youth," "gentleman," or "scholar." Instead of a verb such as "go," use "amble," "stride," "ride," or "fly." To find these more specific and colorful synonyms, use a dictionary or thesaurus—the ones that come with Microsoft Word™ and WordPerfect™ are most helpful.

Research language is standard, not colloquial; it never uses slang. The contracted forms of the negative (can't, won't, didn't) are out of place. The full form must be used. Of the following four levels of English, the proper research language is the standard:

Formal	Standard	Colloquial	Slang
superlative	excellent	first-rate	cool
exasperating	irritating	aggravating	burns me up
deranged	irrational	crazy	nuts

The greatest temptation of theology students is to use sermonic instead of research language. The language of the pulpit is not the language of the thesis. Phrases such as "souls won to the truth" should be replaced with something understandable to the general public: "people baptized into the church."

Another aspect of writing demands attention: inclusive language. The times require sensitivity to gender issues. Without syntactical errors ("everyone did their homework") or excessive recourse to "he or she" (or worse, "he/she"), write in ways that include both genders and do not stereotype sex roles. "Mankind" becomes "humanity"; singular "he" is changed into plural "they," or alternates with "she."

Excellent writing takes time and effort. Mediocre writing is faster and easier. However, it does not usually merit the professor's approval, a reader's interest, or your own satisfaction.

The Paragraph: Smallest Unit of the Paper

The smallest unit of the paper, the paragraph, is somewhat like a link in a chain. And, as in the case of the chain, the paper is only as strong as its weakest paragraph. Therefore, time spent learning how to write strong paragraphs is time well spent.

A paragraph should be all about one topic. Its length is determined by how much has to be said about the matter. If it is too long, it probably includes ideas that do not belong to the main topic. Rule of thumb: If your paragraph fills more than one computer screen, it is suspect. Here short is better than long. On the other hand, a paragraph cannot be extremely short—one sentence is never a true paragraph—because it cannot cover the topic thoroughly.

Many types of effective and interesting paragraphs can be designed. However, certain elements are found in all paragraphs that communicate well and please the reader. Specific elements discussed in this section are unity and coherence. A sampling of paragraphs is also presented.

Paragraph Unity

A good paragraph puts in one place all the material that belongs together and keeps it apart from other items that do not belong. Every well-constructed paragraph has some unifying thought. All the materials included are somehow related to that thought. This precludes the inclusion of extraneous ideas and comments.

One device that fosters paragraph unity is the use of the topic sentence. This sentence, which states the main idea of the paragraph, may come at the beginning, in the middle, or at the end of the paragraph. Its purpose is not only to give the chief idea of the paragraph, but also to provide an anchor, so to speak, for the rest of the sentences in the paragraph. It does so by providing a center to which the rest of the paragraph can relate. Examples of the use of the topic sentence are found in this paragraph and in the majority of paragraphs of this book.

Paragraph Coherence

A strong paragraph hangs together; it coheres. Paragraph coherence is concerned with the order in which the information is presented and with the clear and logical relationship of one statement to the next in the development of ideas. A coherent paragraph conveys information clearly and effectively.

In the following paragraph from Ralph Waldo Emerson's *Self-reliance*, coherence depends on the repeated references to the hypothetical man being described and on the movement from the small, personal, and material, to the intangible and universal.

> The civilized man has built a coach, but has lost the use of his feet. He is supported on crutches, but lacks so much support of muscle. He has a fine Geneva watch, but he fails of the skill to tell the hour by the sun. A Greenwich nautical almanac he has, and so being sure of the information when he wants it, the man in the street does not know a star in the sky. The solstice he does not observe; the equinox he knows as little, and the whole bright calendar of the year is without a dial in his mind.[2]

Sample Expository Paragraphs

The following paragraphs are built around definition, enumeration or classification, comparison, and cause and effect. Other types, such as reiteration, question and answer, and analogy, could also be cited.

Definition

The term *leitourgia* in classical Greek described the performance of a special honorific service for the state, such as, for instance, outfitting a warship or providing a choir for a theatrical performance at a major ceremony. The honor dimension was important to the term. By the second century B.C. the word was used in popular language for priestly service in the worship of the gods. In the Septuagint it was used for the Hebrew *sharath* to designate participation in the divine worship, either as an officiant or as a worshiper. While in the New Testament the more common

---

2. http://emerson.thefreelibrary.com/Essays-First-Series/2−1−2.

term for serving is *diakonia*, by Hippolytus' time *leitourgia* and *munus* were the accepted terms for the performance of Christian worship, especially the Eucharist. These words conveyed the idea of the prestige of the one who could officiate in the church service.[3]

Enumeration or Classification

Women [in the nineteenth century] were not accorded what the twentieth century considers basic human rights. Politically, women were virtual nonentities. Their contributions were confined largely to the domestic realm. They could not secure employment in the occupation of their choice, and higher education was practically closed to them. In addition, they were not only denied the right to vote; they were, socially and individually, perceived as being under the jurisdiction of men. Once married, a woman lost all claim to any property she had previously owned; it was transferred to her husband. She had legal claims neither to her own body nor to her children in the event of divorce.[4]

Comparison/Contrast

In the evangelical Christian community, the issue of headship/submission/equality lies at the heart of the fundamental differences between the two major proactive groups in the ordination debate. The Council on Biblical Manhood and Womanhood, representing those who oppose women's ordination, ultimately bases its biblical argument on the premise that the divine plan in creation affirmed equality of the sexes in spiritual status but included role distinctions involving the headship of man over woman.... Those holding this position have been referred to as "patriarchalists," "hierarchalists," or (their preferred self-designation) "complementarians." The second group, Christians for Biblical Equality, representing evangelicals who support women's ordination, argue that the divine plan at Creation affirmed full equality of the sexes without any male headship or female submission.... Those holding this view have been referred to as "Christian feminists" or (their preferred self-designation) "egalitarians."[5]

Cause and Effect

Even in the religious arena, [nineteenth-century] women were limited. Most churches did not ordain women and either prohibited or frowned upon women speaking in public. Because a large sector of society perceived the church as responsible for the denigration of women, many elements in the women's movement became hostile to it. For example, powerful crusader Elizabeth Gage called the church the bulwark of women's slavery. For her, no entity was more offensive

---

3. Daniel Augsburger, "Clerical Authority and Ordination," in *Women in Ministry: Biblical and Historical Perspectives*, ed. Nancy J. Vyhmeister (Berrien Springs, MI: Andrews University Press, 1998), 83. (Hereafter referred to as *WIM*.)

4. Alicia Worley, "Ellen White and Women's Rights," *WIM*, 357.

5. Richard M. Davidson, "Headship, Submission, and Equality in Scripture," *WIM*, 259.

than organized religion. For this reason, freedom from religious orthodoxy became crucial to feminist leadership.[6]

These samples illustrate good writing. They also show different ways of constructing paragraphs.

Transitions and Introductions

Student writers often have trouble finding an appropriate word to make the transition from one idea or sentence to another. A further difficulty is finding words to introduce quotations. This section suggests some terms for both purposes.

Transitional Words

Following is a list of transitional words and phrases that may be useful in relating sentences and ideas one to another.[7] Using these words can *further* improve your research writing style.

accordingly	however	or
again	in addition	second
also	in like manner	similarly
and	last	so
at the same time	likewise	then
besides	meanwhile	therefore
but	moreover	third
consequently	next	thus
finally	nor	to conclude
first	on the other hand	to sum up
further	on the whole	too
hence		

To sum up, words and phrases such as these can be used effectively to smooth transitions and *thus* make for easier reading. *However*, make sure you are certain what the word means and choose the one that best fits your writing. *Finally*, use a variety of these transition words.

---

6. Worley, "Ellen White and Women's Rights," 357.

7. Kate L. Turabian, *Student's Guide for Writing College Papers*, 3rd ed. (Chicago: University of Chicago Press, 1976), 71.

Introducing Quotations

Quotations are the words and ideas of another author; we borrow them to enhance a position or strengthen an argument. These quotations need to be introduced. Readers are jolted when a quotation comes out of the blue and upset when they have to look at the footnote to find who said such a thing. However, constantly introducing quotations with the phrase "So-and-so wrote that" bores the reader. Here is a list of different verbs that can be used to introduce quotations:

accepts	combats	expresses	points to	states
adds	confirms	indicates	portrays	stipulates
admits	declares	labels	proposes	submits
affirms	defends	mentions	recalls	suggests
agrees	denies	objects	recommends	thinks
argues	describes	opposes	reports	verifies
asks	discusses	points out	reveals	writes
believes				

In introducing quotations, tense usage is important. To refer to an event of the past, use the past: "John Wesley argued that ..." or "Manalo defended...." When referring to stated views and beliefs of present or past writers, the present tense may be used. The idea still stands! In a discussion of the theological understanding of Bultmann, it is correct to say: "Bultmann admits ..., but points out that...." One could even write: "Luther accepts that ... and confirms ...," even when Luther has been dead for centuries. However, you should avoid changing back and forth between past and present. The simplest solution to the tense dilemma is to consistently use the past tense for whatever happened or was written in the past. Whatever the choice, consistency is mandatory; the rationale for using one verb tense over the other should be clear.

Formal quotations may be preceded by a colon or a comma. The setting will determine your choice. Quotations must remain identical to the source, with only the possibility of changing the case of the initial letter. For example, Paul wrote the Corinthians: "Make love your aim" (1 Cor 14:1). The quotation remains intact.

A quotation may also be woven into my sentence. In that case the initial cap will change to a lower case. The syntax of my sentence is the one that counts. For example, if my sentence began "Paul wrote to the Corinthians that," I need to change the quotation. I could write: Paul wrote to the Corinthians that they should make love their aim (1 Cor 14:1). I had to change the person ("you" [understood] to "they"") and the tense ("make" to "should make"). What Paul wrote is now part of what I am saying. This is a paraphrase, but it still needs a reference. As you make quotations fit smoothly into your writing, be especially careful with the person and the tense. Above all, be faithful to your source; use brackets to show any addition or modification.

Quoting Bible texts presents unique problems. We often hear: "First Samuel 3:10 says" (at least the sentence begins with a written-out number!). Obviously, the passage cannot speak. We need to look for another way to quote it. "In 1 Sam 3:10 we read" would be appropriate. Or I could write, "The story reads: 'And the LORD came and stood forth' (1 Sam 3:10)." In the Pauline letters, it is appropriate to write: "Paul wrote." When quoting from Chronicles, I would have to speak of the Chronicler or the author of Chronicles.

American usage calls for double quotation marks around what is quoted. If what I quote contains something in quotation marks, those marks will become single quotation marks within the double quotation marks.

The quotation of longer passages has its own rules. According to Turabian's verdict, when you have eight or more lines, in which there are at least two separate sentences, you have a "block quotation." You will indent the quotation, at least from the left and preferably from both left and right margins, and you will single space. The old rule was to indent half as much as the paragraph. The new rule is to indent the same as a paragraph. Your school will choose for you which rule you must follow; whichever it is, be consistent about it. Naturally, you will need to introduce the quotation. See chapter 13 for details of format.

Be careful to include all the necessary quotation marks and footnotes (or endnotes) to avoid being labeled a plagiarist. Even if you paraphrase, give the reference. The origin of a borrowed phrase or idea must be acknowledged by footnote, endnote, or in-text reference.

The Writing Process

Writing a paper is a process to be achieved in stages: writing, correcting, and rewriting. Two drafts and a final copy may be enough to produce a good paper; often three or four drafts are needed. If your spoken language is not English or if the subject is complex, writing and rewriting become even more necessary. Some students may need to find editorial assistance, since ghostwriting papers is not part of the professor's job description.

First Draft: Write and Rewrite

Writing cannot be done effectively in small segments of time. Set aside enough time to write one complete section of the paper. If you have to stop and start too many times, you will waste time rereading what you wrote before in order to "get the feel of things" again.

In bygone days, teachers always recommended a first, hand-written draft, to be typed later. Today computers make keyboarding the first draft directly a good idea. You can "cut and paste" and edit to your heart's content, all the while working from a rough draft. If you are computer illiterate, now is the time to learn the computer skills needed for scholarship. If you must write your first draft by hand, leave an empty space between lines so you can make legible corrections.

With the notes in hand, you write, one section at a time, following the order of the sorted cards. The wording of the cards suggests the wording for the paper. When you come to a quotation, you may paraphrase it, copy it from your note card (if it is short), or attach it to the paper without copying it (if it is long). If you are working at the computer, you can cut and paste it from the note file to your paper (numbered cards make this easy). In any case, you will need to reference the quotation, citation, or allusion.

How you write will depend on how you have taken notes. If you are writing by hand, you will put the footnote number in the text and make a list of the footnotes on a separate paper. You may also use the computer, with three files: one contains the notes, another contains the alphabetical list of bibliographical entries, the third contains the developing text. Finally, you can use one of the programs that makes automatic footnotes directly from the bibliographical entries you have already entered. Modernizing your work style will spare you sweat and tears.

Once the first writing is completed, allow the draft to rest for a day or so. Then reread and rewrite, making the necessary corrections. A word to the wise: Experience tells me that I see mistakes more easily on a printed page than on a computer screen. Rewriting includes deleting, adding, rearranging, checking spelling and punctuation, completing footnotes, and general editorial work.

Second Draft: Rewrite and Type

After you have corrected the first draft, even you may have trouble reading through the red marks. Rewrite, retype, or — better by far — enter the corrections on the document already in your word processor. This becomes the second draft.

Now is a good time to read the whole paper again, this time aloud or to someone else. Another person who hears or reads the paper usually notices problems you cannot see. Many students find spouses to be excellent critics of their literary work. Students who do not write well in English may need an editor to make corrections.

Whether you input the paper on the computer or hire a typist, you are totally responsible for any mistakes, either in format or typing. Advertisements around schools tout "low prices" for computer work. Saving money is not wise here. You need a computer operator who knows the required format and gives you a perfectly typed paper. Remember, you assume final responsibility for the contents, language, and presentation of the paper.

Revising

In the revision process, the writer needs to look for wrong spellings, bad punctuation, unclear sentences, and anything else that mars the reading. The following is a list of specific areas that may cause problems. Pay special attention to them.

1. Flow of ideas—there should be a natural continuity from one idea and one sentence to the next.
2. Coherence—there should be cohesion (a "sticking together") of ideas and sentences. In order to have coherence, there must be some organizing principle.
3. Bridges—there should be natural bridges from one topic to another; over these the reader may walk from one part of the paper to the next. There should be no abrupt transitions or changes of thought.
4. Logic of organization—there must be a reasonable explanation for the way the ideas and topics are organized. The ideas must also be expressed in logical sentences.
5. Weak spots or omissions—there should be no places where it appears there has been insufficient research or something has been left out. If you discover such a spot, go back to the library and look for something to enrich the poor portion of the paper.
6. Awkward sentences—there is usually a better way to say something. If the sentence does not sound right, change it. The best possible syntax and grammar should be used.
7. Unnecessary words—there should be no more words than needed. Such words as "pretty," "rather," "very," are useless and must be eliminated. The best way to say something is the simplest way.

These seven items provide a good basis for examining and revising the paper. Obviously, this kind of rewriting takes time. But high marks and the satisfaction of having done excellent work should repay your effort.

Help for the Novice Writer

The following books from the University of Chicago Guides to Writing, Editing, and Publishing series provide a wealth of material to help you write better:

Booth, Wayne C., Gregory G. Colomb, and Joseph M. Williams. *The Craft of Research*. 1995.

Chicago Manual of Style. 15th ed. 2003.

Turabian, Kate L. *A Handbook for Writers of Term Papers, Theses, and Dissertations*. 7th ed. Revised by Wayne C. Booth, Gregory G. Colomb, Joseph M. Williams, and the University of Chicago Press Editorial Staff. 2007.

Williams, Joseph M. *Style: Toward Clarity and Grace*. 1990.

Many books on writing could be listed. I have found the following particularly helpful:

Hacker, Diana. *A Writer's Reference*. 3rd ed. Boston: Bedford, 1995.

Henson, Kenneth T. *The Art of Writing for Publication*. Boston: Allyn and Bacon, 1995.

Hudson, Robert. *A Christian Writer's Manual of Style*. Updated and expanded edition. Grand Rapids: Zondervan, 2004.

Lederer, Richard, and Richard Dowis. *The Write Way: The S.P.E.L.L. Guide to Real-life Writing*. New York: Pocket, 1995.

Maggio, Rosalie. *The Nonsexist Word Finder: A Dictionary of Gender-free Usage*. Boston: Beacon, 1988.

Strunk, William, Jr., and E. B. White. *The Elements of Style*. 3rd ed. New York: Macmillan, 1979.

This chapter described English research writing style. Chapter 13 will deal with the format required for research papers and dissertations.

chapter 13

FORMATTING
THE PAPER

So far, this book on writing research papers has discussed the research process, shown how to make bibliographical and note cards, explained ways of organizing the paper, and described English research language. Now it turns to the matter of format, for a paper, thesis, or dissertation must (1) demonstrate careful research, (2) show logical organization, and (3) be presented in perfect format.

There are different systems for formatting a paper. Of necessity, an arbitrary choice of one system rather than another must be made. Because the Turabian style is widely used for academic writing in the field of religion and theology, this book follows *A Manual for Writers*, both for references and for typing format.[1] If your school has a style guide, you will need to follow it.

Chapter 13 gives basic guidelines for formatting the page and specific instructions for preparing different parts of the paper. The instructions assume that you are using a computer or word processor, probably Microsoft Word™ or WordPerfect™, of which any version will work. "Tips for the Typist," in appendix D, summarizes format instructions.

---

1. Kate L. Turabian, *A Manual for Writers of Term Papers, Theses, and Dissertations*, 7th ed., rev. Wayne C. Booth, Gregory G. Colomb, Joseph M. Williams, and the University of Chicago Press Editorial Staff (Chicago: University of Chicago Press, 2007). For excellent advice on formatting your paper correctly in Microsoft Word™, get a copy of this manual: Vincent Kiernan, *Writing Your Dissertation with Microsoft Word: A Step-by-Step Guide* (Alexandria, VA: Mattily, 2005). Following Kiernan's instructions from the moment you start to write will assure a well-formatted paper. He's an expert at Word; I am not.

Page Format

Set up the page format *before* you start typing. You will save yourself untold grief. Measurements are given in inches, but you can use the centimeter equivalent if you prefer (calculate 2.54 cm for each inch). Your word processing program can work with either inches or centimeters.

Body Text

Here are the basic settings for the body text. The page should be letter size (unless you live where A4 is the norm and this size is accepted by your school) and the orientation, portrait. Set the margins at 1 inch on top, bottom, and right (this is default and does not need changing), and 1.5 inches on the left (for proper binding). Set the line spacing for double spacing. Set the justification on left. Make sure you set the tabs you will need. The basic one is at the usual .5 inches from the left margin.

Choose a font that looks like printing (Garamond or Times Roman).[2] Some schools have a rule against a sans serif type such as Arial. Be sure you find out the rules. Generally, fancy fonts are out. Usually you can choose the size, within limits: no larger than 12 points and no smaller than 10 points.

Page Numbers

To simplify things, set the page number for the bottom center of the page. Use the same font as the body text. Put the page number at the bottom of every page, from first through the appendixes.

The first page of the "Introduction" is page 1 (Arabic numeral). In a dissertation, the preliminary pages are numbered in lowercase Roman numerals, at the bottom center of the page, beginning with the title page. Do not type the number, however, on that page.

Titles and Headings

The number of the chapter is typed at 2 inches from the top edge of the paper. The chapter title is typed centered, one double space below the number (some schools may want a triple space). If the title is longer than 4.75 inches, it must be divided, with the longer part on the first line, the shorter part on the second line, and a double space between. If the title takes three lines, use single space. Place the first line of text three single spaces (one double plus one single) below the chapter title. Major headings, such as INTRODUCTION or

---

2. On this page, "Body Text," "Page Numbers," and "Titles and Headings" are in sans serif type. The text is a serif font.

BIBLIOGRAPHY, are typed at 2 inches (13th line) from the top edge of the page, the same as chapter numbers.

Triple spaces are used before any heading, from level one through level five. (Review headings in chapter 11, under "Visible Organization.") To get the right spacing, you will have to do a hard return (the one that completes your paragraph), change from double to single space, do one hard return, and change back to double space. In Word, use ctrl–1 for single space, ctrl–2 for double space. Better yet, write yourself a macro or a style that will do this in one simple stroke.

Titles for appendixes appear on a special title page: APPENDIX A is centered on the page, with the title one double space below. These are the *only* two items on this page. The appendix material appears on the following page.

Preliminary Pages

A table of contents should follow the model provided. When the table is more than one page long, it begins with the phrase TABLE OF CONTENTS at 2 inches from the top of the page. If the table is shorter than one page, it may be centered on the page as it is in the example at the end of this chapter. The table of contents usually includes only chapter titles and the first three levels of subheadings.

Chapter titles are in caps. A double space goes between chapter title and the first heading, which is done in caps and lowercase. Use Arabic numerals for chapter numbers to save yourself grief (if that is fine by your school); otherwise, you need to align the dots after numbers of varying size.

Having set the correct margins, I set the tabs at the top of the page as follows: four left tabs (at 0.25, 0.50, 0.75, and 1.00), then a right tab with dot leaders at 5.25 and a right tab without leaders for the page number at 5.75. Do all this before starting to type.

Each heading must have at least one dot leader before the page number; if not, type it on two lines. What has been said about the table of contents applies also to the lists of illustrations, tables, and figures.

If you have a title page and one page of table of contents, you need not number them. If you have more than that (a longer table of contents, lists, acknowledgments, etc.), they should be numbered with lower-case Roman numerals at the bottom center of the page.

Footnotes and Quotations

The appearance of a paper is easily marred by incorrectly placed notes and quotations. The suggestions given here should help you do it perfectly.

Footnotes

Technology has taken the terror out of doing footnotes. Your word processor will need, however, a little help to do the footnotes as the new rules suggest. In order that the notes will look like those in this book, you will need to follow the instructions given on page 82. Once the footnotes are set up, you simply place the cursor at the end of the phrase or sentence, after the punctuation marks, and insert the note.

Besides the question of the size of the number in the footnote, you need to consider other quirks. So that the gap between the last line of text and the footnote separator is always the same, in Options, select "Below text." Also, watch out for Word's bad habit of putting the last footnote for the page on the following page. Often this is cured by deleting the last paragraph mark at the end of the footnote. If that does not work, lop off a line or two from the page so that the footnote comes to where it belongs. Of course, you may have very long footnotes that start on one page and continue to the next. That is common in a dissertation and is acceptable.

Your school may require footnote numbers to start with 1 on every page. You can change that under Options. However, do not make the change until you are printing your final copy. Having the footnotes in sequential order throughout the chapter is helpful when you do revising and editing—especially if you delete or add a note!

Quotations

Short quotations—one sentence or less—are easily worked into the paragraph. *Double* quotation marks are mandatory for quotations. In American usage, single quotations marks are used only for a quotation within a quotation. Additionally, closing quotation marks are placed *outside* the comma or the period after the word.

Longer quotations—usually two sentences on eight lines or more—are typed as "block quotations." These quotations are single spaced and indented from each margin. The old rule was to indent half as much as the regular paragraph, the new rule is to indent the same as the paragraph. Your school's style guide will determine what you should do. You may also make the quotation one point smaller than the body text (11 instead of 12 point, for example). For both Microsoft Word™ and WordPerfect™ you can set up a paragraph style to make the quotation look like the one in the sample pages at the end of the chapter. When you complete a paragraph in body text, highlight it, click on the style you have created, and the quotation will be just right.

No quotation marks are used for block quotations. When the quotation starts at the beginning of the original paragraph, there is an additional indentation. If following the old rule, the indent will be the same as that of the paper. If following the new rule, the indent should be .25 more than the paragraph indent. If the quotation comes from the middle of the paragraph, there is no indentation. To emphasize a quotation, even if it is not eight lines long, set it off in a block quotation.

You may italicize words or phrases in a quotation in order to show emphasis. Do so sparingly lest you overdo your point. Always make clear to your reader what was italicized by the author and what you italicized. Normally you will indicate this in the footnote, where you will give the reference and the phrase "italics mine" or "emphasis added" in parentheses after the page number: Jones, 37 (italics mine). If you put the phrase *within* the quotation, place it in brackets.

A quotation is followed by its appropriate reference, usually a footnote. However, a Bible quotation may have the reference in parentheses, followed by the period. In the case of block quotations followed by a reference in parentheses, the period precedes the parentheses.

> I appeal to you therefore, brethren, by the mercies of God, to present your bodies as a living sacrifice, holy and acceptable to God, which is your spiritual worship. Do not be conformed to this world but be transformed by the renewal of your mind, that you may prove what is the will of God, what is good and acceptable and perfect. (Rom 12:1–2)

Tables, Figures, and Illustrations

Tables, figures, and illustrations may be used to enhance a paper, thesis, or dissertation. They should be well made, clear, and large enough to be easily read. Colored ink cannot be used for theses or dissertations that are photocopied in black and white. Use instead different kinds of lines or crosshatching. The making of tables is described in chapter 19, which also includes a number of figures to be used as models. Each figure or table must have a number, a title, and a source, if it is not the result of the research being reported.

When the tables or figures are small enough to fit on the page, they may be placed between paragraphs, as near as possible to the text in which they are discussed. It is wise to make a reference to the figure or table in the text: "Figure 4 shows the outline of the walls of Jerusalem in the days of Hezekiah." Leave three empty lines above and below so that tables and figures do not look crowded.

Larger tables and figures are often placed on separate pages, as soon as possible after the text that mentions them. Computer typing often makes this kind of insertion mandatory. Neat appearance and ease of reading are the criteria for designing the pages on which tables and figures are included.

Traditionally titles of tables are typed in capital letters, centered, above the table. Titles of figures are typed in sentence style (first word capitalized, the rest lowercase) below the figure. If these titles are short, they are centered; if they are long, they begin at the left margin. The new usage calls for table titles to be typed sentence style, but still above the table. Again, examples are given in chapter 19.

Spelling, Punctuation, and Other Details

Needless to say, spelling, punctuation, and other small details are important in a research paper. Professors judge by what their eyes see! You, the student, are responsible for all details. You must carefully read the paper, mark any mistakes, and retype or request your typist to make needed corrections. When the paper is handed to the professor, it should be perfect. The professor should not be expected to correct spelling or point out typographical errors.

Spelling

Depending on your school, the spelling will be either British (Saviour, centre, etc.) or American (Savior, center, etc.). Both are correct, but most American schools prefer American spelling. Of course, your quotations will keep their original spelling. Whichever spelling you and your advisor select must be used consistently.

The spelling of foreign words, whether in titles of books and journals or in the text, must be accurate. That means using all the accents and diacritical marks in the original. WordPerfect™ and Word™ include multinational characters such as ç, ø, and é. Of course, foreign words that do not appear in the English dictionary should be italicized. An apparent contradiction to this is the allowance for you to insert a *quotation* in another language without italicizing. If you translate a word, give the English in brackets, as you do with any interpolation to a quotation. For non-Latin scripts follow standard transliteration patterns, such as the ones for biblical languages in appendix B. (Note that a reference to parts of the paper does not capitalize the name of the part, chapter, appendix, bibliography.)

Abbreviations appear in notes rather than in the text. Use standard ones, as given in your dictionary, in Turabian (chapter 24), or *The Chicago Manual of Style* (chapter 15). One abbreviation unique to biblical studies is "v." for "verse" and "vv." for "verses." Abbreviations other than the initials of an author (E. A. Jones) have no space after the period included in them (e.g., A.D.).

Word processors check the spelling for you, thus avoiding most spelling mistakes. Unfortunately, the spell checker cannot distinguish between words such as "there" and "their," but the grammar check should help there. A computer can also automatically divide words properly, but unless your advisor encourages word division, leave it for later publication of your research.

Punctuation

If there is doubt about the punctuation rules of the English language, review them. An English grammar is an important tool for writing research papers.

Besides causing problems by putting periods and commas before the final quotation marks, English punctuation has other idiosyncracies. In English research language, an enumeration needs a comma before the word "and." For example: We like bananas, mangoes, and papaya. At the same time, the tendency to eliminate commas, except as needed for clarity, is evident. An author whose name includes "Jr." or a Roman numeral is written John Jones Jr.—without a comma. When you invert the name, as in the bibliography, you will use commas: Jones, John, Jr.

Lines, short and long, can also cause problems. A hyphen joins two words, as in "twenty-two." An en dash is slightly longer than a hyphen and indicates inclusive numbers: pages 36–39 or the years 1969–1971. An em dash is equivalent to two hyphens. There are no spaces before and after the hyphen, the en dash, or the em dash. Type an em dash as two hyphens: We saw someone--who it was, we have no idea--leaving the house. If your computer program turns the double dash into an em dash—so be it! Distinguish between a line in the middle of the type (a hyphen or a dash) and a line below the letters (underlining). Use the second for the eight-space line used in a bibliography when an author has more than one book. (New usages suggest three em dashes to replace the underlining.)

Current usage puts only one space after the period or full stop. This shows up too in the ellipsis mark, where the dots are always followed by a space. In fact, all punctuation marks are followed by one space, with one exception. When a colon or a period is used to separate parts of books, there is no space after it. For example: *TWOT*, 1:112 means volume 1, page 112; Irenaeus *Against Heresies* 2.2.3 refers to book 2, chapter 2, paragraph 3.

Other Details

Among these details is the use of numbers. In a scientific paper, Arabic numbers are always used. In reporting statistics, Arabic numbers are always used:

for example, 23 percent of the 345 respondents (notice the use of "percent" rather than the symbol) said they preferred bananas. Numbers larger than one thousand have a comma: 4,567. Arabic numbers cannot be used at the beginning of a sentence. Use Arabic numbers for volumes of books or journals. Use Roman numerals only when transcribing a quotation or as page numbers for the preliminary pages (lower case at the bottom of the page).

Ordinal numbers below ten and round numbers should be written out in the text: eighth, one hundredth. In the documentation, however, they are given as numerals: 1st, 2nd, 3rd, 4th. You may use the superscript if you so desire: 1st, 2nd, 3rd, 4th. Be consistent, whichever you choose.

According to Turabian (chapter 23) and Zondervan's *The Christian Writer's Manual of Style* (284),[3] numbers under one hundred are written out (an adaptation of that rule only insists on written numbers below twenty). Likewise, round numbers, such as "five thousand," are written. Fractions are written out: one-half. However, Bible references and page numbers, as well as dates, decimal numbers, percentages, and sums of money are never written out.

These important details are covered in English grammar books and very specifically in Turabian's *Manual for Writers*. Use these works to produce an A-grade paper. However, always take into account your school's rules.

Sample Pages

The next few pages show examples in correct format of the proper appearance of a paper. Unfortunately, these are not the originals on 8 1/2 by 11 paper. However, use your imagination. Be sure to check with your professor to see if these pages conform to your school's rules.

---

3. Robert Hudson, gen. ed., *A Christian Writer's Manual of Style*, updated and expanded ed. (Grand Rapids: Zondervan, 2004).

Andrews University

[2.5 in]

Theological Seminary

[4 in]

THE IMPACT OF *HEILSGESCHICHTE* ON THE
UNDERSTANDING OF THE BIBLICAL
DOCTRINE OF CREATION

[6 in]

A Report

Presented in Partial Fulfillment

of the Requirements for the Course

GSEM 920 Religious Studies Seminar

[8 in]

by

Karen K. Abrahamson

June 2000

TABLE OF CONTENTS

(Note: WordPerfect™ spaces the dots; Microsoft Word™ does not. Let your software determine the format of the leader dots, unless your school has a specific rule otherwise.)

INTRODUCTION

The term *Heilsgeschichte* was coined by Johann Albrecht Bengel (1687-1752). It came to be used to describe "the nature of the Bible as an account of God's working out divine salvation in human history." Proponents of *Heilsgeschichte* or salvation history "rejected the idea that the Bible is a collection of divine 'proof texts' for constructing doctrine in favor of seeing it as a history of God's redemptive plan."[1]

The formal development of the concept in the nineteenth century, according to A. Josef Greig, came in response to the skepticism that emerged in Christianity as a reaction to "the aims of rationalism and pietism, and the results of the historical-critical method."[2] Hans W. Frei points out that for *Heilsgeschichte*, the "saving facts" of the Bible are "real and historical but not in an ordinary way that would open them up to religiously neutral verification."[3]

The concept of *Heilsgeschichte* allows for the reinterpretation of an event from a historical understanding in time to a nonhistorical and experiential interpretation. This hermeneutical concept suggests the question: What impact does this theory have upon biblical doctrine, in particular, the doctrine of Creation?

In order to answer this question, this paper will examine the historical development of *Heilsgeschichte* and analyze its presuppositions and hermeneutical approaches.

---

1. Stanley J. Grenz, David Guretzki, and Cherith Fee Nordling, *Pocket Dictionary of Theological Terms* (Downers Grove, IL: InterVarsity Press, 1999), s.v. *"Heilsgeschichte."*

2. A. Josef Greig, "Some Formative Aspects in the Development of Gerhard von Rad's Idea of History," *AUSS* 16 (1978): 314.

3. Hans W. Frei, *The Eclipse of Biblical Narrative: A Study in Eighteenth and Nineteenth Century Hermeneutics* (New Haven: Yale University Press, 1974), 180.

CHAPTER I

HISTORICAL DEVELOPMENT OF

HEILSGESCHICHTE

Several factors played important roles in shaping the *Heilsgeschichte* concept: (1) rationalism, (2) experiential and inward-turning elements within Christianity, and (3) the implementation of the historical-critical method. These factors later came together to form the basis of Liberal Protestantism.

Rationalism

Immanuel Kant rose from obscurity to provide the "theological watershed between [the] classical and modern (liberal) systems" that would, if accepted, make "the classical view impossible."[4] Kant accomplished this task by reinterpreting reason. His philosophy included two aspects: the timeless nature of God and truth, and the limitation of human reason to the spatio-temporal. Fernando Canale notes that such divergences between God and humanity do not allow for cognitive contact between God, as a "timeless or supernatural object," and human reason.[5] Therefore, the need for some other means of communication arises.

Because Kantian understanding leaned heavily toward the intuitive, rationalism brought uncertainty in regard to history. Since certainty could only be attained through reason, "rationalism stimulated a search for a theology of immediacy and inwardness."[6]

---

4. Class notes, Fernando Canale, THST 619 Principles and Methods of Theology, Andrews University, 1997.

5. Fernando Canale, "Revelation and Inspiration: The Liberal Model," *AUSS* 32 (1994): 170-171.

6. Greig, 314.

2

Speaking of religious theory after Kant, Frei stated:

Religious theory after Kant focused more and more on faith as a distinctive and self-conscious human stance which is reducible to no other. *And faith in this sense qualifies whatever 'reality' it is properly in touch with,* analogous to the way in which for Kant the structure of reason qualifies the transcendental ego's contact with the objects of the sensible world, turning them from things-in-themselves into phenomena for human consciousness.[7]

Experiential and Inward-turning Elements
within Christianity

Thomas Aquinas desired to introduce Aristotle into Christianity in order to lessen the tension between faith and reason. To achieve this, he attempted to differentiate theology from philosophy.[8] Aquinas's views provided the basis for classical scholasticism.

Lutheran Protestantism, though claiming to follow *sola Scriptura*, accepted the hermeneutical presuppositions of classical scholasticism. After the death of Luther, Protestant theologians began the process of rational systematization of doctrine "that often included natural theology, Aristotelian logic and extreme fine-tuning and hairsplitting with regard to doctrinal formulations."[9]

As scholasticism resulted in an increasingly dry and rigid form of religion, nominalism created a new interest in humanity and came to see the human being as more real than the institution. In addition nominalism denied the objective reality of universal principles, which were considered to be "mere concepts with no reality apart from their existence in the mind of the individual."[10] Maintaining the existence of two realms of truth (scientific and theological) led some nominalists to exalt the experimental method as the main path to truth, while others began to move in the direction of mysticism "as a way by

---

7. Frei, 32 (emphasis supplied).

8. John W. Baldwin, *The Scholastic Culture of the Middle Ages: 1000-1300* (Lexington, MA: D. C. Heath, 1971), 93.

9. Roger E. Olson, *The Story of Christian Theology: Twenty Centuries of Tradition and Reform* (Downers Grove, IL: InterVarsity Press, 1999), 475.

10. Grenz, Guretzki, and Nordling, s.v. "nominalism."

which the individual could come directly into the presence of God."[11] In Greig's words, "The failure of rationalism to attain its theological goals tended to turn the theologian's attitude inwards, toward religious experience." This resulted in the development of the Pietistic movement within German Lutheranism.[12]

German Pietism

Pietism stood "between the controversies of orthodoxy and the more innovative approaches to theology."[13] Olson defined Pietism as "a renewal movement that aimed at a completion of the Protestant Reformation begun by Martin Luther."[14]

Through Pietism Lutheranism was refreshed and revived as three elements in the life of the believer were emphasized: the study and application to daily life of the Bible and the development of a pious life. An additional emphasis on missionary activity caused some, however, to develop an indifference to biblical doctrine and led them into idealism.[15] This idealism found the nature of reality "more in terms of spirit or mind than matter or material."[16] It attempted to "retain the comprehensiveness of vision in Romanticism and Transcendentalism while avoiding their subjectivism. . . . At the same time, it retained an allure for philosophy by attempting to build on rationality rather than intuition."[17]

---

11. Earle E. Cairns, *Christianity through the Centuries: A History of the Christian Church*, rev. and enl. ed. (Grand Rapids: Zondervan, Academie Books, 1981), 239-240.

12. Greig, 315.

13. Ibid., 314.

14. Olson, 473.

15. Cairns, 381.

16. Grenz, Guretzk, and Nordling, s.v. "idealism."

17. Steve Wilkens and Alan Padgett, *Faith and Reason in the 19th Century*, Christianity and Western Thought, vol. 2 (Downers Grove, IL: InterVarsity Press, 2000), 63.

SUMMARY AND CONCLUSIONS

Heilsgeschichte has been defined in this paper as a hermeneutical principle within the historical-critical method. Its development was simultaneous with the growth of the Liberal Protestant movement and came about as a result of the need to bridge the gap between the historical veracity of the Bible and the new theologically oriented method of interpretation.

Several factors played roles in bringing about the concept of *Heilsgeschichte*: (1) rationalism, as developed by Immanuel Kant; (2) experiential and inward-turning elements within Christianity, such as German Pietism, Schleiermacher's concept of *Gefühl*, and Hegel's dialectical philosophy; and the historical-critical method.

The paper began with the hypothesis that the Liberal Protestant concept of *Heilsgeschichte* impacts the doctrine of creation by allowing for the reinterpretation of the event from a historical understanding of the event in time to one of nonhistorical and experiential interpretation. This allows for the rejection of the first eleven chapters of the book of Genesis as historical documentation, while preserving the theological integrity of those passages.

An examination of the presuppositions upon which the *Heilsgeschichte* concept is built shows that this hypothesis is true. Furthermore, the nonhistorical and experiential interpretation is problematic on five counts: (1) It uses subjective methods of interpretation, (2) it dissects Scripture, (3) it denigrates the concept of propositional truth, (4) it questions faith, and (5) it does not use consistently its own hermeneutical method–the scientific method.

BIBLIOGRAPHY

Baldwin, John W. *The Scholastic Culture of the Middle Ages: 1000-1300*. Lexington, MA: D. C. Heath, 1971.

Cairns, Earle E. *Christianity through the Centuries: A History of the Christian Church*. Revised and enlarged edition. Grand Rapids: Zondervan, Academie Books, 1981.

Canale, Fernando. "Revelation and Inspiration: The Liberal Model." *Andrews University Seminary Studies* 32 (1994): 169-195.

Frei, Hans W. *The Eclipse of Biblical Narrative: A Study in Eighteenth and Nineteenth Century Hermeneutics*. New Haven: Yale University Press, 1974.

Fretheim, Terence E. *Creation, Fall, and Flood: Studies in Genesis 1-11*. Minneapolis: Augsburg, 1969.

Greig, A. Josef. "A Critical Note on the Origin of the Term *Heilsgeschichte*." *The Expository Times* 87 (1975-1976): 118-119.

————. "Some Formative Aspects in the Development of Gerhard von Rad's Idea of History." *Andrews University Seminary Studies* 16 (1978): 313-331.

Grenz, Stanley J., David Guretzki, and Cherith Fee Nordling. *Pocket Dictionary of Theological Terms*. Downers Grove, IL: InterVarsity Press, 1999.

Grenz, Stanley J., and Roger E. Olson. *Twentieth Century Theology: God and the World in a Transitional Age*. Downers Grove, IL: InterVarsity Press, 1992.

Hasel, Gerhard. *Old Testament Theology: Basic Issues in the Current Debate*. Revised edition. Grand Rapids: Eerdmans, 1972.

Hegel, G.W.F. *The Phenomenology of Mind*. 2 vols. Translated by J. B. Baillie. New York: Macmillan, 1910.

Lichtenberger, F. *History of German Theology in The Nineteenth Century*. Translated and edited by W. Hastie. Edinburgh: T. & T. Clark, 1889.

Lundin, Roger, Clarence Walhout, and Anthony C. Thiselton. *The Promise of Hermeneutics*. Grand Rapids: Eerdmans, 1999.

chapter 14

BIBLICAL EXEGESIS AS RESEARCH

Biblical exegesis is not usually listed as a type of research; it is, however, a study that uses research methods. You must think carefully, develop a bibliography, read books and journals, take notes, organize the topic, and write the paper.

This chapter describes a research-oriented exegetical process at an intermediate level. It also lists commonly used sources and describes an acceptable final form for the exegetical paper.

Steps in the Exegetical Process

Many different schemes of exegesis exist. The one described here starts with the biblical text in its canonical context.[1] It assumes the authority and unity of Scripture and seeks to ascertain the meaning of the Bible, both for its original readers or hearers and for the life of the church today.

Step 1: Determine the Canonical Context

Read in its canonical setting the passage you want to study. Find out what it is a part of and how it functions within that setting. Look for the markers that

---

1. See Grant R. Osborne, *The Hermeneutical Spiral* (Downers Grove, IL: InterVarsity Press, 1993), 19–40; Lee J. Gugliotto also begins with the context; see his massive *Handbook for Bible Study* (Hagerstown, MD: Review & Herald, 1996). Another excellent guide for NT exegesis is Gordon Fee, *New Testament Exegesis: A Handbook for Students and Pastors*, 3rd ed. (Louisville: Westminster John Knox, 2002). See also George H. Guthrie and J. Scott Duvall, *Biblical Greek Exegesis: A Graded Approach to Learning Intermediate and Advanced Greek* (Grand Rapids: Zondervan, 1998). Finally, consider Michael Gorman, *Elements of Biblical Exegesis: A Basic Guide for Students and Ministers* (Peabody, MA: Hendrickson, 2001). For doctoral students I recommend Stanislaw Bayliński, *A Guide to Biblical Research: Introductory Notes*, Subsidia biblica 28 (Rome: Editrice pontificio institutio biblico, 2006).

indicate its limits, as well as its relation to what precedes and what follows. Outline your passage within the context of the genre and structure of the section of the book or even of the whole book.

After you have studied the Bible text—your passage and its context—you may want to see how other authors have understood the organization of the chapter and of the book of which it is a part. This information is part of what is given in an Old Testament or New Testament introduction (used in the technical sense of a work that tells *about* a Bible book) or in a Bible commentary. However, because authors' presuppositions may cause them to see things in a particular light, you need to be careful about accepting their explanation at face value. Read with care and thought. At this point, do not read interpretations of your passage—only gather information on the canonical context.

The following introductions may be valuable:

Arnold, Bill T., and Bryan E. Beyer. *Encountering the Old Testament*. Grand Rapids: 2nd ed. Grand Rapids: Baker, 1999.

Carson, D. A., and Douglas Moo. *Introduction to the New Testament*. 2nd ed. Grand Rapids: Zondervan, 2005.

Elwell, Walter, and Robert W. Yarbrough. *Encountering the New Testament*. Grand Rapids: Baker, 1998.

Guthrie, Donald. *New Testament Introduction*. 4th rev. ed. Downers Grove, IL: InterVarsity Press, 1990.

Longman, Tremper, III, and Raymond Dillard. *An Introduction to the Old Testament,* 2nd ed. Grand Rapids: Zondervan, 2006.

Step 2: Establish the Text

After demarcating the passage to be studied, that is, determining its beginning and ending, establish the text. This means determining as accurately as possible, by means of textual criticism, the original text. No variant reading in the entire Scripture changes the basic biblical message. However, there are textual variants of significance. An example of these is the *Comma Johanneum* (1 John 5:7–8), used for generations as a New Testament proof of the doctrine of the Trinity, which has now been shown to be a late addition (eleventh century) to the Bible text. There is no point in doing exegesis on a doubtful variant.

In order to find the oldest form of a Bible text—or at least locate the most trustworthy one—the original languages must be used. For the Hebrew Bible, the following are reliable texts:

Biblia Stuttgartensia. Stuttgart: Deutsche Bibelstiftung, 1990.

Rahlfs, A., ed. *Septuaginta*. 8th ed. 2 vols. Stuttgart: Württembergische Bibelanstalt, 1965.

Two editions of the Greek New Testament are recommended. The first is easy to read and use, but its restricted textual apparatus only includes problems that could affect Bible translation. The second has a more complete, yet difficult-to-use, textual apparatus.

Greek New Testament. 4th rev. ed. Stuttgart: Deutsche Bibelgesellschaft, 1994. (Commonly called UBS4 text)

Nestle, Erwin, and Kurt Aland, eds. *Novum Testamentum Graece.* 27th ed. Stuttgart: Württembergische Bibelanstalt, 1993.

A companion of the United Bible Societies, *A Textual Commentary on the Greek New Testament,* clarifies the decisions on textual criticism made by the Committee of New Testament Scholars. The certainty attributed to the authenticity of a phrase or word is designated by the letters A, B, C, and D. Reasons for the choice are given for each passage. The volume is a useful tool for determining New Testament text:

Metzger, Bruce. *A Textual Commentary on the Greek New Testament.* 2nd ed. Stuttgart: Deutsche Bibelgeschaft, 1994.

For those whose biblical languages are poor, a comparison of different Bible versions can help. This comparison — together with a study of notes to the text — will suggest which is considered the most authentic text. Naturally, serious Bible translations, rather than popular ones, should be used for this comparative study. Modern versions constitute an improvement over the King James Version (prepared in 1611), because they use manuscripts not available at that time. The following English versions are suggested:

New American Standard Bible. Published in 1971, revised in 1995, the NASB uses formal but clear English. There are abundant notes and references.

New International Version. Revised in 1984, the NIV uses clear and simple English. Although it may oversimplify some text problems, the NIV is a sound, modern translation. *Today's New International Version* follows the same high standard.

Revised Standard Version. First published in 1952, the RSV has come to occupy an important place among scholarly modern Bible translations.

New Revised Standard Version. This revision of the RSV by a committee of scholars was completed in 1989. The NRSV incorporates later discoveries and research and uses inclusive language.

Reading the text in other modern languages is useful if the version you read was translated from the original languages. If it was not, you are one additional step removed from the original.

Step 3: Establish the Translation

Now you ask: What does the original text say? To establish the translation, take into account vocabulary and grammar.

Some reliable dictionaries and lexicons are the following:

Bauer, Walter. *A Greek-English Lexicon of the New Testament and Other Early Christian Literature.* 3rd ed. Revised and edited by Frederick W. Danker. Chicago: University of Chicago Press, 2000.

Brown, Francis, S. R. Driver, and C. A. Briggs. *The New Brown, Driver, and Briggs Hebrew and English Lexicon of the Old Testament.* Grand Rapids: Baker, 1987.

Holladay, William L. *A Concise Hebrew and Aramaic Lexicon of the Old Testament.* Grand Rapids: Eerdmans, 1993.

Koehler, L., W. Baumgartner, and J. Stamm. *Hebrew and Aramaic Lexicon of the Old Testament.* 2 vols. Leiden: Brill, 2001.

Liddell, Henry George, and Robert Scott. *A Greek-English Lexicon.* Oxford: Clarendon, reprint, 1996.

Some helpful grammars are:

Blass, Friedrich, and Albert Debrunner. *A Greek Grammar of the New Testament and Other Early Christian Literature.* Translated by Robert W. Funk. Chicago: University of Chicago Press, 1961.

Gesenius, W., and E. Kautsch. *Gesenius' Hebrew Grammar.* 2nd English ed. Revised by A. E. Cowley. Oxford: Clarendon, 1970.

Joüon, Paul. *A Grammar of Biblical Hebrew.* Translated and revised by T. Muraoka. 2 vols. Subsidia Biblica. Rome: Pontificio Istituto Biblico, 1996.

Moulton, James Hope, Wilbert Howard, and Nigel Turner. *A Grammar of New Testament Greek.* 4 vols. Edinburgh: T. and T. Clark, 1906–1970.

Wallace, Daniel B. *Greek Grammar beyond the Basics: An Exegetical Syntax of the New Testament.* Grand Rapids: Zondervan, 1996.

The Greek and Hebrew grammars you have used in class can also help you. You may also use electronic tools, such as Logos Libronix and BibleWorks. Try also the Internet, at http://www.biblestudytools.com.

Those who are "Greek and Hebrew challenged" still have valuable tools:

Fields, Lee. *Hebrew for the Rest of Us.* Grand Rapids: Zondervan, 2008.

Mounce, William. *Greek for the Rest of Us.* Grand Rapids: Zondervan, 2003.

———. *Interlinear for the Rest of Us.* Grand Rapids: Zondervan, 2006.

Step 4: Establish the Meaning

Establishing the meaning goes beyond the simple translation of the text. Now the question is asked: What does the passage mean? In order to determine the meaning of a text, study the syntax of the sentences. In addition, investigate the meaning of important words.

Syntax

In studying the syntax of a passage, look at the structure of the sentence and the function of the words. Look for idiomatic phrases and hard-to-translate prepositions. In Hebrew, look for constructs showing possession or other relations. In short, look for any element that might modify the first, direct, and obvious translation of the passage. For step 4, the following books are useful (see also the grammars noted above):

Brooks, James A., and Carlton L. Winbery. *Syntax of New Testament Greek*. Washington, DC: University Press of America, 1988.

Moule, C. F. D. *An Idiom-book of the New Testament Greek*. 2nd ed. Cambridge: Cambridge University Press, 1978.

Waltke, Bruce K., and M. O'Connor. *An Introduction to Biblical Hebrew Syntax*. Winona Lake, IN: Eisenbrauns, 1990.

Word Study

Look up important nouns and verbs in a concordance to see how they are used in other passages. Start with other occurrences of these words in the same book, then in other passages by the same author, then in other authors of the same period. Afterwards, study these same words in theological dictionaries.

Concordances

Using a concordance in English is not as accurate as using one based on Hebrew or Greek words. English concordances list the words that appear in a given English version; Young and Strong work from the King James Version. Young's *Concordance* does show for each English word what the original language word is, but a given Greek or Hebrew word is not always translated in the same way. To find all the uses of a certain word, you need to use a Greek or Hebrew concordance, either in book form or in one of the Bible software programs.

Even-Shoshan, Abraham, ed. *A New Concordance of the Bible*. Jerusalem: Kiryat Sefer, 1983.

Hatch, Edwin, and Henry Redpath. *A Concordance to the Septuagint and Other Greek Versions of the Old Testament*. Graz: Akademische Druck, 1954.

Kohlenberger, John R., Edward Goodrick, and James Swanson. *The Exhaustive Concordance to the Greek New Testament*. Grand Rapids: Zondervan, 1995.

———. *The Greek-English Concordance to the New Testament*. Grand Rapids: Zondervan, 1997.

Kohlenberger, John R., and James Swanson. *The Hebrew-English Concordance to the Old Testament*. Grand Rapids: Zondervan, 1998.

Wigram, George. *The Englishman's Greek Concordance of the New Testament*. Peabody, MA: Hendrickson, 1996.

———. *The Englishman's Hebrew Concordance of the Old Testament*. Peabody, MA: Hendrickson, 1996.

Theological dictionaries

Theological dictionaries and books containing word studies are useful to the process of exegesis. However, their authors—as well as their users—have certain presuppositions that must be taken into account.

The following are good for the Old Testament:

Botterweck, G. J., and H. Ringren. *Theological Dictionary of the Old Testament (TDOT)*. Grand Rapids: Eerdmans, 1974–. (As of 2007, only 15 volumes are available.)

Harris, R. Laird, Gleason L. Archer, and Bruce K. Waltke. *Theological Wordbook of the Old Testament (TWOT)*. Chicago: Moody Publishers, 2003.

VanGemeren, Willem A., gen. ed. *New International Dictionary of Old Testament Theology and Exegesis (NIDOTTE)*. 5 vols. Grand Rapids: Zondervan, 1997.

TDOT is being translated from the German, at a very slow pace. *TWOT* is a condensation and conservative adaptation of the German work on which *TDOT* is based. It keys the words to Strong's *Concordance* numbers, thus permitting someone who knows little or no Hebrew to benefit from its contents. *NIDOTTE* has a Scripture index and an English topical index that allow those who may not be strong in Hebrew to take advantage of a wealth of information. It uses the Goodrick-Kohlenberger numbers, which are used in their concordances noted above.

The following are good for the New Testament:

Balz, Horst, and Gerhard Schneider. 3 vols. *Exegetical Dictionary of the New Testament*. Grand Rapids: Eerdmans, 1990.

Brown, Colin, ed. *The New International Dictionary of New Testament Theology (NIDNTT)*. 4 vols. Grand Rapids: Zondervan, 1978–1986.

Kittel, G., and G. Friedrich, eds. *Theological Dictionary of the New Testament (TDNT)*. 10 vols. Grand Rapids: Eerdmans, 1964–1976.

Verbrugge, Verlyn D., ed. *The New International Dictionary of New Testament Theology: Abridged Edition*. Grand Rapids: Zondervan, 2003. (Abridgment and reorganization of *NIDNTT*; uses Goodrick-Kohlenberger numbers.)

TDNT is a classic, indispensable to biblical scholars. The single most important book of the set, volume 10, contains indexes by Greek, Hebrew, and English words, and also by texts that are referenced. *TDNT* comments on families of words and on words of theological importance. *NIDNTT* is to *TDNT* what *NIDOTTE* is to *TDOT* (see above): less complicated, more conservative, and easier to handle. It also contains much less information.

A basic, almost elementary, but useful tool is:

Mounce, William, ed. *Complete Expository Dictionary of Old and New Testament Words*. Grand Rapids: Zondervan, 2006.

At the end of this step, you should have a clear, accurate, and smooth translation of the passage—the cumulative result of the first four steps. On the basis of this translation—which should be arrived at quite independently of any existing Bible translation—the next three steps should be undertaken.

Step 5: Establish the Historical and Geographical Context

This step of exegesis considers the historical and geographical context of the passage. It asks: What was happening at the time this passage was written that might explain the text?

Historical information is needed to clarify the text and suggests explanations for what was said or happened. Knowledge of the socio-political and economic situation of the time is important to understanding the passage. Also, knowledge of the geography and climate of the region, as well as of the customs of the people, helps bring the biblical text to life.

For historical and geographical information, the following sources are useful:

Aharoni, Yohanan. *The Land of the Bible: A Historical Geography.* 2nd ed. Philadelphia: Westminster, 1979.
Aharoni, Yohanan, and Michael Avi-Yonah. *The Macmillan Bible Atlas.* Rev. 3rd ed. Toronto: Maxwell Macmillan, 1993.
Bromiley, Geoffrey, ed. *International Standard Bible Encyclopedia.* 4 vols. Rev. ed. Grand Rapids: Eerdmans, 1979 – 1988.
Freedman, David Noel, ed. *Anchor Bible Dictionary.* 6 vols. New York: Doubleday, 1992.

See also the two *Encountering* books from step 1.

A related type of information is obtained from biblical archaeology. The excavations and their interpretation provide interesting data on the way people lived. Information concerning ancient languages has also come from archaeological discoveries. Some material on biblical archaeology is found in the dictionaries listed above. Many books have been written on the topic; these four are among the most useful. Your professor may have additional suggestions.

Bimson, John, ed. *Baker Encyclopedia of Bible Places: Towns and Cities, Countries and States, Archaeology and Topography.* Grand Rapids: Baker, 1995.
Blaiklock, Edward M., and R. K. Harrison, eds. *The New Dictionary of Biblical Archaeology.* Grand Rapids: Zondervan, 1983.
Kaiser, Walter C., Jr., ed. *Archaeological Study Bible.* Grand Rapids: Zondervan, 2006.
Stern, Ephraim, ed. *The New Encyclopedia of Archaeological Excavations in the Holy Land.* 4 vols. New York: Simon & Schuster, 1993.

Step 6: Establish the Original Theological Meaning

In this step of exegesis the question is: What did the passage mean to those who first heard or read it? On the basis of the previous steps and informed by your own biblical and theological understanding, bring out the deeper meaning.

Once you have established a clear understanding of the theological meaning of the passage, you can read what commentators say, to check or confirm your conclusions. Now you should be ready to read others' opinions without danger of being carried away by the postures of scholars. To read commentaries prior to this step could prejudice the outcome of your research. Reading them now gives the opportunity of corroborating what you already know, of broadening your knowledge, or even of defending your position against that of other authors who do not see things as you do.

Step 7: Establish the Application for Today

Once the meaning for the people who received the message or sang the psalm or heard the prophecy has been determined, the basic biblical meaning can be extracted. The last step of exegesis applies theological meaning to today's church or individual Christian. This application forms the basis of preaching and teaching.

This step of exegesis is difficult but necessary if Scripture is to speak to our times. It may not be required in a theoretical paper, but it is an integral part of biblical interpretation, especially for preaching.

By carefully following these seven steps of exegesis I can be reasonably sure of coming to a correct interpretation of Scripture. Naturally, biases and presuppositions can lead me astray. However, careful study of the Bible, starting from the text itself, allows the Bible to speak for itself to tell me what it wants to say (exegesis), without having me read into it (eisegesis) what I would like it to say.

Presentation of Exegesis

Not all of the search and study undertaken in these seven steps of exegesis is reported. Much of what you do is important to your research but irrelevant to the reader. The written report will not contain the parsing of the verbs or a list of all 59 occurrences of *dechomai* in the New Testament.

In any exegetical study there must be sufficient detail to make clear to the reader how I came to certain conclusions. To ask the reader to accept by faith that I know what I am saying falls short of the rigor demanded of research. If the tense of the verb is important to the interpretation of the verse, the study must point that out and give a clear explanation of why it is important. If knowing Jewish marriage customs clarifies the passage, I must describe and document those customs. If an aspect of the climate explains something in the text, I must note it.

The written presentation may be made in seven parts: one for each of the steps. However, there may be little to say about some of these steps. Another possibility is to do a phrase-by-phrase commentary. It is easier to work in small units than to deal with a whole passage. A weakness of this system, however, is that it tends to blur the unity of the passage. A strength of this system is that it gives equal importance to all details in the passage being exegeted.

A better solution might be to divide the study into three sections. The first is the introduction, stating the purpose of the research and giving the context of the text studied. The next section provides a translation of the passage, with notes explaining how I arrived at that translation. The third interprets the text, giving the theological meaning of the passage and its present application. I must present evidence of having answered all seven questions. The following outline, given as a model to Intermediate Greek students, illustrates this approach.

INTRODUCTION
    Passage selected
    Reasons for choosing this passage
    Setting of the passage
    Author
    Date
    Audience
    Literary interrelations
    Historical/geographical/socio-economic context
THE TEXT
    Translation
    Information on
        Textual problems
        Grammar and syntax
        Important words
INTERPRETATION
    Meaning for original readers
    Application for today's Christians
BIBLIOGRAPHY

When we write exegetical papers we often need to quote Greek or Hebrew words. These may be transliterated (see a reasonable transliteration scheme in appendix B) or typed in the original language. WordPerfect™ and Microsoft Word™ have Greek and Hebrew fonts. You may also use the fonts that come with Bible software or download fonts from the Internet.

As was noted at the beginning of the chapter, exegesis as a form of research may be frowned on by some who think of research in terms of surveys, experiments, or archival searching. Nevertheless, an exegesis paper following the seven steps outlined in this chapter allows the exegete to show excellent research techniques and style. It also contributes to the fund of biblical knowledge. And if that is not research, what is?

Another special form of research is descriptive research. It is discussed in chapter 15.

chapter 15

DESCRIPTIVE RESEARCH

Descriptive research does exactly what its name says: it describes, usually one or more characteristics of a group of people, technically called a population. This is not a literary or poetical description, but a concrete and concise depiction of reality. Sometimes the information gathered is strictly quantitative — numbers and percentages; other times it is qualitative, including the "why" along with the "how many." This chapter presents the steps of descriptive research as well as techniques for conducting surveys and interviews.

Within the pastoral setting, descriptive research could portray a congregation: how many members there are, what age groups they belong to, what their professions and occupations are, whether they live in apartments or houses, how often they attend church, whether they tithe, and so on. Descriptive research could also be employed to study the population of an area where a church is to be planted or the way pastors perceive the usefulness of their seminary training.

The purpose of descriptive research is to make reality known. As a result, conclusions may be reached and decisions made. In the times of the Roman Empire, the census was not merely intended to let Rome know how many citizens there were. Rather, on the basis of a census, taxes were levied and armies were organized. Today, descriptive research is used to find out how many people watch a certain television program in order to decide what the best airing time is. A marketing company of a particular soap product surveys a large group of teenagers to discover not only how many are washing their face with their product, but to determine the best way to get more of them to use this particular soap. Descriptive research on the preschool children in a certain town may be useful in deciding whether or not the school needs to add another classroom in the next three years.

Descriptive research may have first been used to document need for change by John Howard, who began to fret in 1773 over the inhumane conditions of the prisons in Bedford, England. In order to prove what he was saying, he traveled all over England, visiting jails and noting the exact number of prisoners, what crimes they had committed, the conditions under which they were held, and other matters concerning the prison system. After completing his descriptive study, he stood before the House of Commons and gave a detailed and precise report that became the basis for important prison reforms. Howard later compared English prisons with jails in other European countries. His book *The State of Prisons* (1777) was one of the first comparative-descriptive studies. After studying the prisons of the land, he went on to investigate the conditions in hospitals. In one of these places he contracted an illness and died, a martyr for research.

This interesting story aside, it is evident that the report Howard prepared did not resolve any problem. It only provided the information necessary to set change in motion. This is the usefulness of descriptive research.

In technical language, the purpose of descriptive research is to:

1. Collect detailed factual information that describes existing phenomena
2. Identify problems or justify conditions and practices
3. Make comparisons and evaluations
4. Determine what others are doing with similar problems or situations and benefit from their experience in making future plans and decisions.[1]

Obtaining precise data is not always easy. A little boy, asked if he loves his mother, will normally answer: Yes! Human beings want to please the people who ask them questions. Personal observations may not provide accurate data either; what you see may be tainted by your personal bias. If neither respondent nor observer is trustworthy, how can you be sure you are really seeing all there is to see?

Use as many different methods as possible to get information. To describe a congregation, get information from the church membership records, the church treasurer's records, the Sabbath or Sunday school attendance records, the lay ministries records, and any other records that may be appropriate. In addi-

---

1. Stephen Isaac and William B. Michael, *Handbook in Research Evaluation* (San Diego: EDITS, 1971), 18.

tion, survey the members, getting specific information from them. Interview former pastors or other persons who may have important information. Finally, add personal observations. The secret for obtaining a complete and accurate description lies in using several approaches, tapping into different sources.

Descriptive research usually studies a situation at a given moment in time. A specialized type of descriptive research studies a person, case, or situation over time. A study of the growth of a church over ten years is an example. Some descriptions over time may prove difficult or impossible for theology students, except as dissertations. See chapter 21 on D.Min. projects.

Steps in Descriptive Research

The descriptive research process may be divided into four steps: defining the objectives, designing the approach, collecting the data, and writing the results. Usually the first two steps take most of the time.

Defining the Objectives

Within the framework of the purpose of the study, what is the information to be obtained? And from whom is it to be obtained? What facts and characteristics are to be uncovered? These questions must be answered in order to accomplish the first step.

In research on the function of deacons in a church, the objective of the survey might be to discover who the deacons are—how old they are, where they live, where they work, how long they have been church members. One might also wish to find out what they do in the church—visit members, take care of the church property, keep order during services, etc.—and how they consider their responsibilities—whether they feel needed, adequately prepared, or satisfied. Knowing exactly what you need to find out is the foundation of good descriptive research.

Designing the Approach

Once you know what you need to find out, the second step is to decide on the best way to obtain the different kinds of information. Personal interviews may be appropriate to gather some data. Other information is best obtained by using a questionnaire. Still other data can be obtained from records. Personal observation is valid as well.

For each of these different approaches a strategy must be developed. Will all of the deacons be interviewed? If not, how will I choose the ones to be interviewed? When and where will I do the interviews? Will the survey of church members' impressions of the deacons' work be anonymous? How can I get the greatest number of members to reply to my survey? Techniques for surveying, sampling, and interviewing are important enough to be considered under separate headings.

Before designing my own instruments, strategies, and procedures, I must read widely, both on the topic or situation to be studied and on possible methodologies to use. For example, if I am planning to survey the personal devotional habits of young people, I should read everything written about the topic and especially look for studies already done about this topic. The *ATLA Religion Index* is an excellent place to look for this information.

After extensive reading on the theory, the methodology, and the situation to be studied, consultation with the professor guiding the study is in order. Since some of the techniques of descriptive research are foreign to theological education, students should look for professors in education, sociology, or psychology who may be willing to assist in the process.

If at all possible, find instruments (collective name for surveys, questionnaires, interview outlines, etc.) that have already been prepared by a credible researcher. Finding them may take time, but preparing good ones will probably take longer. D.Min. projects, reported online in *Research in Ministry*,[2] should provide some examples.

Once the instruments have been designed, some form of validation is appropriate. A pilot study, using a small number of respondents, may be used to find out if the questions are well worded, clearly understandable, and easy to answer. A panel of experts might also be used to study the instruments and advise on their appropriateness. Even better, both methods can be used.

Collecting the Data

Collecting the data is the exciting part of the research. After all the hard work of preparing, it is fun to send out questionnaires and get them back. It is interesting to go through the interview process. It is satisfying to be nearing the goal.

This elation, however, brings with it a major danger. You may trust your memory and not write down precisely and accurately the findings. It then becomes impossible to reconstruct the information obtained. The only antidote to this problem is to set up the easiest possible way to record in an

---

2. http://rim.atla.com/star/rimonline_login.htm.

organized and orderly fashion every piece of data. The importance of clear notes or recordings cannot be overemphasized.

Writing the Results

As in all other research papers, there must be an introduction. This gives the background, the definition of the problem, the purpose, the limitations and delimitations, and the definition of terms.

Following the introduction, a descriptive research paper or thesis needs to have what is termed a "review of literature." This section or chapter reports on the preparatory reading, both on the topic or population investigated (youth, deacons, women administrators, etc.), the methodology used (surveys, scales, ranking, etc.), and the theoretical framework, if appropriate. See more on the review of literature in chapter 20.

The review of literature is followed by a section or chapter on the research method employed: how the questionnaire was developed, tested, and applied; how the sampling was done; how the interview was designed and carried out. This description of the method explains to the reader how the research was accomplished. It helps the reader judge the quality of the study and may assist in future research design.

Then comes the description of the results. What was discovered? The topics are organized in some logical way and described in turn. Often the questions of the survey are taken one after another, or, if the questionnaire is long, by related groups of questions.

Finally, the whole process is summarized. On the basis of this summary, conclusions are drawn. Pastoral research usually ends with recommendations for action. Recommendations for further study may also be made.

The language of the report must be clear and precise. Generalities have no place. The following examples give precise data: how many, what percent. They also use language that only affirms what the subjects said—not what they are assumed to have done or believed.

Nearly half of the 140 pastors surveyed (48.5 percent) said they had completed a four-year theology course, while 42 (30 percent) responded that they had taken a three-year course. Seventeen individuals (12 percent) reported completing a two-year course, while 13 of those surveyed (9.5 percent) stated that they had no college training before entering the ministry.

In response to a question on their perception of the pastor's sharing of administrative responsibilities with the lay leaders, the largest group of elders (12, or 40 percent of the total of 30 elders) noted that the pastor shared well. The smallest group (4 elders, or 13.3 percent) stated that he did not share at all. Eight elders

(26.6 percent) checked the answer "Undecided." Six elders (20 percent) did not reply. If one takes those who did not answer as being undecided, the number of elders who did not feel qualified to answer the question, or who had doubts about their pastor's sharing of responsibilities, was 14 (46.6 percent).

Sampling

When Gallup polls want to know which candidate the citizens are going to elect, they do not ask every registered voter. Rather, they sample the population. That is, they poll a representative group. Regardless of the kind of instrument used to get information—survey, interview, checklist—sampling is a way to get a lot of information from not so many people.

When a seamstress wants to buy thread for a sewing project, she takes to the store a small piece of the cloth she will sew. That sample does not show the pattern or the design, only the color; it is enough to buy thread. For a sample to represent the total population—not just the color of the cloth—it must have all the characteristics of that population. A sample must be large enough to represent the population and it must contain the same types of people in the same proportion in which they appear in the total population. Random, representative, and cluster sampling are ways to get the information you need.

Random Sampling

Random sampling is a technique used to ensure—as far as possible—an unbiased representation of a population. Here "random" does not mean "chance." The researcher designs ways to achieve a fair representation by polling every tenth name on the list or interviewing every fourth candidate. However, before random sampling is applied, the population must be studied to ascertain that the method used guarantees, as nearly as possible, a representative sampling.

Random sampling can be applied to the total population. For example, every sixth member of the church—regardless of age, sex, or other factors—receives a questionnaire. Random sampling avoids the possibility of choosing only one's friends (or enemies) to answer the questions. It can be a safeguard for the research and the researcher.

Statistical theory indicates the correct size of samples. You will find information on this in a statistics textbook. You can also get help from a statistician or professor of statistics. The rule of thumb is that the larger the population, the smaller the percentage of people who must be surveyed.

Representative Sampling

To represent the population, the sample must include all the different kinds of people in the group. And it must include them in the proportion in which they are found. Thus, a representative sample (often called stratified sample) will include men and women, old and young, rich and poor, black and white, and whatever other kinds of people are in the larger group. If there are more women than men in the church, the sample must contain more women. If there are more old ladies than young ladies, the sample must also represent this characteristic of the total group.

Stratified sampling can be added to random sampling. Perhaps every sixth man between 20 and 40, every sixth woman between 41 and 60, and every sixth unmarried female receives a questionnaire. The benefits of both kinds of sampling are compounded.

Cluster Sampling

Cluster sampling selects sample clusters or groups out of the population and studies all members of those groups. For example, Betty wants to study third-grade children in her city. She finds that there are 56 third-grade classes, of which 40 are in public schools, 10 in church-related schools, and 6 in private schools. She also notes that 25 have between 20 and 30 children, 15 have fewer than 15 children, 10 have between 31 and 40 children, and 6 have more than 40 third graders. Once the classrooms are divided into categories, she can randomly choose one room from each category. Betty will then study all the third graders in the clusters (classrooms) chosen.

This approach to sampling could be appropriate for studying churches, Bible classes, or young people's groups. Proximity of the subject makes the study easy to conduct. The dynamics of group interaction, the sharing in the study, may also enrich the study.

Surveys

Surveys have become increasingly popular in recent years. People are asked what kind of toothpaste they use, for which political candidate they will vote, or how they feel about interracial marriage. Some surveys are done orally—the poll on the street before elections. Some use questionnaires to which a person must respond in writing. All share the same intention: to obtain information. While information obtained from a questionnaire is extensive, it tends to be shallow. Many people are polled, but not at great depth. This type of research is called quantitative and depends to a great extent on numbers.

A well-prepared questionnaire can obtain data that describes reality. A poorly prepared one may be useless or, even worse, give distorted information. Preparing questionnaires that will elicit the information needed is difficult and takes time and expertise. The tips given below can help you, but if you are serious about your research, please get help from a professional.

Tips for Preparing a Questionnaire

1. Know exactly what information you want to obtain. Know also what you are going to do with the information you get.
2. Make the questionnaire as brief as possible. No one wants to take any more time than is absolutely necessary to answer questions. The chances that a questionnaire may be thrown in the waste basket increase in direct proportion to its length and complexity.
3. Ask only for information not available elsewhere. For example, do not ask members to give their address or date of baptism if the church clerk has that information. Ask only for what you need.
4. Be sure the topic of the survey is important enough to justify the respondents' time and effort to complete it. A survey on the local church school will be more important to a mother of small children than a questionnaire about retirement homes.
5. Ask questions so that they elicit precise, factual data rather than impressions or opinions. A question such as "How many hours do you spend each week reading?" will get better information on reading habits than "Do you like to read?"
6. Formulate the questions in a clear, straightforward manner, with little possibility for misunderstanding. This will mean writing the questions, trying them out on people of similar background to those who will be surveyed, and rewriting until they are clear. Use language familiar to those who will be surveyed.
7. Put the items in a logical order. Make one thing naturally follow the other. People asked to answer a survey get frustrated when the questionnaire does not make sense to them. And frustrated people may throw the paper away or answer carelessly, rendering the results useless.
8. Make the format simple and convenient to answer. Doing this enhances the chances that respondents will complete the questionnaire accurately and promptly. Consideration for the respondent translates into better data for the researcher.

9. Give clear instructions for filling out the form. Start out the page with instructions on how to answer correctly. An example may be helpful to the respondents.
10. Leave demographic questions, those about the respondent's age, gender, education, etc., to the end of the questionnaire.

Survey Questions

Many kinds of questions appear in questionnaires. However, they can all be classified as open or closed.

Open Questions

An open question allows respondents to answer, without prompting, however they wish. Because answers vary so greatly, the tabulating of open answers is long and involved. However, if the survey is attempting to discover the favorite hymns of a congregation or the training most needed by the elders, the question has to be open, in order to allow real freedom.

For example, in a survey on theological education, respondents were asked: "What course or courses, which you did not study as part of your ministerial training, do you now wish you could have taken?" The responses were tabulated and ranked to provide the overall answer to the question.

Closed Questions

In a closed question, possible answers are given; from these the respondent must choose. These questions are easy to answer, easy to correct, but the answers may not be totally accurate. If the options do not include all possibilities on the continuum, the respondent may not be able to give a correct response or may skip the question. Here is an example of a closed question:

On the average, how much time do you spend each day in personal, private Bible study and reading? Do not count time spent in family worship or studying the children's Bible lesson.

( ) More than one hour a day
( ) From 45 minutes to one hour a day
( ) From 30 to 45 minutes a day
( ) From 15 to 30 minutes a day
( ) Less than 15 minutes a day

This question is worded in such a way that it is impossible to discover how many church members are not studying the Bible at all. To find that out—embarrassing as it may be to the members—one needs to add another category: ( ) No study at all.

Another form of closed question is the scale, which reduces the answer to a numerical value. For example, a question seeking to evaluate a certain aspect of a training program could offer these three options:

1= Very valuable
2= Of some value
3= Of little value

Respondents may be asked to agree or disagree with a statement. To the assertion "Deacons should give a good example by paying a faithful tithe," the options could be: (1) Disagree; (2) Not Sure; (3) Agree. Asked about the preparation of elders to lead the congregation, the options might be: (1) Not prepared; (2) Little prepared; (3) Acceptably prepared; (4) Well prepared; (5) Very well prepared. Usually these scales are prepared with an uneven number of options. The gradation must be clear and the continuum obvious.

Survey Returns

The ideal is to have a 100 percent return, that is, to have every one of the questionnaires completed and returned in time for the tabulation. This rarely happens. Either a letter gets lost, or a respondent fails to return the paper, or a questionnaire is not correctly filled out—and the survey results give information on a limited part of the population.

A researcher must plan well and work hard in order to get maximum cooperation. If the questionnaire is prepared according to the tips given above, if anonymity is guaranteed, and if there is some type of follow-up, the possibility of reaching a fairly high level of response is good.

In most areas of the world, anonymity is an important factor in obtaining responses. People want their opinions to be known, but do not want others to know what they think. In one survey on a sensitive issue, respondents mailed their returns from other cities so that not even the postmark could give them away! Even in a small survey, it is wise to make provision for anonymity, thus providing respondents the chance to speak up without having to sign their name.

Student researchers may have difficulty getting responses to their surveys and questionnaires. For this reason, a cover letter written by their faculty sponsor—especially if he or she is well known—can be helpful. This letter points out the importance of the study and urges people to participate. It can definitely raise the percentage of return.

Making it easy to return the survey is important. A sheet of paper given out to the congregation during the church service should be picked up as soon as it is filled out. If the people are merely asked to leave the papers on a table on the way out of church, they may forget. Pencils or pens should be provided. If the questionnaire is mailed, a stamped, self-addressed envelope encourages respondents to answer and mail the survey. (This, of course, functions only within the same country.)

Follow-up is not easy; it takes time and (sometimes) money. Insistence may be the only way to get a complete picture of reality. It is well known that the first ones to answer are those who are totally for or against something. Those who are moderate in their views may need to be prodded to divulge their opinions. Without a fair representation, the results could be skewed.

The second request for answers to a questionnaire may be general—"to all those church members who did not turn in the form last week"—but this system is not accurate. Some may have forgotten what they did and turn in a second form! To be more precise, you need to know to whom the question-naires were given and who did not respond. Using a code number on the form sent out will permit resending the survey to those who did not answer, with-out compromising anonymity. Consult with a statistician on how to accom-plish this.

Using the best techniques should assure a good return—perhaps not 100 percent, but certainly well above 60 percent. A student's advisor or thesis com-mittee often determines the minimum percentage acceptable. Make an effort to achieve as high a percentage as possible.

Interviews

Interviews permit a deeper and fuller understanding of the attitudes of a respondent. Whereas the survey may have room only for "agree" and "dis-agree" answers, an interview can tell the researcher why the person disagrees or agrees. Interviewing takes time but provides information not available through a survey.

In order for an interview to afford the most information possible, the interviewer should record the conversation. An audio recording can only be made with the express permission of the person interviewed. Usually, the person interviewed will be happier to have the conversation recorded than to risk distortion.

The interviewer should explain clearly what information is needed and why. Ethical behavior demands that the interviewer obtain permission to use materials from the interview in the research report. If the name of the interviewed person is given in the thesis, the person has the right to see and approve these portions before they are published. If the person interviewed is unhappy, far better to modify a quotation or remove it from the paper than to anger someone who has cooperated in the study.

Go to the interview with a written outline of the questions to be asked. The conversation may depart from this outline, but at least you will have a framework for your interview. If you are interviewing several people on the same topic, fill out the same outline for each one. Then you can put your information into a table, which will help to organize the information obtained.

Interviews with a purpose, an outline, and a recording system will give good information. They should be interesting as well. For in-depth information on opinions and attitudes, interviews are superior to surveys. Because of the depth and volume of information obtained in an interview, the number of persons interviewed is much smaller than the number of those surveyed.

Qualitative research does not deal with numbers, but with ideas and people. Students who wish to do purely qualitative research would do well to consult the following books as well as a person who teaches qualitative research:

Cresswell, John W. *Qualitative Inquiry and Research Design*. Thousand Oaks, CA: Sage, 2000.
Denzin, Norman, and Yvonna Lincoln. *The SAGE Handbook of Qualitative Research*. Thousand Oaks, CA: Sage, 2005.
Silverman, David. *Doing Qualitative Research: A Practical Handbook*. London: Sage, 2000.

Researching and recording the history of a congregation could be an excellent topic. Very little information will come from church papers. Most of it will come from the recollections of members. This kind of descriptive research is called oral history. On this topic, please see:

Ritchie, Donald A. *Doing Oral History: A Practical Guide*. Oxford: Oxford University Press, 2003.

Descriptive methods are often used in pastoral research. Knowing how to obtain and report information is vital to the process. Tables and graphs can enhance your report. See chapter 19 for information on how to create and use them.

Another kind of pastoral research is program development. It is described in the next chapter.

chapter 16

PROGRAM DEVELOPMENT AS RESEARCH

Program development, also called product or curriculum development, is another specialized form of research. This chapter explains the application of this type of research to the pastoral setting. In program development research, the researcher determines the need for a program or intervention, establishes its theoretical basis, sets its objectives, designs it, implements it, and evaluates the results.

In an educational setting, program development often has to do with curriculum and classes. In real church life, the program is whatever steps you deem necessary to solve a problem, such as a low percentage of tithe paying or deaconesses who do not know how to be deaconesses. Classes or seminars may be involved, but the "program" may just as well be a mentoring plan or one-on-one training program.

For example, Pastor Bill arrives at Valley Church, which belongs to a conservative, mission-minded worldwide fellowship of churches, in early March. He soon observes that most of the three hundred members are spectators and the pastor is expected to do all the work. In conversation with the elders he asks questions about how members understand the doctrine of spiritual gifts. The answer is quick: "Pastor, this is not a tongue-speaking church!" Pastor Bill realizes he has a problem; he needs to design and implement a program to change the situation. He can also use this opportunity to meet a course requirement in his seminary program.

Steps in Program Development

For the development of a program or intervention to be considered as research, specific steps must be followed. The steps presented here are designed especially for pastors.

1. Define the Problem

Decide what is wrong or needs fixing. Start with your own observation. Then ask questions of others. Pastor Bill's problem can be stated in this way: "At Valley Church, only 70 of 300 members take any part in the church's ministries, internal or external. Responses to questions indicate that the topic of spiritual gifts has not been considered in recent years."

2. Describe the Population

Pastor Bill needs to describe the church for which he is preparing the program: membership, finances, ministries, participation. He needs to find out about the members: age, education, income, how long they have been church members, where they live. He will pay special attention to those who hold church positions. To document these needs and his church (steps 1 and 2) he will use descriptive research. These techniques are described in chapter 15.

If a program is to fit the needs of a whole church, the place to begin could be a church assessment. Christian Schwarz and associates offer a Natural Church Development survey to be applied to a local church to determine where the church stands on eight different markers.[1]

3. Set Goals and Objectives

The first two steps describe reality. This third step describes the ideal: What do we want to happen? What will things look like when the problem is solved? Goals (the final destination) and objectives (smaller goals along the way) point the way, keeping a researcher on track. They also serve as norms against which to measure performance.

To be useful, goals and objectives must be expressed as outcomes. Pastor Bill's objective is not to teach the members about spiritual gifts, but to get them to recognize their giftedness and apply the gifts to useful ministry. In the process members may acquire understanding, skills, attitudes, or appreciation. But

---

1. Schwarz's landmark work on Natural Church Development is showcased at http://www.ncd-international.org. His latest book, *Color Your World with Natural Church Development* (St. Charles, IL: ChurchSmart, 2005), has already been translated into several languages.

the question related to goals is: What will the church members know, feel, and do because of having gone through Pastor Bill's program? How will they show the knowledge, understanding, skills, and attitudes they have acquired?

To set goals and objectives, Pastor Bill and his elders—who are already part of the team—will first brainstorm, writing down all the possible desirable outcomes, regardless of importance. Once this brainstorming is done, the objectives may be prioritized, that is, ranked according to perceived importance.

Although they do express positive outcomes, objectives such as the following are too general and do not help to measure achievement:

- Valley Church members will understand the importance of spiritual gifts.
- Valley Church members will participate in the life of the church.

Questions arise: How will I know that the members understand? How will I know they are participating? How will this be visible? More measurable objectives would read somewhat as follows:

- Valley Church members who attend the workshop will evidence knowledge of the doctrine of spiritual gifts by explaining it to those who did not attend.
- Valley Church members will evidence participation in the life of the church by taking part in at least one church ministry or activity every month.

Once set by the group, the objectives should be validated by the pastor (researcher) and other experts, such as experienced pastors of another church or seminary professors. One could determine that objectives considered acceptable by four of the five consulted would be retained.

4. Review the Literature

In this step the researcher must establish an acceptable basis for the project. The review of literature should generally include three aspects: (a) a theoretical basis for the program; (b) a review of other, similar programs; (c) a study of people such as the ones for whom the program or intervention is being developed.

The information gathered in the three areas may become three chapters or three sections of one chapter, depending on the length of the paper.

Theoretical Basis

For Christians, the basis of bases is the Bible. What do Scriptures say about the thrust and/or content of the program or intervention? What have other scholars and/or pastors written about the topic — in this case, the doctrine of spiritual gifts together with its implications for church life? What is the tradition of the particular church body on this topic?

Similar Programs

Books do not yield as much information on the development and implementation of programs as does the periodical literature. Examine the *ATLA Index, Research in Ministry,* and *ERIC* for sources. Look also in denominational literature; you may find what others are doing in local churches about common Christian problems. If the program being developed is entirely new, there may be little information on what others have already tried. Although little may be found, the search must be made and documented. Pastor Bill finds several spiritual gift inventories and reports on how other churches have implemented gift discovery and application to ministry.

The Population Involved

While the information obtained in step 2 says a lot about Valley Church members, the literature will give information on members in other churches, their understanding and application of spiritual gifts, and how people are mentored. If people in a study are of a certain age or ethnic group, those groups need to be studied. What do they value? How do they learn? What are their major concerns? Since a program (or intervention) cannot be carried out apart from people, knowing about them is important.

5. Design the Program

Once the contents of the program have been determined — on the basis of the objectives chosen, the theoretical literature studied, and a clear understanding of the people for whom the intervention is intended — the program can be designed. The nature of the learners, the material to be presented, and the setting in which the learning experience will take place must be taken into consideration in the design. Since program development is being done as research, all of these aspects must be documented.

The design of the program includes deciding on the length and frequency of the meetings, the audiovisuals, the handouts, as well as the speakers or presenters. The program designer determines the steps to be taken in preparation for the meetings — such as obtaining permission from the church board, advertising, and making physical arrangements for the meetings. Even the evaluation, which will take place after the program is completed, must be designed at this time. Nothing is left to chance. Everything is planned, organized, and written down.

Pastor Bill has important decisions to make: What will be the formal aspects of his program? Whose help will he get? What will be the informal aspects of the intervention? He finally decides to have a series of sermons on discipleship, followed by a weekend workshop on spiritual gifts. At the same time, he will train counselors and mentors within the church to help those who attend the workshop and take the test to find a place to minister and to develop their gift in ministry.

6. Prepare Materials and Resources

Write out lectures or talks, even if you are used to preaching from only a brief outline. Written materials will become part of the research; together with copies of visual aids and handouts, they will go into the appendix of the paper. A good rule to follow is to include in the written paper everything someone else would need to replicate the program.

Make all necessary arrangements for additional resources, human or material.

Get a second opinion from a trusted mentor. This could be your academic advisor or an experienced pastor.

Pastor Bill writes his sermons, prepares PowerPoint^{TM} presentations, gets the needed copies of the gifts assessment questionnaires, invites his professor, and makes physical arrangements for every aspect of the program. He also prepares a test on spiritual gifts to use before and after the workshop, to see what people learn.

7. Implement the Program

After going through all the preparatory steps—permission from the church board, presentation to the church members, advertising, etc.—present the program according to your plan. It may be wise to make a first presentation of your program on a reduced scale, in a small church, or with a small group. Once you have learned how to do it, you can involve a large group.

Keep a journal, complete with dates, times, and names, as well as impressions—yours and those of the participants. Take note of everything that happens during the sessions. This information will be useful in evaluating the program and in presenting the written report.

8. Evaluate the Program

The evaluation must be multifaceted—several kinds of evaluation made by different people. For example, the church members involved in the program can be surveyed to find out how they felt about the program. A test on the doctrine of spiritual gifts, given before and after the program, may give objective information on acquisition of knowledge. The church officers can be interviewed. The participation of members in ministry can be monitored to see if the program made any difference. Finally, Pastor Bill is entitled to make a subjective evaluation of what has happened.

Successful evaluation must be planned early and with care. Questions must be asked thoughtfully. If people think the pastor wants to hear that the program was successful, they may say exactly that, regardless of how they perceive what happened. Design evaluation questions that minimize this danger. For example, rather than asking whether they liked the program or not, ask what the participants liked most and least, or what should be added or deleted the next time the program is presented.

Program development demands weeks and months of reading, planning, preparation, presentation, and evaluation. It is, therefore, difficult to do for a class paper, unless you, like Pastor Bill, are in a hands-on educational program. Program development is more appropriate for a thesis or major project, planned to take a longer period and under the direct supervision of a thesis or dissertation advisor.

Pastor Bill starts thinking in March, has the workshop in September, and completes his paper in January of the following year. He has killed two birds with one stone: His paper got an A and his church is vibrant.

9. Write the Paper

After the program has been produced, presented, and evaluated, it must be written up in a formal report. The next section deals with the writing and organization of the project or dissertation.

Organizing and Writing the Report

The organization of the paper will closely parallel the steps of the research. A conventional report of program development research has five chapters.

The first chapter—the introduction—should contain the same elements as any other introduction: the background, the statement of the problem, the purpose of the paper, an overview of the contents of the paper, and items such as the definition of terms and delimitations. The need and the objectives, as expressed in steps 1 through 3, must also be included. (In a short paper, this section may be called INTRODUCTION and not have the status of a chapter.)

Chapter 2 is a review of literature that includes the materials in step 4. If the program has an extensive biblical or theological basis, this may need to be written up in a separate chapter. If, however, the biblical and/or theological basis is evident in the talks or sermons of the program itself, and if footnoting is done there, the supervising professor may consider its exposition in that part of the paper to be sufficient.

Chapter 3 describes the group for whom the program was designed.

The development of the program is presented in chapter 4. This includes a report of everything from setting the goals, through obtaining the church board's permission, to the presentation of the program. Actual dates and places are reported. People participating are usually not mentioned by name but by position. The outline of events for the program is presented. The evaluation occupies a prominent place. In this chapter, reference is made to items that appear in the appendixes. This section is a complete history of the entire program and could be divided into three parts: preparation, presentation, and evaluation.

Chapter 5 contains the summary and conclusions. It may also provide suggestions for future implementation of such a program or for further research. Should the introduction not be given chapter status, the summary and conclusions will not have a chapter number either.

The appendixes present a variety of materials, each in its own section. For example, there will be correspondence, invitations and publicity, the content of the presentations, illustrations (including PowerPoint and overheads), handouts, and evaluation questionnaires. Because the materials in the appendixes are vital to replicating the project, they must be complete, well organized, and carefully labeled.

The bibliography is the last item in the paper. However, last is not least; the bibliography may be the first thing a reader peruses.

Program development can be useful in pastoral work for preparing workshops, special weeks, weekend programs, lesson series, or training programs for church officers. Naturally, in the church setting they may not be followed as precisely as these steps for a research project. However, following the suggestions given here will enhance the pastor's presentation of special programs in the church.

Chapters 14 through 16 have dealt with special forms of research: exegesis, descriptive research, and program development. Chapter 17 deals with the case-study method of research, an alternative form of research often used in practical or applied theology.

Chapter 17

THE CASE STUDY AS RESEARCH

Another method of research, often used in law and the social sciences, is the case study. This kind of research study is also prominent in advanced levels of pastoral studies, especially in pastoral care and counseling classes. This chapter contains a minimal description of the social science case-study method and a detailed explanation of the pastoral-theological case study.

The Case Study in the Social Sciences

A case study in social science research involves an intensive study of the background, current status, and environmental interaction of a given social unit: an individual, a group, an institution, or a community. An example of this kind of study would be a school counselor's in-depth research on a pupil with a learning disability or the study of a family unit undergoing counseling.

The in-depth investigation of the case study results in a complete, well-organized picture of the person or group studied. The scope of the investigation may be limited in time, or it may follow the development of the person or group studied for weeks or even years. It may concentrate on specific factors, or it may cover all elements and events. In comparison with the survey, which usually examines a small number of variables in a large group of people, the case study examines a large number of variables in one person or one small group.

Case studies are useful as background information in planning for further investigation; they bring to light variables that need further study. Case studies often provide hypotheses that guide additional research. They also give useful anecdotes to illustrate generalized statistical findings. However, as case studies deal with individuals or small groups, they may not be representative of the total population. They do not lend themselves to generalization. In addition, case studies are often vulnerable to subjectivity. This happens because the cases chosen may be dramatic or highly emotional, or the researcher may become personally involved with the subject or subjects being described, thus failing to view the whole process in an objective manner.[1]

The Case Study in Pastoral Research

In pastoral research, the case study is similar to what was described above. It studies one situation, the activities of one group, or one incident. Naturally, a pastor's case study looks at an event or person or situation related to ministry. It must analyze the background of the incident, all of the factors that contribute to the interplay and interaction, and what actually happens.

A pastoral case study is different in that it brings into the study a biblical-theological point of view. Such a case study begins with a narration and ends in a theological understanding of how such an event should be handled. It is a tool for reflection. Since the case is usually taken from the pastoral researcher's own ministry, it leads to self-analysis and assists in establishing theological guidelines for handling future episodes of the same nature.

The case-study method for pastoral-theological reflection described in this chapter is used extensively in doctoral programs in ministry. The version here described owes much to the Doctor of Pastoral Studies Program (DPS) of the South East Asia Graduate School of Theology (SEAGST).[2]

Definition of Terms

Some terms are used in a technical or specific sense. Definition of these words or phrases is important.

---

1. See Stephen Isaac and William Michael, *Handbook in Research and Evaluation* (San Diego: Knapp, 1971), 20; Robert K. Yin, *Case Study Research: Design and Method*, rev. ed. (Newbury Park, CA: Sage, 1989); an excellent and recent book on the topic is Dawson R. Hancock and Bob Algozzine, *Doing Case Study Research: A Practical Guide for Beginning Researchers* (New York: Teachers College Press, 2006).

2. Special thanks to Tjaard Hommes, former director of the DPS program for SEAGST. The case-study method was for years the only one accepted by SEAGST for the DPS dissertation (*Handbook* [Manila: Association for Theological Education in South East Asia, 2000], 123).

Case

A case is an objective description of a pastoral situation or relationship about which theological reflection will be done. The written case is the basis of a case study. "Fructuoso" (in this chapter) is an example of a written case.

Case Study

A case study is the process of pastoral-theological reflection about a given case. Based on the original case, it analyzes, reflects, theologizes, and prescribes action. As far as this book is concerned, the case study is a written paper, the length of which is determined by the complexity of the case, the level of the student, and the demands of the professor. The fact that the word "study" is used to describe this way of thinking suggests method, effort, and discipline in reflection.

Case-Study Method

The case-study method is a way of doing pastoral-theological reflection. Such a method normally starts from a case and proceeds, via critical analysis of the data, to a constructive interpretation of the pastoral-theological issues implied in the case. It culminates in guidelines for action.

Purpose of the Case-Study Method

The case-study method is used in pastoral education to enable pastors to enhance their critical and creative ability for doing theology. Being able to *do* theology in ministry helps answer the nagging question "Why?" Why do I direct worship in this particular way? Why do I handle a broken relationship in the congregation in the way I do? Why do I preach in a certain way? It also helps answer the question "How?" How can I do this better? How can the church handle situations such as this one?

The method helps pastors (and student pastors) learn from a situation, either their own or someone else's. The case-study method is a tool to enhance awareness of the individuals involved, of the situation, of the message of Scripture, and of the pastor's own religious tradition. Doing a case study is doing theology—applying God's Word to everyday life.

This way of doing theology, of thinking theologically, is not simply a tool. It is an experience. However, it is a disciplined experience. Reliving and rethinking a case brings theology out of experience. The result is a theologically sound and contextually viable pastoral action.

Parts of a Case Study

The case study for pastoral theology is divided into four major areas: observation, analysis, interpretation, and action. In a case study, these areas will be chapters; in a dissertation, they will be parts, divided into chapters.

Observation: What the Senses Capture

The first activity involved in developing a case study is careful observation of the case. This demands effort to listen, see, hear, and even experience. Everything that is said and done in relation with the incident or case must be noted. Close observation is the basis for understanding.

Once a case has been observed, it should be written down. Simple sentences that clearly tell the story must be used. The words, activities, and gestures of the people involved are written into the case. What a person *said* should be recorded, not how the researcher thinks the person felt. Body language—a raised eyebrow, a frown—is also recorded for later analysis and interpretation. Observable facts and activities are written into the case; they will form the basis of the study.

Details are important insofar as they are related to the incident. If a detail does not appear in the case, the feelings it suggests cannot be analyzed, the theology it calls for cannot be interpreted. On the other hand, irrelevant items cloud the picture. For example, a lady's wearing a red dress may not be essential—unless the case deals with the elder's feelings about a woman who wears a red dress the day she does the Scripture reading in church! The rule is to include all details necessary to the case and exclude all those that do not explain what people do or think.

To protect the privacy of the individuals involved in the case, personal names are usually changed. No one should be hurt or embarrassed by the contents of a case study. The precise town where the case took place may not be mentioned, but the general location must be given because of the importance of socio-cultural factors involved in the case.

An introductory section containing important background information often precedes the written case. Of special interest is the writer's relation to the case. Other matters, such as location and time, may also be included.

In a paper or thesis, the case is presented in double-space format, with numbered lines. The following example comes from Mindanao, in the southern Philippines.[3]

---

3. Reuel Almocera, "Christianity Encounters Filipino Spirit-world Beliefs: A Case Study" (DPS dissertation, SEAGST, 1990). This dissertation is available at the library of the Adventist International Institute of Advanced Studies, Silang, Cavite, Philippines, or from the James White Library, Andrews University, Berrien Springs, Michigan.

FRUCTUOSO

1   Fructuoso did not receive much of an education. His parents were poor
2 and his home *barrio* was far from a town where a government high school
3 operated. But he could read and write. He used to say that this was almost
4 enough to satisfy his hunger for knowledge and truth.

5   When the second world war broke out, Fructuoso joined the guerilla
6 resistance movement. Since most of the guerillas had only bolo-knives for
7 weapons, many of them, Fructuoso included, relied heavily on *anting-anting*[4]
8 for protection, defense, and survival. Fructuoso testified that these amulets,
9 claimed to have originated from the spirits, were powerful and effective. He
10 insisted that he survived the war largely because of their power. He often
11 expressed his belief in these supernatural beings.

12   After the war Fructuoso became a Seventh-day Adventist Christian. The
13 American pastor, who instructed him in preparation for baptism, told Fructu-
14 oso that although the Bible speaks of devils and demons, the spirits he feared
15 were mostly a product of human imagination and animistic influences. So,
16 when Fructuoso decided to be baptized, he abandoned his amulets by throw-
17 ing them into the sea. He ended his allegiance to his *abyan*[5] and devoted his
18 loyalty to Jesus Christ.

19   Fructuoso's economic life flourished after his baptism. He transformed a
20 choice piece of land into a coconut plantation and, by a moderate standard,
21 he was rich. He became influential in the community and in the church. In
22 fact, he was a church elder for twenty years.

23   At sixty years of age Fructuoso contracted a strange disease. He went to
24 the best hospitals and secured the services of notable physicians. He submit-
25 ted himself to modern diagnostic tests. He was declared normal and healthy.
26 Fructuoso knew, however, that something was wrong. More than once his
27 stomach bloated when the tide was high. Besides, his stool looked like mud,
28 smelled like rotten fish, and yielded unidentifiable creeping creatures.

29   Unsatisfied with the physicians' diagnosis, Fructuoso consulted a *manan-*
30 *ambal*,[6] who explained that an unidentified sorcerer had cast a spell on Fruc-
31 tuoso, causing his disease. The *mananambal* suggested that the spirits must

---

4. *Anting-anting* is a talisman, usually a piece of paper soaked in "holy oil" inside a small bottle. This is tied to the user's body and is carried by the individual most of the time. For a more extensive treatment of the subject, see Ben E. Garcia, *Diwata ng Anting-Anting* (Cebu City: Sto. Rosario Parish, 1982).

5. An *abyan* is believed to be the patron spirit or the supernatural being that gives magical powers to the *anting-anting*.

6. A *mananambal* is a practitioner of the spirit world for healing and casting out spirits. He is believed to be able to heal because of his own powerful contact with the spirit world.

32 be appeased or Fructuoso would die. He prescribed a ritual that included the
33 sacrifice of three pigs.
34   Fructuoso solicited some counsel from his fellow church members regard-
35 ing the prescription of the *mananambal*. Some encouraged him not to sub-
36 mit to such a ritual. But some of the older church members urged him to go
37 ahead; however, they counseled him to first resign from his eldership.
38   Finally, Fructuoso went through the ritual. Soon after, he got well. After
39 attending church services in other places far from his home for some months,
40 he resumed regular church attendance despite the accusing looks of some
41 members.

Analysis: The Horizontal Dimension

Once the case has been written out, the next step is to carefully analyze the
events, interactions, and reactions of the person or persons involved in the
case. Of special importance are the views expressed by those involved. Obviously, the work done at this stage presupposes a well-written case that includes
all the elements on which to base an analysis.

The task of analysis is to understand, not to make judgments regarding the
rightness or wrongness of anyone's actions. What makes people do what they
do? Key questions to be asked in the analysis of the case are:

- What kind of dynamics affect the way people think and feel,
  about themselves, about others, about life?
- What kind of views, feelings, relationships, interactions, reactions, expectations, and priorities seem to motivate the persons
  involved?
- What kind of power plays, external influences, likes or dislikes,
  self-understandings or misunderstandings seem to color the
  case?
- What kind of psychological, social, cultural, political, economic,
  spiritual, and religious factors seem to play a role in the case?

The analysis is a description of the factors that make people think and act
the way they do. The analysis must be done critically, yet with imagination. It
must look behind the words used to the feelings expressed. The analysis must
be aided by disciplines such as sociology and psychology. The analysis takes
into account those local, cultural values that shape life and give it structure. It
also values the religious understanding of the people involved in the case.

The research for the analysis of the case is done in the areas of local history, sociology, psychology, religion, values, and more. Some of the informa-

tion may be obtained from one's own experience as well as the experience of others who know the situation where the case took place. However, a great deal of research must be done in the library. One must investigate what others have thought and written about the dynamics seen in the case. At this point, the research procedure is the same as that described throughout this book.

In Fructuoso's case, the most obvious societal factors had to do with beliefs regarding the spirit world, illness, and healing. Also important was the American pastor's worldview that clashed with the local understanding.

Interpretation: The Vertical Dimension

The third activity, called interpretation, has a vertical dimension—it involves interpreting the case in the light of theology. The key question is: What do the Bible, theology, and the church's tradition and doctrine say about the case? Of prime importance in the interpretation is the theology of the case: What is biblically and theologically right or wrong about the issue?

The interpretation must be based on Scripture and informed by the study of the Christian faith and tradition. The writings of theologians, the church's teachings, and the church's practice must be taken into account. In addition, the insight of pastoral counselors, the research of psychologists or sociologists of religion, and the comments of students of relationships between church and culture should be explored as sources of materials contributing to the interpretation.

In Fructuoso's case the theological issue was evil spirits. Do they exist? What or who are they? How powerful are they? What does the Bible say about them? How do Christians relate to the evil powers?

Some cases are very complex and bring up many theological issues. To deal with all of them may force the writer to be superficial. To choose the most important and to focus on it is the better part of valor and intelligence. The questions asked in narrowing and delimiting a research topic may well be applied here.

Action: What Needs to Be Done

The fourth activity is that of action planning. Here one evaluates any action already taken and outlines appropriate future pastoral strategies for responding to the case.

The strategy should include not only what one proposes to do but also the rationale for choosing that strategy. The strategy planned must be realistic, contextual, and appropriate to the local situation. Furthermore, it must be correct in the light of principles derived from the research of the interpretation section.

The key questions to ask are: Which action is most appropriate and creative in the light of Scriptures, Christian faith and tradition, and the local situation? Why is this course of action best? These questions must be answered with great pastoral creativity based on theologically sound principles.

In a real-life situation involving a complex case, more than one action plan might be possible — even desirable. However, a case-study writer should resist the temptation to deal with all likely action strategies. In the normal case study a student should pursue only one action plan in response to the key issue or problem of the case. Alternative suggestions could be mentioned, but need not be developed. If the case describes pastoral action already accomplished, what has been done might be discussed and evaluated.

The Fructuoso case concluded with a plan for giving biblically sound teaching on the spirit world, with emphasis on their reality and Christ's power over them. The action proposed a Christian exorcism ceremony, in which lay leaders and pastors would participate to show Christ's triumph over evil spirits.

Writing the Case Study

Writing a case study is much the same as writing a research paper. The normal methodology for research is used. The format for research papers, as described in this book, is employed. While following academic rigor, the case study provides some room for creativity and imagination.

The four activities described above form the outline for the written case study. Class papers and doctoral theses do, however, have differences between them.

Case-Study Papers

The written case — the product of *observation* — together with the introduction (purpose, background, etc.) becomes the first chapter in the case study. The case will probably be no more than two pages (double spaced). Each line is numbered, to facilitate reference to it in later parts of the paper. Names of places and people must be disguised to preserve the confidentiality of those involved.

The *analysis*, a study of the horizontal dimensions of the case — socio-cultural, psychological, economic, religious, and political factors involved — constitutes the second chapter of the case study. It is written as a research paper, with subheadings as needed to organize the material. Footnotes are also used to document information brought in from sources other than the case itself or the imagination of the researcher. For example, the case from the Philippines might require an explanation of Filipino values. Information on that way of thinking might be gleaned from the journal *Philippine Values Digest* and would need to be footnoted.

The format of the *interpretation*, which is chapter 3, is similar to that of the second chapter. Its content is different, in that it looks at the vertical dimensions — the theological, biblical, church-related aspect of the question. Again, footnoting should be used to reference biblical, theological, or church polity sources.

The final section of the case study is the *action*. It is prefaced by a synthesis/summary of the analysis and interpretation, which serves as the basis for the action. This summary brings into focus the factors affecting the case and establishes the appropriate theological response. It is also useful for those who only read introduction, summary, and conclusions of research work. The action plan uses an essay format and describes pastoral action already accomplished and yet to be done. An outline format (see chapter 5) may be used if a procedure is outlined.

The bibliography presents a list of materials consulted, whether quotations or citations from the items were used or not. The purpose of this list is not only to impress the professors and free one's self from charges of plagiarism, but also to provide future researchers with a starting point for their endeavors.

Case-Study Dissertations

When a case study is developed into a dissertation for a professional doctorate in theology, the parts can be outlined as follows.

Part One: Presentation

Chapter 1 includes introductory remarks and the written case — the product of *observation*. The case will probably be no more than two pages (double space). Each line is numbered, to facilitate reference to it in later parts of the paper.

Chapter 2 contains the introduction, that is, pastoral theological issues, methodology, delimitations, significance, definition of terms (if needed), and overview of the dissertation.

Part Two: Analysis

The *analysis*, a study of the socio-cultural, psychological, economic, and political factors involved in the case, will have as many chapters as needed to discuss the different problems. "Fructuoso" had two chapters: socio-cultural and psychosocial dynamics, and the dynamics of Filipino folk religion as expressed in the case.

Part Three: Interpretation

The *interpretation* studies the theological, biblical, and church-related aspect of the question. The number of chapters depends on the number of issues investigated. No more than three chapters should be allowed. "Fructuoso" had a chapter on spirits and demons in the Bible and a chapter on healing rituals.

Part Four: Action

The *action* section of the study is prefaced by a synthesis/summary of the analysis and interpretation, which serves as the rationale for the action. This summary brings into focus the factors affecting the case and establishes the appropriate theological response. This section usually has two chapters.

Bibliography and appendixes (as needed) close the study.

To summarize, the case-study method requires observation of a situation, analysis of what is happening, interpretation of the dynamics of the case in the light of the Bible and Christian faith-tradition, and a plan for action, dealing with the key issue or problem. When all of these parts are carefully put together, this practical way of doing theology becomes a method of research.

Chapters 1 through 13 gave general instructions concerning research thinking and writing. Chapters 14 through 17 presented specific — and slightly different — research methods, especially designed for pastors and theology students. Chapter 18 deals with two more variations on the theme of research in religion.

MISCELLANEOUS THEOLOGICAL WRITING

In addition to the research and exegesis papers that are required as part of theological education, professors may request papers that relate theology to the practice of ministry. These are often called papers on theological issues in ministry. In addition, professors commonly assign critical reviews of books or articles. This chapter deals with these two types of writing.

Papers on Theological Issues in Ministry

A paper on a theological issue in ministry is a research paper in applied theology. A theological issue in ministry study applies the results of the study of a theological issue to a human reality, usually to a situation in the pastor's own ministry. It is "doing theology" at its best.

The Usefulness of Papers on Issues in Ministry

Throughout theological training, papers on theological issues in ministry are helpful to students. Writing them helps you gain a broader and deeper knowledge of theology. The exercise equips you for better, more thoughtful, and more creative ministry. In addition, the information and insights gathered can be useful to help other pastors and churches minister more effectively. The study of theological issues in ministry is designed to help writers develop skills in: (a) accurate and objective observation, (b) imaginative analysis, (c) theological reflection, (d) statement of a pastoral-theological point of view, (e) planning effective pastoral strategies, and (f) writing about all of the above.

A major study of the theological and practical implications of an issue in ministry can become a master's project or a dissertation for a professional degree in theology, such as the D.Min. See chapter 21.

Writing a Paper on a Theological Issue in Ministry

The basic rules on researching, organizing, and writing papers, as they appear in this book, should be followed. All aspects of format and documentation must also be respected. The parts of the paper are the same: preliminary pages, introduction, chapters of the body, summary and conclusion, and bibliography.

The study of a theological issue in ministry is a careful analysis of a particular aspect or problem encountered in a specific situation. For example, in a certain church, some members may find it offensive to have laypersons preach because, they say, the pulpit is sacred and only an ordained minister should occupy it. The issue is practical, but since the reason given is theological, the concern takes on theological dimensions.

To solve the dilemma, you will need to carefully study the biblical passages bearing on the topic. You will also want to examine the history of lay preaching, especially in your own denomination, along with the writings of church leaders on the topic. You will also take into account the cultural situation of the specific church. After careful consideration of the theoretical bases for what should or should not be done, you will come to a Bible-based, theologically informed conclusion. After that, you will draw conclusions and suggest an action plan. In some ways this type of study is similar to a case study, but the case is not spelled out in detail.

Parts of a Study on a Theological Issue in Ministry

The introduction must include the background of the problem, the situation addressed, and the identification of the theological issue involved. Do not give the names of people involved, although they may be at the center of the predicament. If the issue discussed is sensitive, it may be best not even to identify the church. People must be protected by proper anonymity.

The body of the paper will contain the theoretical foundation for the application to ministry. The number of sections or chapters will depend on the topic. The first area to be researched is normally biblical and theological. In addition, there may be sections on the history of a doctrine or idea and on the church's stance on this issue. If psychological or sociological factors need to be taken into account, they must also be discussed.

The final section of the paper, corresponding to the summary and conclusions of a regular research paper, is called "Application to Ministry" and should be made up of three parts: (a) a brief summary or synthesis of the theological discussion, (b) the writer's own conclusion on the topic, and, based on these, (c) a suggested course of pastoral action to apply the conclusion to a real situation in ministry. Depending on the length, these parts may be sections in a chapter or separate chapters.

Individual professors may give further information regarding their own requirements for pastoral theology papers. In any case, as long as you are a student, they are the final authority on your work.

Book Reviews

In today's world, so many books are written and published that I cannot hope to read everything, even in my own field. In order to have an idea of the content of those I cannot read, I read book reviews. They give the thrust of the work, an evaluation of its contents, and an assessment of its importance.

Professors often assign book reviews to force students to read carefully and write thoughtfully. In some seminars, students read different books, then report on them in class, so the group benefits, almost as if each had read every item.

As you can see from the preceding paragraphs, there are professional, critical book reviews, such as you find in scholarly journals, and student-written reviews. While they are different, they require similar skills. In fact, you might have an in-between review — one written for a doctoral-level seminar.

Writing the Review

Preparing a book review entails reading, taking notes, evaluating what has been read, and writing out a summary, assessment, and comments concerning the book or article. That sounds like research, does it not?

A student's book review should contain four main parts: (1) a complete bibliographical entry; (2) information regarding the author and his or her academic training, position, and other books authored; (3) a summary of the book, which, depending on the length of the review, should be not shorter than one paragraph or longer than two hundred words; and (4) an evaluation of the book.

Bibliographical Entry

The format of the bibliographical entry is the same as is used in a bibliography. Complete instructions on preparing this entry appear in chapter 6.

Include the number of pages in the book. For publication in journals, the price of the book is normally included.

Author Information

Information on the author may be obtained from the book itself, from biographical files many libraries keep, and from other sources, such as those mentioned in chapter 8. *The ATLA Religion Index One* is also a good source of information. Search Google Scholar by author to bring up the articles the person has written, as well as reviews of books he or she has published. These listings let you know how much he or she has written, on what topics, and how his or her books have been received.

Summary

The summary should synthesize the thrust of the book and its main arguments. Take care not to distort the emphasis given by the author. The length of the summary will depend not only on the length of the material, but on the complexity of its contents. Unless requested otherwise, for a class, keep the summary to three or four paragraphs.

Evaluation

The evaluation of the book should be made first of all on the basis of the author's own objectives, as stated in the introduction. This mandates a careful reading of the introduction or preface. If the author said this book was a "simple sketch of the doctrine of the immortality of the soul," he should not be faulted for omitting a record of the theological controversies of the Middle Ages on the subject. Likewise, if an author states that the book deals with New Testament Christology, she will not be expected to deal with the topic in the subapostolic era.

The evaluation is often based on comparison. The content of a religious work may rightfully be evaluated by the Bible. It is correct to point out agreements with biblical teaching and deviations therefrom. However, this must be done carefully, with due documentation, and recognizing that the differences may be in matters of interpretation and presuppositions.

At times it is appropriate to compare the book or article with another item written by the same author. This comparison points out differences, similarities, and changes over time. The review of a book or article may compare the work of one author to that of another on the same topic. When making comparisons, one must describe the two concepts or items, then compare them. It is not enough to merely note that they are different.

The careful book review must document the author's statements, giving in parentheses the page where the item was found. Sometimes a review quotes paragraphs that show the author's position. Be sure to keep in mind the author's context in order not to distort the ideas.

Although one may disagree with the author and with the position he or she espouses, the language of a book or article review must be courteous. A well-documented analysis will be more convincing than a heated, emotional tirade. The language of a review written for a class assignment should be similar to that of research—cool, calm, and collected. Think of meeting the author of the book at a professional meeting and having him say in dismay, "So are you the reviewer who hit me so hard?"

Questions to Guide Evaluation

Broad questions to be answered are the usual journalistic queries:

1. *What* is the basic thrust of the author's work? In a nutshell, what is he saying? You are given the chance to summarize the work in a few paragraphs.

2. *Why* does the author say what she does? What is in her training and background that leads her to the conclusions she expresses? It is important to place a book or article in its context; a person writing from a background of poverty and oppression will not write as would someone from a rich and privileged position. You need to be sensitive to the differences.

3. *To whom* is the writing directed and for what purpose? Is this work intended for children or scholars? What is the author trying to achieve? Usually the author does not keep you guessing. Of course, the audience of the writing is vital to the tone and content of the piece.

4. *For whom or what* (or against whom or what) does the author stand? Answering question 1 should help answer this question. If the author states a position, you have no trouble repeating it. If the author does not, be careful not to attribute to him what your thought might be his position. You know how you feel when someone accuses you of having said something you did not say—or mean.

5. *How well* has the author met her own objectives? Do not judge an author by what you think should have been said as much as by what she has set out to do. You will usually find that in the introduction of the book or article. If the idea was to write a brief introduction, you should not expect an in-depth treatment of the topic.

6. *How* does this work *compare* with other writings—either by the same author or of another author in the same field? You will have to read carefully and widely to answer this question. You may want

to compare what the author wrote ten years ago and what he has written now, or you may compare one author's work with another author's work.

7. *What is your opinion* of this work? What is it good for? Who will benefit from reading it? When you take on a well-known author, this kind of evaluation requires careful thought.

These questions are designed to help you analyze and evaluate thinking and writing. To evaluate content, you must be conversant with the topic. Perhaps professors assign reviews to motivate students, not only to read but also to study the topic under consideration.

A Sample Review

Since "a picture is worth a thousand words," an example of a book review may be more useful than further explanation.

Hoppe, Leslie J. *There Shall Be No Poor among You.* Nashville: Abingdon, 2004. 197 pp. Paper, $22.00.[1]

Leslie Hoppe, Professor of Old Testament Studies at Catholic Theological Union in Chicago, states in his Introduction that the purpose of this work is "to determine how the Bible can help individual believers and communities of faith shape their response to the poor and poverty today" (7). His further intent is for the reader to be come "engaged in direct communication" with the texts under study (16). His approach is to examine issues of the poor and poverty in the canonical, apocryphal, and pseudepigraphal texts, as well as Rabbinic tradition and Catholic and Protestant documents. Hoppe then proceeds to reference every text in the sacred writings in which a word having "the poor" in its semantic field occurs. However, he goes beyond the classic word-study approach. He is appreciative of the larger social issues that cause poverty and thus is able to recognize the biblical writers' concerns regarding the problem, even if they did not use the words "poor" or "poverty."

This study examines the issues and texts in their historical, political, and economic settings. It takes cognizance of socioeconomic realities and does not simply treat "the poor" and "poverty" as literary spiritual symbols, detached from the physical and literal social circumstances of the times. Thus, in contrast to Albert Gelin's classic *The Poor of Yahweh,* Hoppe argues that "the poor" and "poverty" in the Bible are not religious metaphors for "poverty in spirit." The biblical tradition sees poverty as a social and economic problem that the community of faith can ignore to their own destruction.

---

1. If you were citing this review, the bib entry would read: Maynard-Reid, Pedrito U. Review of *There Shall Be No Poor among You,* by Leslie J. Hoppe. *Andrews University Seminary Studies* 43 (Autumn 2005): 352–353.

There Shall Be No Poor among You is an excellent introductory survey on poverty and the poor in biblical times. It adequately and concisely summarizes the social situation and carefully addresses all the issues surrounding both the problematic and straightforward texts regarding the poor. The book is ideal as an introductory text or supplementary reading material for a university or seminary class. It is not burdened with footnotes, yet the minimal well-chosen endnotes give credence to the work. However, the more serious researcher of the sociological/political/economic backgrounds will find the book less helpful. But this is not the main purpose of the work. It is the biblical text that drives its ultimate purpose. Hoppe wishes the reader to hear the text and the text alone.

This work is not only valuable as an academic text, but it can also serve as an excellent study guide for the local church or for small-group discussions. Of special benefit in this regard is the list of questions for reflection that concludes each chapter. In addition, Hoppe occasionally relates the biblical material to contemporary events. For example, the pre-Exodus servitude of the Hebrews is equated with Jim Crow laws of the South, antiunion practices of the industrial North, and the oppression of the indigenous population of Chiapas, Mexico, by the government.

Although my commendation of this book is overwhelming, I find its treatment of the NT material quite inadequate. I can only hope that a second edition will give more space to this area.

Walla Walla College   *Pedrito U. Maynard-Reid*
College Place, Washington

As you see, Professor Maynard-Reid has not followed the four-part scheme prescribed for student reviews, but then, experience allows a person some leeway!

chapter 19

STATISTICS, TABLES, AND GRAPHS[1]

For many the word "statistics" brings to mind numbers and more numbers, devoid of all relation to reality, unintelligible to most mortals. Others may imagine vast computers that perform complicated operations, impossible to do by hand and head. This leads to attitudes that range from admiration to skepticism. Statistics are an instrument in the hands of politicians, business people, bankers, and others who must manage large quantities of information. They may also be a tool used by a researcher to turn small bits of information into interesting and reasonable conclusions.

Although many people shy away from statistics, in daily life they are used more than one realizes. For example, Christian Schwarz says that "the factor with the strongest correlation to the overall quality and growth of a church is the readiness to accept help from the outside."[2] This is statistical language and Schwarz used statistical method to reach this conclusion. Or, when Win Arn notes that one year after a Billy Graham crusade, of 100 converts, only 15 percent were active in the church, and 82 percent of those had a friend or relative in the church before joining, he is using statistics.[3] Whether or not you use statistics in your papers, you should be able to read and understand statistical information.

---

1. Thanks to professor Edward Maiorov, Professor of Mathematics and Statistics, River Plate University, Argentina, for his help with the section on statistics.

2. Christian A. Schwarz, *Natural Church Development: A Guide to Eight Essential Qualities of Healthy Churches,* 3rd ed. (Carol Stream, IL: ChurchSmart Resources, 1998), 23.

3. Win Arn and Charles Arn, *The Master's Plan for Discipling* (Pasadena, CA: Church Growth, 1982), 134, 135.

Some Basics of Statistics

Chapter 15 described sampling, one of the techniques of statistics. Here we consider basic ideas such as grouping of data, measures of central tendency, measures of dispersion, distribution, and correlation.

The first and essential idea of statistics is that of the list or inventory. History tells of the listing of population and economic data for planning wars or levying taxes. Egyptians and Assyrians recorded systematic and periodical censuses. In the Bible, there is record of a census of men older than twenty years (Num 1:18) and of male Levites over one month of age (Num 3:15).

Grouping of Data

Numerical data may be organized from large to small, or vice versa, in ascending or descending order. *N* (in italics) is shorthand for the number of persons or entries.

Suppose that the ages of the 50 members of a church are the following: 12, 12, 14, 14, 14, 15, 15, 16, 16, 18, 18, 18, 18, 20, 20, 20, 22, 22, 23, 23, 23, 25, 25, 25, 25, 27, 27, 27, 30, 30, 30, 32, 32, 32, 32, 32, 32, 32, 32, 36, 41, 41, 46, 46, 50, 55, 55, 65, 69, 69. Putting these numbers in order shows the distribution of ages in the membership.

The same information is given below in a frequency chart (where frequency shows how many persons are of a certain age). This step of statistical calculations is not part of the final report and is only done in a rough draft.

Age	Frequency
12	2
14	3
15	2
16	2
18	4
20	3
22	2
23	3
25	4
27	3
30	3
32	8
36	1
41	2
46	2
50	1
55	2
65	1
69	2

Especially when N is very large, the data are grouped by intervals. Generally speaking there should be no fewer than five intervals, no more than twelve. The number of intervals will depend on the size of N. The same information as presented above is now grouped by intervals.

Age	Frequency
10-19	13
20-29	15
30-39	12
40-49	4
50-59	3
60-69	3

This kind of statistical treatment may be used by a pastor to divide the church members by age groups: youth, adults, and seniors. Limits must be set for each group; for example: youth, 12-19; adults, 20-59; seniors, 60 and above.

Graphic Representation of a Frequency Distribution

The frequency distribution may be graphically shown by a histogram, a frequency polygon, or a frequency curve. Each graph has its special use.

Histogram

The histogram represents a frequency distribution. The width of its bars (or rectangles) is determined by the intervals. The height of the bars is given by the frequency. The scale need not be exactly the same for both dimensions. The histogram should be a little wider than it is tall.

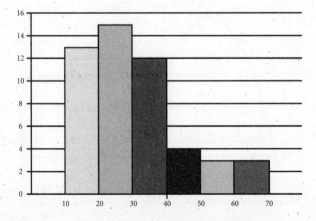

Fig. 1. Members of Church X, by ages

Frequency Polygon

Figure 2 shows the same data as the histogram. The points that shape the frequency polygon are given, on the horizontal axis, by the midpoint of each interval. On the vertical axis the points simply represent the frequency. The line is brought to the horizontal axis at the midpoint of the intervals before and after those used in the graph.

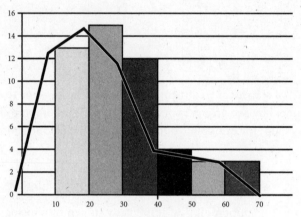

Fig 2. Members of Church X, by ages

Frequency Curve

When N is very large (for example, if the church had 1,500 members), more intervals are used, and the polygon becomes a curve. If the imaginary church of the previous examples had a similar age distribution, but a much larger membership, the graphical representation would be approximately that of Figure 3.

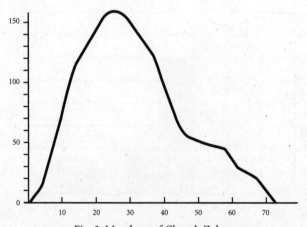

Fig. 3. Members of Church Z, by ages

Measures of Central Tendency

One might ask, How much mission offering does a member give each week? There are three ways of calculating the "average offering." These are called measures of central tendency.

Average or Arithmetic Mean (m)

The mean is the result of dividing the sum (in this case, the total offering) by N (the number of members present). So, if an offering of 200 dollars was given by 40 people, the mean offering was 5 dollars.

If the calculation is made from a frequency chart, using grouped data, these steps must be followed:

1. Find the midpoint of the interval.
2. Multiply that midpoint by the frequency of the interval.
3. Add all of these.
4. Divide by N.

Using the example of the fifty-member church, let us calculate the mean age of a church member. This step is merely a rough draft and not part of the final report; it needs no figure number.

Age	Frequency	Midpoint	Frequency x Midpoint
10-19	13	14.5	13 x 14.5 = 188.5
20-29	15	24.5	15 x 24.5 = 367.5
30-39	12	34.5	12 x 34.5 = 414
40-49	4	44.5	4 x 44.5 = 178
50-59	3	54.5	3 x 54.5 = 163.5
60-69	3	64.5	3 x 64.5 = 193.5
			TOTAL = 1505.0

1505/50 = 30.1 years. The mean age of a church member is a little more than 30 years.

Median

The median is the middle value, halfway from either end of the listing. Consider the mission offerings for one quarter (13 weeks). In order to find the median, the sums must be placed in order: 534, 560, 580, 590, 595, 598, **600**, 602, 605, 610, 612, 620, 630. The median is 600 pesos, because there are six numbers (values) larger than it, and six smaller than it.

If the number of values were even, one would have to average the two middle values in order to determine the median. For example: If the number of persons baptized after studying with six Bible instructors were 20, 22, 24, 30, 32, 38, the median would be halfway between 24 and 30, the two central values. Thus the median would be 27. The arithmetic mean is 27.7 candidates per instructor.

It is possible to obtain a median from grouped data. If you need to do it, see a statistician.

Mode

The mode is the value that appears most often, the one with the greatest frequency. In the imaginary church of fifty members, the mode is 32 years of age. This age was given 8 times.

Mean, Median, and Mode

The mean or mathematical average is the most commonly used of the three. However, it is easily affected by extremes. For example, if the salary of five persons were $12,600; $4,500; $4,400; $4,300; and $4,200 a year, the average salary would be $6,000. This would not give a true picture of wages earned, because only one of the five is earning that much. The median would be $4,400 and would give a more accurate picture of the five persons' earnings.

The mode is the least precise of these measures, but it is the easiest to calculate. A book seller is far more interested in the mode than the mean or median. He wants to know which is the most popular book in his store so he can order more copies. To find out, he only needs to count the number of each book sold.

Each of these measurements has its place. However, when you read or present statistics, be careful to note which of the three is being used.

Measures of Dispersion

These measures look not so much at what happens at the middle of the listing as at what happens at the ends. Measures of dispersion focus on differences rather than similarities.

Two church classes have five members each. The ages of the members of Class A are: 60, 63, 21, 15, 11. The ages in Class B are: 34, 40, 28, 30, 38. The mean (average) age in both classes is 34 years. But in Class A there are two seniors, one young adult, and two adolescents. On the other hand, Class B is more homogeneous, as far as age is concerned. One could say that the ages of the members of Class A are more varied or more disperse.

Range

Range is the simplest measure of dispersion. It is the difference between the highest and lowest values. In Class A, the range is 63-11 = 52; in Class B, the range is 40-28 = 12. The wide range shows that in Class A there is more variance than in class B.

Standard Deviation

Although the range is easier to figure, this measure is not very precise. A more precise measure is the standard deviation or S, which is the square root of the mean of the square of the variances from the arithmetic mean. The formula is:

$$S=\sqrt{\left(\frac{\Sigma d^2}{N}\right)}$$

Σ is the symbol for sum; d is the difference between a value and its arithmetic mean (x-m). The standard deviation is more easily computed when the numbers are arranged in a table form.

Class A				Class B		
Age	d=x-m	d²		Age	d=x-m	d²
63	63-34= 29	841		40	40-34= 6	36
50	60-34= 26	676		38	38-34= 4	16
21	21-34=-13	169		34	34-34= 0	0
15	15-34=-19	361		30	30-34=-4	16
11	11-34=-23	529		28	28-34=-6	36

$$\Sigma d^2 = 2576 \qquad\qquad \Sigma d^2 = 104$$

$$S=\sqrt{\left(\frac{2576}{5}\right)}=\sqrt{515.22}=22.69 \qquad S=\sqrt{\left(\frac{104}{5}\right)}=\sqrt{20.8}=4.56$$

The steps for this calculation are:

1. Find the arithmetic mean.
2. Find the variance, subtracting each value from the mean.
3. Square the value of the variance.
4. Add the square of the variances.
5. Divide by N.
6. Obtain the square root.

The larger the S (standard deviation), the greater the range or the variance, and the smaller the homogeneity.

Distribution

Graphic representations have already been used to give a picture of how values are distributed. Figures 2 and 3 show how the church members' ages are distributed. A frequency polygon shows the distribution of a small N (fig. 2), whereas the frequency curve represents a large N (fig. 3).

The distribution of values may be normal or skewed. These concepts are explored in the following section.

Normal Distribution

If we measure the height of a large number of people, we will find that these measurements form a symmetrical frequency polygon. There are about the same number of very tall individuals as very short ones. The majority are somewhere in the middle. The same happens with the measurement of a large number of leaves from the same tree, or the shoe size of men 25 years old in a given place. The larger the number, the more bell-shaped is the curve, similar to the one in figure 4. Theoretically, in a total population, the distribution of tall and short people should form a perfect curve, such as that in figure 5.

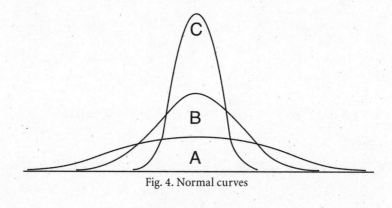

Fig. 4. Normal curves

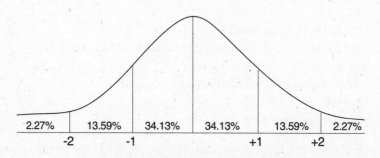

Fig 5. Percentage of area in each standard deviation

In one standard deviation (to either side of the mean), we find about 34 percent of the cases. Approximately another 14 percent fall in the second standard deviation, whereas only some 2 percent fall in the third standard deviation. As an example of this, let us use the measurement of IQs, where the arithmetic mean is 100 and the standard deviation is 15. These figures tell us that approximately 68 percent of the population may be expected to have an IQ between 85 and 115. Only about 2 percent will have an IQ of more than 130 or less than 70.

Skewed Distribution

If a population had a larger percentage than expected of higher extreme IQs or lower extreme IQs, the distribution — and hence the curve — would be skewed as the ones in figure 6. Curve A shows a population with more high IQs than normal, while curve B shows more low IQs than expected. A skewed curve shows a distribution of characteristics different from what would normally be expected.

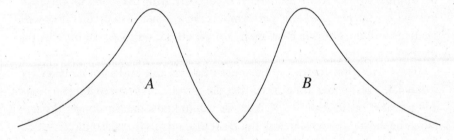

Fig. 6. Skewed curves

Correlation

An example of correlation is provided by the work of researcher Bert E. Holmes, who counted cricket chirps. Holmes counted the chirps made by 115 crickets in a minute. He also measured the temperature when the crickets were chirping. He discovered that when he counted the chirps for 15 seconds and added 37 to that number, the result was quite close to the Fahrenheit temperature — as long as it was not too cold or too hot, that is, between 45 and 80 degrees — at the time of counting.[4]

Without discussing whether the higher temperature caused more chirps or more chirps caused higher temperatures, we can state that there is a positive

---

4. Bert E. Holmes, "Vocal Thermometers," *Scientific Monthly* 25 (September 1927): 261–67.

correlation between the temperature and the number of cricket chirps per second. The more temperature, the more chirps. In fact, Holmes found this positive correlation to be very high: 0.9919. A perfect positive correlation is r = +1.00.

In 1975 Mike Scofield studied the relation between the size of a church and the quantity of offerings that entered the treasury per member during the year. He found that when the church grew, the mean per capita offering diminished.[5] This is an example of negative correlation: more members, fewer offerings. A perfect negative correlation is expressed: r = -1.00.

When the correlation coefficient (r) is close to 1.00 (either plus or minus), correlation is said to be high (positive or negative). When the correlation coefficient is close to 0, correlation is low or nonexistent. In fact, a very low coefficient (positive or negative) might sometimes be considered a product of chance.

Used in a regression equation, the correlation coefficient may be employed for predictions. Given the value of one variable, the other may be predicted. Thus, without reading the thermometer, one could tell the temperature by the number of cricket chirps. After years of correlating the scores on entrance tests with students' academic performance, researchers can predict how well students will do. On this basis many universities require a certain score on these examinations.

The correlation coefficient becomes more meaningful as more pairs are studied. If a researcher announced that the correlation between long sermons and member satisfaction is r = -0.80, we would know that the longer the sermon, the shorter the satisfaction. But if she also told us that she only consulted four people, we would not pay too much attention. On the other hand, if 100 members were consulted, even if the r = -0.60, we would give credence to the report.

Once again: correlation does not mean causality. The crowing of roosters does not make the sun come out; neither does sunrise make roosters crow. But both do happen at approximately the same time. If a high correlation between two items is consistently reported many times, it becomes difficult to doubt a cause-and-effect relationship. Smoking and cancer, notably lung cancer, are a good example. But even in this case, tobacco manufacturers admit correlation, but try to deny causality.

The calculation of r is complicated. If you undertake a correlation study, get help from a statistician. Statistical calculators can do the calculations, but the design of the research demands professional help.

---

5. Quoted in Gottfried Oosterwal, *Patterns of SDA Church Growth in America* (Berrien Springs, MI: Andrews University Press, 1976), 83–87.

Statistical Graphs and Tables

Statistical information is sometimes written into the text of a research report, often in tables and graphs. Tables contain rows of numbers. Graphs represent the numbers by lines and spaces; they are visually more interesting. Tables and graphs allow much information to be given in an organized manner in little space. The rules governing the presentation of tables and graphs in research writing are explained in the following pages.[6]

Tables

All tables must have a number and a title. They must also be listed in a list of tables, which comes after the table of contents in the preliminary pages. As in this book, if there are only a few tables, these may be listed together with the illustrations.

If the table is too large to fit across the page, it may be placed lengthwise on a following page. If it is too large to fit either way, it may be prepared on a larger page that is then folded to fit into the paper. A smaller font or photographic reduction may also be used to make a table small enough to fit on the page.

Reference should be made to the table in the text. This draws the reader's attention to the location and contents of the tables or graphs. A reader should be able to get a clear idea of the results of the research without having to examine every table and graph, even when all details are not in the text. The following example is taken from a description of pastors in South America.

> Table 1 shows the contact of pastors with well-educated people. From the pastors' report, it appears that for the entire division the largest group (155, 45.9 percent) has some contact with educated people, and that the next largest group (112, 33.1 percent) reports little contact with them. A comparison between the Spanish-speaking and Portuguese-speaking respondents shows that although a larger group of Portuguese-speaking pastors (38, 23.0 percent) said they have much contact with educated people, more Spanish-speaking pastors than Portuguese-speaking pastors reported some interaction with educated people (Sp.: 94, 54.3 percent; Port.: 61, 37.0 percent).

Tables should be placed as soon as possible after they are mentioned in the text. However, they should not break a paragraph. If a table needs to be on a separate page, it should still appear as soon as possible after the reference to it.

---

6. On graphs and tables, see Turabian, *A Manual for Writers*, 7th ed., 82–97, 359–371.

TABLE 1

REPORTED CONTACT OF PASTORS WITH
WELL-EDUCATED PERSONS

Pastor's Contact	Spanish-Speaking Pastors		Portuguese-Speaking Pastors		South American Division	
	N	%	N	%	N	%
No answer	1	0.6	1	0.6	2	0.6
Much	20	11.6	38	23.0	58	17.2
Some	94	54.3	61	37.0	155	45.9
Little	54	31.2	58	35.2	112	33.1
None	4	2.3	7	4.2	11	3.2
	173	100.0	165	100.0	338	100.0

While they are not identical, all three tables are acceptable variations in style. Vertical lines (not allowed in some schools) are used in table 2. Do not mix different styles in one paper. The titles of the left-hand column are typed flush left. The titles of the other columns are centered over the numbers. Numbers are right aligned. The three dots represent nul or zero. The vertical spacing and the font size vary to fit the space available; the vertical spacing should be between one and two lines. The font may be small, but it must still be readable.

Use the table feature of your word processor. Once the table is complete, with all the information, decide which lines you will keep and which you will erase. Some schools have rules about the appearance of tables. Be sure to inquire.

TABLE 2

TIME SPENT WEEKLY IN SERMON PREPARATION AS REPORTED BY
PRESIDENTS, DEPARTMENTAL DIRECTORS, AND PASTORS

Weekly	Presidents		Departmental Directors		Pastors			
					Graduates		Non-grads	
	N	%	N	%	N	%	N	%
No answer	1	2.8	2	3.3	2	0.9	...	...
No time	...	...	...	...	...	...	2	7.1
0-2 hours	16	44.4	24	40.0	13	6.2	13	46.4
3-5 hours	13	36.1	26	43.3	91	42.7	10	5.8
6-9 hours	6	16.7	4	6.7	76	35.7	2	7.1
10-14 hrs.	...	...	4	6.7	29	13.6	1	3.6
Over 15 h.	...	...	...	...	2	0.9	...	...
Totals	36	100.0	60	100.0	213	100.0	28	100.0

When the information portrayed in the table comes from one's own research, no source is needed. Table 3 shows how to handle the reference to other sources.

TABLE 3

AGES OF POPULATION IN COUNTRIES OF
THE SOUTH AMERICAN DIVISION

Countries in the South American Division	5-19 %	20-29 %	30-44 %	45-59 %	60-74 %
Argentina	34	17	22	16	11
Bolivia	44	19	20	11	6
Brazil	39	21	22	12	6
Chile	33	21	24	14	8
Ecuador	43	21	20	11	5
Paraguay	42	21	22	10	5
Perú	41	21	20	12	6
Uruguay	29	17	22	18	14

Source: *1991 Demographic Yearbook* (New York: United Nations, 1992), 164-167.

An alternative format for the titles of tables is to start the title flush left and use sentence-style capitalization, as follows:

Table 1. Reported contact of pastors with well-educated persons

Table 2. Time spent weekly in sermon preparation as reported by president, departmental directors, and pastors

Table 3. Ages of population in countries of the South American Division.

Neatness and clarity are hallmarks of well-made tables. Sufficient white space around them sets them off. Normally, three empty lines precede and follow each table and graph. Work until you produce a pleasing effect.

Graphs

A simple, attractive, carefully presented graph stands out in the paper. A table may present more information, but a graph is a more effective communicator. The limitations of graphs are evident: (1) they do not show as much data as a table; (2) they represent approximate values; (3) they take time and some artistic talent to create.

All graphs should be typed or drawn in black ink. Computer-generated graphs are excellent; however, this specialized technology is not indispensable to create clear, accurate, and appealing graphs. The most common are bar, line, and circular graphs.

Bar Graphs

These may be simple, compound, or double (sometimes triple).

Simple Bars

The bars may be drawn vertically or horizontally; here they are vertical. Care must be taken to achieve a pleasing appearance while maintaining maximum clarity.

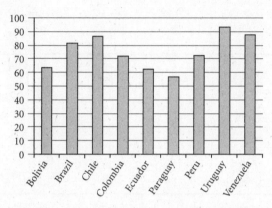

Fig. 7. Percentage of urban population in South American countries
Source: United Nations, *Demographic Yearbook, 2003* (New York: United Nations, 2004), table 6, Urban and total population by sex, 1994-2003.

Compound Bar Graphs

Figure 8 is a compound bar graph showing the same information given in table 3. It is visually more interesting, but not as precise.

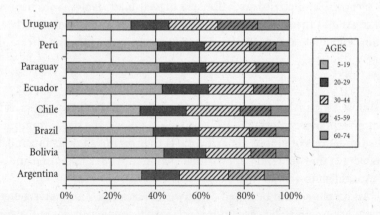

Fig. 8. Age distribution in countries of the South American Division
Source: *1991 Demographic Yearbook* (New York: United Nations, 1992), 164-167.

Figure 9, another compound bar graph, compares the tithes and offerings in the Seventh-day Adventist Church worldwide from the years 1960 to 2000. It is visually attractive, but does not give specific sums for each kind of offering. This type of visual aid is useful in the oral presentation of research. If the graph is shown in colors on an overhead projector it can be particularly eye-catching. Unfortunately, color is generally not used in graphs in a thesis or dissertation.

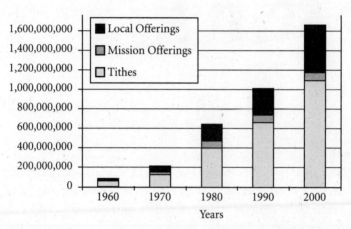

Fig. 9. A comparison of tithes, mission offerings, and local offerings from 1960 to 2000
Source: *Annual Statistical Report* (Silver Spring, MD: General Conference of Seventh-day Adventists, 2005), 4.

With compound bar graphs, one must be especially careful to make the colors (in the original) or the crosshatching sufficiently distinct. The distinctions can be lost in printing. Obviously, all figures will need to be done over more than once until they are done just so.

Double Bar Graphs

Double bar graphs are used to compare at least two variables. Figure 10 shows the languages spoken by students of the Adventist University of Africa at the university's three extension centers in 2006. The three-dimensional bars are interesting but fail to show the exact number of students who speak each language. If numbers are important in your research, use a table.

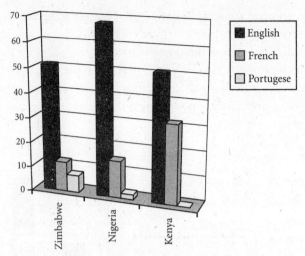

Fig.10. Languages spoken by students in the three extension campuses of the Adventist University of Africa in 2006

Line Graphs

A line graph usually portrays change over time. The horizontal axis represents time; the vertical, another variable, which in figure 11 is the number of workers sent out of their home division by the Adventist Church between 1901 and 2000. Here a computer-generated graphic displays a visually interesting figure.

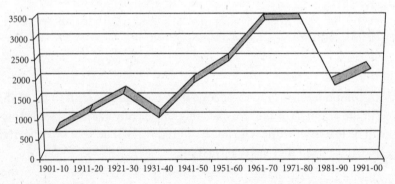

Fig. 11. Adventist workers sent from one world division of the Seventh-day Adventist Church to another, by decades
Source: *Annual Statistical Report,* 1992 and 2001.

The scale on each axis does not need to be identical (that is, the same for one missionary as for one year), but care must be taken not to distort the impact of the information. For example, should the year line in figure 11 be shorter, the increase of church workers would appear to be truly astronomical.

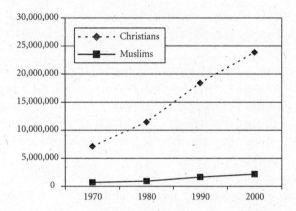

Fig. 12. A comparison of the growth of Christianity and Islam in Kenya, 1970–2000
Source: *World Christian Encyclopedia*, 2nd ed., vol. 1 (Oxford: Oxford University Press, 2001), s.v. "Kenya"; *World Christian Encyclopedia* (Nairobi: Oxford University Press, 1982), s.v. "Kenya."

Line graphs may compare one phenomenon to another over time. The lines must be different to avoid confusion. Figure 12 shows a comparison of the growth of Christianity and Islam in Kenya between 1970 and 2000.

Circular Graphs

Also called pie charts, circular graphs represent the total divided into its parts.

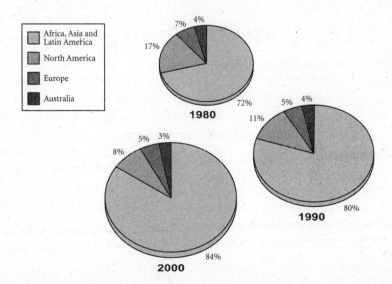

Fig. 13. Membership of the Seventh-day Adventist Church on different continents 1980–2000
Source: *Annual Statistical Report*, 1980, 1990, 2000.

The figures are usually expressed in percentages, although actual figures may also be given. Figure 13 shows examples of pie graphs. These were made with Excel™.

If you have no access to a computer program that makes circular graphs, you may still construct your own. A percentage protractor is useful for this task. It will give you percentages rather than degrees of the circle. However, you can also calculate the areas of your circular graphs. Remember that 180 degrees is the same as 50 percent; 90 degrees is equivalent to 25 percent, and so on.

Divide the circle to represent the percentages. Then label each section with the percentage of the whole and the exact number, if you like. Make the differences between sections show by using different crosshatchings.

As with other graphs, the pie charts are eye-catching. However, they do not convey precise information as a table would. You must decide whether you need precision or interest.

Experts produce figures in a matter of minutes, using Microsoft Excel or some other computer program. Unless you are a whiz at computer graphics, you may want to ask someone else to make the figures for you too. You can also stay with old-fashioned tables—simpler to make, easy to understand, but not quite as exciting as computer-prepared charts and figures. (Thanks to my eighth-grade grandson Erik, who used Excel to produce these figures.)

Statistics and Honesty

Disraeli, the great English statesman, is reported to have quipped that there are three kinds of lies: lies, damned lies, and statistics.[7] By contrast, H. G. Wells stated that "some day it will be as necessary for an efficient civilization to think statistically as it is to read and write."[8] Both statements may exaggerate, but both contain some truth. Statistics form a part of modern life, but their use demands honesty, not only in telling the truth, but in not stretching facts to suit one's own purposes.

Figures 14 and 15 show how a graphic representation may distort information. The first one shows the growth of the world population between 1950 and 2000. The second modifies proportions, giving a distorted impression of reality.

---

7. D. Huff, *How to Lie with Statistics* (New York: Norton, 1954), 1.
8. Ibid.

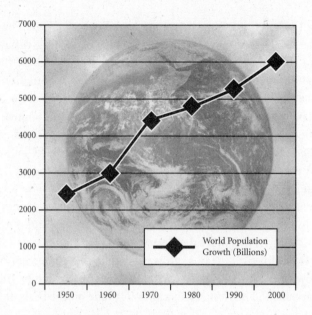

Fig. 14. Growth of world population, 1950–2000
Sources: *United Nations Statistical Yearbook* (New York: United Nations, 1997), 95; and *Time Almanac 2000* (New York: Time, 2000), 153.

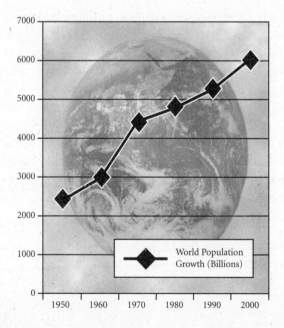

Fig. 15. A distorted view of the growth of world population, 1950-2000

In figure 15 the proportions on axis Y have been changed. The growth appears more accelerated, but the distorted image of Earth gives away that change. Were there no Earth to show the distorted proportions, the visual impact could fool the observer into panic over world overpopulation.

Percentages may also be used to convey erroneous information. A physician could state that only three of his patients had died, while someone could argue that the same physician had lost 75 percent of those he had cared for. Both could be telling a half truth. If there were four patients, three would be 75 percent. A percentage figure should be given along with the total number (N) on which it is based.

The base number for calculating percentages is important, as may be seen from the following example. If the manager reduces the employee's salary by 20 percent, and the original salary was $100, the employee would now be getting $80. If on this sum the boss gives his employee a 20 percent raise, the unlucky fellow would only be getting $96 (20 times 80 divided by 100 equals 16). What happened? The first calculation was made on the basis of 100; the second on the basis of 80.

When reading statistical reports, do not accept every piece of data without considering the total picture. All too often distortion for convenience is used by authors. It is necessary to apply critical thinking even to the numbers you read.

Many ways of lying with statistics could be mentioned. None of them is appropriate to research. Let total honesty prevail! Research reports must be accurate and precise. Pastoral research must be even more ethical and honest.

This chapter has presented some basic notions of statistics and instructions for preparing and presenting different kinds of tables and graphs. Further help in statistical design should be procured from a qualified professional on the subject. The calculation of statistics has become much more simple with the advent of the computer and appropriate software. In fact, tables and graphs may be computer generated from raw data or calculations in a database or spreadsheet. For this type of assistance, look for a computer expert!

To complete the picture of theological-biblical-pastoral research, chapters 20 and 21 turn to dissertations or doctoral theses.

chapter 20

THESES AND DISSERTATIONS

A first theological degree is usually earned by passing courses and examinations. The second culminates with major research, often called a thesis, at the master's level. At the doctoral level, the same kind of work—but longer and more complex—is known as a doctoral thesis or dissertation. Theses and dissertations have many common elements; one of these is the review of literature, important enough to deserve a separate section of this chapter before the discussion of theses and dissertations.

Review of Literature

A review of literature, which often appears in the first or second chapter of a thesis or dissertation (and sometimes also in the proposal), reports what has already been written, in books and journals, about the topic under research. It provides, so to speak, the background for the painting. In large strokes, the review of literature paints a backdrop against which the research will be done. One professor described the review of related literature as a salute to the past—a recognition of the research and study already done on one's topic. After a gentlemanly tip of the hat, one goes on to further research of the topic. Another description of a review of literature puts it this way: Before inventing a new typewriter, an inventor looks at all existing typewriters—IBM, Smith-Corona, Brothers, Royal, Olivetti, and so on. This survey becomes a starting point for the inventing process.

A review of literature shows your advisor or committee that you have made a thorough investigation of the topic and have read the main works already written on it. It guarantees that there will be no going over the same ground others have covered, no "reinventing of the wheel." A thorough review of the literature shows you know whereof you speak.

If the proposal has a review of literature, it will reflect extensive reading; however, it certainly will not embody the total reading for the thesis or dissertation. More items that belong in the review of literature will appear in the course of your reading. They may be added later. Conversely, you may decide to remove some item from the final version of the review of related literature.

This summary of the status of research is not a series of book reviews or critiques (see chapter 18). It synthesizes information from many sources about the issue, its background, and previous attempts to resolve the problem. Not only does the review of literature consider information on your problem, it also looks at studies that have used a similar methodology to solve a different problem.

The style of writing is descriptive. Synthesis is key: putting ideas together to present a big picture. Normally, the review of literature does not include interaction or discussion with the authors reviewed. Evaluation is at a minimum. For example, imagine part of a review of literature on the theological significance (tongue-in-cheek, of course) of the durian, that Asian fruit that has only lovers and haters:

> Professor Adriel Sandoval, in agreement with Yeng Ka Seng and Komarno, states that durian will be the fruit of the tree of life. (References for all three) Sandoval goes so far as to suggest that only the durian could have been tempting enough to Adam and Eve to cause them to disobey God's instructions. (Reference) In clear opposition to his position is that of Vasinee Suvonapong, who claims that durian came into being only after the fall, once decay and decomposition had set in. (Reference)

Students often ask how long the review of literature should be and how many items it should contain. There is no precise answer. Simply put, the full picture should be given; as many items as are needed to show familiarity with the topic of the research should be blended into the review of literature. This aspect of the thesis or dissertation is assessed both qualitatively and quantitatively. Usually, professors tend to be more impressed by quality than by quantity. In spite of that, more is usually better. The omission of an item considered important by an examiner at the thesis defense may be embarrassing and force rewriting.

The amount of research already done on the topic will, to a certain extent, determine the scope and breadth of the review. If there is little research on a topic, every item available needs to be included. If much has been written on the topic, the reviewer may take a selective approach.

When a review of literature is selective rather than comprehensive, a clear rationale for the selection and omission of materials must be given. In a 1990 thesis on preaching, an M.Th. student chose a time limitation; he reviewed "text books written on preaching since 1970." The rationale followed: "This time limitation was chosen because it is unlikely that books written and copy-righted before that date would still be in print and available for use as text-books." One might also choose to limit the authors by nationality, gender, or approach.

At times the literature on a specific aspect of the problem is reviewed. An M.Th. student writing on "Christian Freedom in Colossians 2:6–23" did a comprehensive review (all available commentaries on Colossians and Gala-tians) of literature but focused only on the answers to the question: "From what did Christ's death on the cross free Christians?" The review of literature for a comparative study on soteriology in Theravada Buddhism contained only works that compared Christianity and Buddhism; an appropriate and convincing rationale for this selection was presented.

A review of literature needs to be organized. If there are few studies, one might follow a chronological or alphabetical order for the presentation. This is not usual, however. Most reviews of literature need to be organized topi-cally, with headings and even subheadings. As he read, the student writing on Christian freedom noticed that the answers given by Protestant, Catholic, and Seventh-day Adventist scholars differed significantly, so he divided the review into three parts. The first of these sections was then divided according to what the authors said. Forty-seven items were reviewed under the follow-ing organization.

I. Protestant Authors
  A. Authors Who Perceive Christian Freedom as Freedom from Law
    1. Freedom from the Moral Law
    2. Freedom from the Ceremonial Law
  B. Authors Who Understand Christian Freedom as Freedom from Condemnation
II. Roman Catholic Authors
III. Seventh-day Adventist Authors

A review of literature may be exhaustive or representative. In the first case, every item is described; in the second, only specific items are described. These items are chosen as representative of a larger group, all of which are carefully referenced in the footnotes. When a representative review is written, the student must be sure that the item described does, in fact, accurately represent the others.

You are responsible not only for writing the review of literature, but also for designing the rationale for excluding some materials and including others and for organizing the review. Yet, your thesis or dissertation committee has the final word. Work closely with your advisor or committee to avoid surprises.

In different types of theses or dissertations, the review of literature includes different materials. For example, in descriptive research, the review of literature includes information on other research done on the same topic, on studies using the same procedure or methodology, and on the theory that undergirds the research. In program development research, the review of literature includes literature on the undergirding theoretical basis, on the group for whom the program is to be developed, and on similar programs already developed. In a dissertation on one aspect of *Heilsgeschichte*, the review of literature might contain a history of the concept and evaluations of *Heilsgeschichte*.

At times, a thesis advisor or committee may allow alternatives to the review of literature. Two options are the annotated bibliography and the bibliographical essay. The annotated bibliography briefly describes the item, thus showing that the researcher has examined it already; an example appears in chapter 6. The bibliographical essay notes what has already been written on the topic and evaluates the usefulness of the sources listed. Some thesis or dissertation committees — especially in Ph.D.-in-religion papers — may prefer to have you put into footnotes a vast amount of information regarding previous studies and opinions on the topic instead of writing a separate review. The thesis or dissertation produced by this method may have as much space dedicated to footnotes as to text. Make sure you know what your advisor and committee want from you before you spend weeks doing what you think is appropriate.

Theses

The Master of Arts in Religion degree often requires a thesis; the Master of Theology degree always does. A thesis is generally a long and complex research paper. Instructions given on research methodology in chapters 1 through 13 apply also to the thesis. In fact, the research method must be even more strictly applied to a thesis than to a class paper.

The M.A. thesis is expected to be about 80–100 pages long. For an M.A. in Religion, the thesis usually is a bibliographical research paper. The student's thesis advisor or committee may give permission for the student to do a major exegetical paper. Professional master's degree programs may allow descriptive research, program development, or a church-growth study as a thesis. Other possibilities are the case study and the theological issue in ministry.

The M.Th. thesis will normally be from 100 to 150 pages long. The choice of topic will depend on the student's area of concentration. This thesis is a half step between the M.A. and the Ph.D./Th.D.

A thesis—either M.A. or M.Th.—is expected to contribute something new to the fund of general knowledge. It cannot be a mere rehash of old materials. Since the thesis allows more space in which to develop the research, the topic will naturally be more complex than the topic for a term paper. However, you should select a problem that is amenable to treatment within the available time and resources and within the allotted pages.

Thesis writing is directed by an advisor or supervisor, often with others who form the thesis committee. You must work closely with your advisor in choosing the topic and in writing the thesis proposal, which is then approved by a committee. Each school has its own way of doing theses. Please follow instructions carefully!

The thesis process may be divided into three main segments: proposal, writing, and defense. These three aspects are described in turn.

Proposal

The thesis proposal should contain the same elements as the proposal for a paper (see chapter 5). However, each part must be developed in greater detail. Whereas in a paper proposal, two pages might suffice, an M.A. or M.Th. thesis proposal may be eight to ten pages long.

Writing a proposal is not a waste of time. What goes into the proposal eventually goes into the thesis. By the time your proposal is presented and accepted, you will have completed a large part of the reading and research.

A proposal has a title page and a table of contents. It begins much as does any normal research paper; however, the similarities with a regular paper end soon. The whole of the proposal is an explanation of what the thesis will contain—a prophetic description, perhaps.

Your M.A. or M.Th. proposal should begin with a background for the study and the statement of the problem. You should also present the purpose and objectives of the research, as well as its significance. Any delimitations should be explained. (In a thesis, limitations such as lack of time or knowledge are not acceptable; they are considered excuses for poor work and their presence may suggest you need a different topic!) Define any terms that may not be clear to your readers. State your presuppositions, if it is appropriate. Explain the method you are using. If the study is historical or bibliographical, a description of the methodology is fairly short, yet each step of the procedure must be carefully delineated. Describe the kinds of sources you will use, how you will go about your search for information, and how one part of the research will relate to another. If the thesis follows another form of research, an appropriate description of its steps must be included.

The proposal of descriptive research demands additional information. The instrument or questionnaire forms part of the proposal, and the way in which it will be applied is fully described. Information on the population to be surveyed, proposed sampling techniques, data to be obtained, and the statistical treatment of the data must be provided. In some cases this section will be sufficiently long to merit a place as an independent chapter. The advisor usually makes this decision.

Proposals for other kinds of research have their own characteristics. A proposal for an exegetical thesis will state the problem in the text; it will also take into account how others have tried to solve the problem. It will clearly delineate the method to be used. In a case-study proposal, the introduction will give the case, together with its background, the topics that will be examined to explain the dynamics of the case, both sociological/psychological/cultural and theological. In a program development thesis, the steps to be taken must accompany the statement of the problem and the other basics noted in the first paragraph of this section.

Following the methodology or procedure section, a detailed tentative outline is presented. This may be done in either format indicated in chapter 5. The outline is prepared in close cooperation with the advisor, who usually makes sure the whole committee (if there is one) agrees on the proposed organization of the thesis. The tentative outline forms part of the proposal.

The last part of the proposal is a working bibliography that lists all items already considered. It will not include all the materials you will eventually use, for it is tentative and subject to change. However, the committee expects to see a promising list that includes all the best and recognized sources for the research.

A search for sources for a thesis must go beyond the library of the school where you are enrolled. You will get some materials through interlibrary loan; other items you must find at other libraries. Then, there is the Internet. Learn to use the latest technology. Plan on becoming a library addict before you finish your work.

The student's advisor or thesis committee meets with the student to finalize the proposal. The student presents his or her views, and the professors stipulate their requirements. The proposal is either accepted as it is, accepted subject to certain changes, or rejected. A final copy of the thesis proposal is usually filed with the program director, not only to certify that you have fulfilled this requirement, but to serve as a model for students who will follow you.

The proposal serves you and your advisor or committee as a guide to your writing. It is something of a contract made between the two sides. Departing from the path laid out in the proposal can be dangerous: "There is a way which seems right to man, but its end is the way of death" (Prov 14:12).

Once the proposal has been approved, thesis research and writing begin in earnest. From now until you finish it, the thesis will dominate your life. Some suggestions for the writing and research of a thesis are given in the following section.

Thesis Writing

After your proposal has been accepted, you will continue reading, researching, and taking notes. The greatest part of the time needed to prepare a thesis is dedicated to these activities. Only when you complete this process should you begin to write. There is no point in writing a chapter without having all the information.

Perhaps the most important advice for a thesis writer is to work closely with the thesis advisor and/or committee. Be sure the advisor agrees with any deviation from the original plan. If the work is guided by a committee, make sure you have a committee decision on what you are to do rather than one member's opinion. If your professor is one who writes out the comments on your work, you are indeed blessed. It is acceptable for you to nudge your advisor to give you comments in writing. Suggest that you need to be sure you are doing the right thing. You need not mention that you are trying to make sure the professor does not have a change of heart and mind and ask you to do something different!

Plan time for the advisor and committee members to read all the parts of your thesis. Remember that professors are usually too busy to read your chapter overnight, simply because you have handed it in and are in a hurry to graduate. It is imperative to develop—and follow—a chronogram that allows time for reading and corrections. This goes for both you and the advisor.

Thesis typing is a major enterprise. Finding a thesis typist may be almost as hard as writing the paper, though you are still held responsible for typing and format errors. With today's technology, students usually do their own typing—on the computer. Once more, learning to touch-type and use a word processor is highly recommended. See additional comments on word processing in chapter 13.

The quality of English required for a thesis demands special attention to editing. You are responsible for getting the necessary editorial help to polish the English. The advisor or committee chair may improve the language and style of writing with his or her corrections, but the advisor's main task is to direct in matters of content. The institutional thesis editor will indicate format corrections necessary, but does not have time to rewrite problematic English.

Generally, the thesis must be given to the examiners at least one week—or as much as four weeks—before the defense date. While the examiners read your thesis, you will have time to check for any mistakes in the paper and to prepare the abstract, vita, and any acknowledgments you wish to include.

The preliminary parts of a thesis include an abstract of the thesis and the approval sheet, prepared according to the school's obligatory format. A model used in several schools appears at the end of this chapter. The abstract is a brief summary of the problem studied, the findings of the research, and the conclusions reached. Its normal length is from 150 to 350 words, depending on the degree and the school.

The acknowledgments contain a personal note of gratitude to whomever thanks are due. Some theses are dedicated to a special person, but this is not necessary. In any case, wisdom suggests moderation and reserve in the expressions of thanks.

The order of the preliminary pages is fixed by each school. However, the following is considered normal: blank page, abstract title page, abstract, thesis title page, blank page, approval sheet, dedication, table of contents, list of illustrations (including figures and tables), list of abbreviations, acknowledgments.

The vita, which gives the student's personal information, as well as academic and professional history, follows the bibliography. This is the last item in the thesis. Check the format customary for your school and degree.

Oral Defense

When all the chapters of the thesis have been written, the conclusions have been drawn, and the bibliography is ready, the thesis advisor sets a date for the defense, if there is one. The student must make complete copies of the thesis for all the members of the committee, including the external examiner, if there is one. Each school has specific guidelines regarding the number of copies needed.

The oral examination or defense usually deals with the thesis and matters related to it. Usually you are given the chance to make a brief presentation of your research. Use visuals to impress the examiners: overhead projection or, even better, PowerPoint™ computer graphics to add luster to the presentation.

When you come to the oral defense knowing that your thesis is well written, you need not fear. Professors are glad to "show off" a good student! Again, the need for working closely with the advisor and the committee cannot be overemphasized.

Even as late as the oral defense, changes in the thesis may be requested. Once these are completed and certified by the advisor, you are responsible for turning in the original to the dean or program coordinator. From this, as many copies as the school requires are made, always at your expense. These are bound, again at your expense, and kept as a permanent record of your intellectual achievement.

Dissertations

Most of what has been said about theses applies also to dissertations. The main difference is in the scope and length of the required work. A doctoral-quality dissertation takes time, effort, and finances. A student must plan on sufficient time for completing the dissertation—months or even years.

A Doctor of Theology or Doctor of Philosophy dissertation is a major research project. It investigates a complex or difficult problem in the area of the candidate's major emphasis. This dissertation will be at least 250 pages long and may be as long as 500 pages.

The writing of a Th.D./Ph.D. dissertation takes for granted that the candidate has the language tools needed to do exhaustive research in the chosen area. A knowledge of biblical languages is presupposed. Normally, the candidate must pass examinations in French and/or German. Other languages may be needed, depending on the topic. For example, a study on early church fathers would demand a knowledge of Latin; a study of a particular unreached people group might demand knowing their language.

As with the thesis, the main stages of a dissertation are three: proposal, research and writing, and defense.

Proposal

Divergent philosophies guide the proposal process in various schools. Some prefer to have a proposal that contains as many as three chapters of the dissertation.

Others want a short and succinct presentation of no more than ten to twelve pages. Some schools require students to take a class in which they receive specific instructions on preparing the proposal and writing the dissertation. Be thankful if your school is one of these.

Schools that require a long proposal usually require that the topic be approved before the student is given the green light to write the three chapters. The required three chapters are the introduction, the review of literature, and the methodology. A bibliography is also required. All of this work is done in close association with the advisor and the dissertation committee.

A short proposal shows, in a few pages, that you know exactly what you are going to do and how you are going to do it. The Ph.D. proposal required at Andrews University is an example of the short version. The brief review of literature is built into the proposal, mostly in footnotes, especially in the background, justification, viability, and methodology sections. The proposal has three main parts: research proposal, outline, and bibliography. The outline includes chapter titles and two levels of subheadings. The short proposal is no longer than twelve pages, excluding the tentative bibliography.

> RESEARCH PROPOSAL
>> Background of the Problem (as needed)
>> Statement of the Problem
>> Purpose of the Research
>> Justification for the Research
>> Viability of the Research
>> Scope/Delimitations
>> Methodology
> OUTLINE OF THE PROPOSED DISSERTATION
> TENTATIVE BIBLIOGRAPHY

Research and Writing

All that has been said about research and writing applies here, when a Ph.D. student lives, breathes, and sleeps dissertation! If meticulous care in taking notes and organizing them was important in a research paper, it is triply so in the dissertation.

The relationship between doctoral candidate and advisor is of paramount importance. After you graduate, you will be your own boss. Until then, you need to practice submission to your advisor's wishes. Writing and defending a dissertation is not only a matter of dogged research and painful writing, it is a political feat as well. In fact, at the termination of the process congratulations for a game well played are often in order.

Each school has its own rules for the interaction of candidate and dissertation advisor and committee. Obtain the handbook from your school and follow it closely, perhaps even blindly. There will be time to celebrate when the process is over.

Defense

What has been said about the defense of a master's thesis holds for the Th.D./Ph.D. dissertation. After having written a masterpiece, you will be confident and your advisor will be thrilled to show you off! The defense will be a joyful exercise in which your achievements are made public. However, if your work is merely acceptable and you have had uneasy moments with your advisor, you can expect the defense to be difficult. Given a choice, you will obviously take the first route.

Specific guidelines for the defense procedure and the handing in of final copies of the dissertation are provided by individual schools. Become familiar with these instructions and follow them closely. You will be spared tears and grief.

At the defense, a Ph.D. candidate usually makes a brief presentation summarizing the research done. Practice this presentation as you did your first sermon! Make the presentation clear yet agile. Touch the high points, what the observers at the defense need to know in order to understand the dissertation without having read it. Use technology if it can make the presentation clearer and more enjoyable.

Asking and answering questions takes up the better part of the defense. Your examiners want to know how well you know the topic and its ramifications. If you are not absolutely clear on the question (or its answer!), ask the examiner to rephrase it. This will give you a few seconds to think. Of course, the ploy cannot be used for every question. Answer the specific question asked, not one you wish the professor had asked. Refer to pages in your dissertation, especially when it is evident that the examiner did not read the document with great care. Whatever you do, do not argue with the examiners or contradict them. It is much better to say with a smile: "You may have a point there; I will be happy to consider it." When the questioning is over and the examiners sit in executive session to decide your fate, they may not remember what you said as much as how you said it.

In conclusion, may your dissertation months be short and your joy at finishing your work be long!

[2 in]   LIBERATION THEOLOGY'S USE OF THE EXODUS

AS A SOTERIOLOGICAL MODEL

[3.5 in]   A thesis presented

in partial fulfillment of the requirements

for the degree

Master of Theology

by

[5 in]   Atilio Rene Dupatonga

APPROVAL BY THE COMMITTEE:

_____   _____

Advisor: Ernesto Ramos   M.Th. coordinator: Samuel Suen

_____   _____

Committee member: Cho Young Mo Dean, Theological Seminary: Tekito Tumoto

_____

Committee member: Mary Masok

_____   _____

External examiner: Tim Zarate   Date of approval

[Modifications are made to suit the number of signatures needed on the approval sheet. If so
desired, the position and/or degree of each person may be added.]

chapter 21

DOCTOR OF MINISTRY PROJECTS

The Doctor of Ministry and Doctor of Pastoral Theology are professional programs with an emphasis on practical theology. The variations between the two degrees are more likely to represent the differences between schools than between degrees. Both require theological reflection applied to a pastoral situation. Although D.Min. papers represent doctoral-level work, they are usually called "projects" rather than dissertations. Their aim is not so much to enlarge the fund of knowledge as to solve a problem in ministry and to provide the pastor-researcher an opportunity for personal growth.

The accrediting association to which a seminary belongs has a clear say in defining the form and content of the D.Min. project. Current standards of the Association of Theological Schools point to a "written doctoral-level project that addresses both the nature and the practice of ministry." This "ministry project should demonstrate the candidate's ability to identify a specific theological topic in ministry, organize an effective research model, use appropriate resources, and evaluate the results, and should reflect the candidate's depth of theological insight in relation to ministry."[1]

In a 1999 article in *Theological Education*, Timothy Lincoln reported a survey of D.Min. final papers in schools accredited by the Association of Theological Schools. He found that the D.Min. project constitutes a genre of its own, "an exercise in *phronesis*, practical Christian wisdom." He summarizes: "Written for an audience of persons engaged in ministry, the project should

---

1. The Commission on Accrediting, Association of Theological Schools, "Degree Program Standards," standard F.3.1.3, 2005, 21, hrrp://www.ats.edu/accrediting/standards/DegreeStandards.pdf.

address an issue arising out of ministerial practice, use an appropriate research model informed by the social sciences, and interpret itself from the point of view of a Christian minister."[2]

D.Min. projects are as varied as the ministries of those who write them. Some are more practical; others can be more theoretical. Ministry always figures prominently.

A common model is the "in-ministry" project, described in chapter 16 as program development. In this kind of paper a student develops a program and applies it in his or her ministry setting. Preparation, presentation, and evaluation are all parts of the process and the paper. The program may be as short as a weekend seminar or as long as a one-year church revitalization program. In the first case, the advisor or the D.Min. committee may require that the program be repeated, possibly at another location.

The "in-ministry" project requires hours and hours of thinking and doing; writing it out will take less time and fewer pages than writing other types of projects. Descriptive research may be needed to demonstrate a need for such an intervention (chapter 15). Normally the seminary requires that the advisor or mentor visit the place where the candidate is carrying out the program, often at the candidate's expense. Find out what requirements your school has regarding advising of "in-ministry" projects.

The case study (chapter 17) or the study of a theological issue in ministry (chapter 18) are also acceptable as D.Min. projects. This type of study is more theoretical. There is no actual application or evaluation of a program, but ministry is at the heart of the research. In the same category one could include church-growth studies or strategies to reach an unreached people group. Again, descriptive research may be necessary (chapter 15). The application to ministry is clear.

Occasionally a D.Min. project may be even more theoretical than the projects described in the three previous paragraphs. The history of a denomination in a certain country or region may be an acceptable research topic. Biographies of ministers or missionaries could also be done. However, this type of project requires exceptional writing skills and special permission from your school's authorities.

Two important parts complement each other in this type of writing project. There must be theory (the "why") and there must be practice (the "how to"). The proportion of each depends on the topic, the candidate, the doctoral committee, and the school. The theory includes the biblical and theological bases for the practical application as well as any explanations

2. Timothy D. Lincoln, "Writing Practical Christian Wisdom: Genre and the Doctor of Ministry Dissertation," *Theological Education* 36 (1999): 171.

from the social sciences—sociology, psychology, education, economics, history, geography, culture—that may undergird the intervention. Practice is what you do, on the basis of the theory studied, to solve the problem addressed.

The D.Min. project, just as the master's thesis or doctoral dissertation, is done in stages: proposal, research and writing, and defense.

Proposal

The project proposal can be completed only after many hours of reading, thinking, and observing. Regardless of the shape of the study, the proposal is the initial and required step toward the coveted degree. Its indispensable parts are:

1. Background information on the problem to be addressed to make the proposal clear to the readers and examiners
2. A statement of the problem
3. A statement of the task or purpose of the study
4. The justification for the study: the need for it and the contributions it will make
5. Any delimitations that affect the study (even your presuppositions, if they qualify)
6. The methodology or procedure to be followed, showing not only the areas to be researched in the library but the practical application of the chosen intervention or program—the how; this part describes the candidate's war plan
7. A detailed tentative outline
8. A preliminary bibliography

Normally a proposal for a D.Min. or D.P.Th. does not exceed ten carefully written pages. Some schools may have different or additional requirements, such as length, a statement of intent, or a vita. Clear the requirements of your school with your advisor or program director.

The Written Paper

The project for a professional degree in theology demonstrates the ability to think creatively and to act decisively. The time spent in carrying out a plan, program, or intervention in ministry is usually not reflected in the number of pages written for the project. How can you translate the hours you spent in evangelism, teaching, or administration into pages? The writing is important, but the doing usually takes precedence.

Most schools set a limit to the number of pages a D.Min. project may contain. Usually, the body of the text (excluding appendixes and bibliography) should be under 150 pages. Again, professors are looking for quality rather than quantity. Be sure to follow the guidelines of your seminary.

The organization of the paper is similar to that of a doctoral dissertation. The first chapter introduces the topic, presenting the problem or issue, the task (or purpose) of the project, the benefits of solving the problem (justification), the approach being followed, a definition of terms (if needed), and an overview of the rest of the paper. Chapter 2 normally is theoretical: biblical, theological, sociological, psychological. In fact, there may be two theoretical chapters, if needed. Other chapters depend on the topic. The last chapter is always the same: summary, conclusions, and recommendations.

Bear in mind that sometimes the committee reads only the first and last chapters of a dissertation or project. Thus, everything of vital importance must be in those two chapters: where you intended to go and what you found when you arrived there. Appendixes vary according to the project. For a seminar, for example, include the outlines of the presentations, together with copies of the handouts and illustrations used. If there were questionnaires, they also belong in the appendix. A bibliography closes the paper.

Each D.Min. project is to be accompanied by an abstract, a 350-word summary of the project. The abstract includes the problem or issue, the findings, and the conclusions. The approval sheet, of which a modifiable model is given at the end of chapter 20, follows the title page.

Procedure

The candidate's project committee is composed of an advisor and at least one reader or second member of the committee (different schools have different rules). Fortunately, the student is usually involved in the selection of the committee. The task of the advisor is to counsel and to supervise the candidate in the preparation of the project. The advisor reads, marks, and returns the material to the candidate, who then rewrites and returns the material to the advisor, who reads, marks, and returns. Normally a candidate rewrites at least three times. The reader (or readers) usually does not read a chapter until the advisor has approved it. Thus the advisor is far more involved in the preparation of the written portion of the project than the readers.

In working together, student and advisor should avoid pitfalls that might sour relations or delay the work. One of the dangers is that either party may forget what he or she said. A workable solution to this problem is for you to take notes of what your advisor said and write up a synthesis of the instructions. Give a copy of this summary to your advisor to make sure that you heard correctly. If you do this with a nice spirit, your advisor will probably thank you for making sure you both know what is happening.

Another issue that blights the project procedure is delays, either by the advisor or the student. Suppose you work hard to complete a chapter, take it to the advisor, only to be informed that he has gone to Outer Slobovia for a series of evangelistic meetings. Likewise, instead of finishing chapter 3 in April, you complete it at the end of May — and the advisor is up to her ears in a major writing project. The solution to this problem is for you and your advisor to set up a timetable — when you will turn in your materials and how long you will have to wait for your advisor to read and return them. Obviously, there may still be glitches, but if you two agree, half the battle is already won.

Once the project is deemed ready for defense by the advisor and reader(s), a date is set for the oral examination, and copies are made available to the examiners. At the oral examination you will make a brief and lively presentation of your research. You will then be asked questions about the research, its methodology, its findings, and your own conclusions. The project may be approved as submitted, approved with revisions to be made and certified by the advisor, or rejected. When the work has been carefully done, there is little danger of rejection!

After the defense, you and your advisor make the necessary adjustments to the paper. Then you submit the appropriate number of copies to the appropriate office — each seminary has its own rules — at the appropriate time, in preparation for graduation. Most seminaries in North America cooperate with ATLA in the preparation of *Research in Ministry*, an index to D.Min. projects available online at http://rim.atla.com/star/rimonline_login.htm. Your school submits your abstract so that future students can refer to your work.

Specific Kinds of D.Min. Papers

This chapter has proposed general directions for D.Min. papers. In addition, specific information appears in other chapters. Chapter 15 has instructions on descriptive research; chapter 16 explains program development; and chapter 17 has information on the case study. In chapter 18 you have materials on theological issues in ministry. Three other possibilities are given as examples:

a church-growth study, a church-planting project, and a strategy for reaching unreached peoples.

Church-Growth Study

A church-growth study may become an appropriate D.Min. project when it carefully studies the growth of a given church over time, analyzes the factors involved in its growth (or lack thereof), and designs appropriate strategies to enhance the church's growth. Occasionally, the study could include a group of churches.

Procedure

1. Become familiar with church-growth literature, both theoretical and narrative. Pay special attention to materials about churches similar to the one you are studying.
2. Investigate the growth patterns of the church over the past ten years. Get information from church records and other sources.
3. Study the climate and activities of the church during the past ten years. Read newsletters and reports; survey and interview as needed.
4. Analyze the community in which the church is located. Find out about its people, institutions, industry, schools, socio-economic life, and traditions.
5. Come to tentative conclusions regarding the reasons for growth (or nongrowth).
6. Applying sound, biblical principles of church growth, design a program for optimum growth for a specific church.

Written Presentation

The following chapters would constitute the study:

Chapter 1: Introduction

This should include a statement of the problem, justification for the study, definition of terms, and methodology used. A bibliographical essay or review of literature on church growth and church-growth studies pertinent to the study is appropriate here. This will give the reader the assurance that the candidate is indeed aware of what the literature says. (The scope of the review should be defined. For example, one might set limits on the time of writing or the type of church.) Your advisor may prefer this review of literature to constitute a separate chapter, which would make the description of the church chapter 3.

Chapter 2: History and description of the church

The patterns in growth and finances are described, together with the history of the church during the ten years. Descriptions of current facilities, programs, activities, and membership demographics are also presented.

Chapter 3: Description of the community

This should include demographics, economics, religion, traditions, institutions, and so on.

Chapter 4: Analysis of the situation

This chapter analyzes the current church situation and possibilities for growth in light of church-growth theory, the history and statistics of the church, and the characteristics of the community.

Chapter 5: Strategy for growth

This chapter designs a strategy for sustainable growth by applying missiological and church-growth principles to the local situation.

Chapter 6: Summary, conclusions, and reflections

Appendixes

Bibliography

Church Planting

A church-planting project will take the planting of a new church from design through realization. This type of D.Min. project will naturally take much longer than bibliographic research.

Procedure

1. Study the literature on church planting.
2. Choose a location for the new church.
3. In collaboration with the advisor, design the plan and chronogram for the church planting, together with the criteria for evaluating the final result.
4. Obtain support of church administration and members to be involved in the church planting.
5. Carry out the plan.
6. In collaboration with the advisor, evaluate what has been done.
7. Write the dissertation or project.

Written Presentation

The body of the paper (excluding bibliography and appendixes) should be less than 100 pages long. The bulk of the work is in doing, not in reading or writing.

Chapter 1: Introduction

Task, justification, plan, and chronogram, criteria for evaluation (all taken from the proposal).

Chapter 2: Theoretical basis

A discussion of biblical and theological principles and assumptions relevant to the project. Review of literature on church planting under similar circumstances.

Chapter 3: Narrative of the church planting

A careful narrative of the steps taken to plant the church includes dates, activities, programs, and participants. This chapter shows how the objectives described in chapter 1 were met.

Chapter 4: Evaluation of the project

A narration of the evaluation process and the presentation of its results.

Chapter 5: Summary, conclusions, and reflections

The summary is provided for those who read only chapters 1 and 5. The conclusions and reflections give opportunity for subjective evaluation of the process and suggestions for someone who might attempt to plant a similar church.

Strategy to Reach an Unreached People Group

This type of doctoral project is more common for a concentration in missions than for other types of D.Min. programs. It is theoretical rather than practical. Such a writing project is especially significant for those whose ministry brings them in contact with non-Christian peoples but are currently studying in areas other than their own.[3]

Procedure

1. Read the literature on reaching unreached peoples.

---

3. My thanks to Bruce Bauer, missionary and mission professor, for this outline. Useful to this type of study are books such as the following: John D. Robb, *Focus! The Power of People Group Thinking: A Practical Manual for Planning Effective Strategies to Reach the Unreached* (Monrovia, CA: MARC, 1989); Bill Stearns and Amy Stearns, *Catch the Vision 2000* (Minneapolis: Bethany, 1991).

2. Select a target group.
3. Study this group, its customs, beliefs, and socio-economic situation.
4. Analyze any contacts the group has had with Christians in general and with your particular denomination.
5. Design a strategy for the specific group.
6. Write the project/dissertation.

Written Presentation

Chapter 1: Introduction
   Statement of the problem, naming the group and its location, justification for the study, definition of terms, methodology, and so on.

Chapter 2: Description of the unreached people
   Location, culture, religion, history, socio-economic status, health, education, and so on. Description of the people's interaction with Christianity in general and with your denomination in particular.

Chapter 3: Analysis of deterrents and bridges to evangelism
   Study of factors that seem to make evangelism difficult. Inquiry into possible natural bridges from the group's culture and religion to Christianity.

Chapter 4: Proposed strategy
   An application of sound, biblical, missiological principles to design an implementable strategy for creating a Christian presence among the group.

Chapter 5: Summary, conclusions, and reflections.
   The summary is provided for those who read only chapters 1 and 5.

Appendixes

Bibliography

Now and then I hear people denigrate the D.Min. project, comparing it unfavorably to a Ph.D. dissertation. Such comments rankle my soul! Rightly done, this project has all the earmarks of research: It is based on solid theory — biblical, theological, and otherwise — and it contributes to the welfare of God's people as well as to the growth of ministry. May your D.Min. project bring satisfaction to you and glory to God.

CONCLUSION

This book has described several different types of endings for papers and dissertations. There is the summary-conclusion ending or the summary-conclusion-recommendations finale. You have also read about the theological issue in ministry with an "application-to-ministry" ending. The ending for this book does not follow any of these patterns.

In fact, it is not for me to conclude this book. It is for you, the student, to do so. The work you have produced following these guidelines summarizes, concludes, and applies any conclusion that I could have written. Your work will speak for me as well as for you.

May the skills you have honed and the abilities you have developed, to say nothing of the masterpiece you have produced, satisfy you and your professor. May this have been a battle well fought, a victory won with honor.

If you have written a good paper, I shall be content. My motto has long been: ἐκ χαοῦ κόσμος (lit., "out of chaos, order"). If your paper is well done, beauty and order have come out of chaos. I am satisfied.

And as you and I strive to bring order and beauty out of that which is unclear, confused, or unknown, may it be *soli Deo gloria*.

Appendix A

APA CITATION STYLE

Each discipline prefers its own citation style. While history and religion tend to use the Chicago style (Turabian), the social sciences adhere to the style known as APA (American Psychological Association), not to be confused with Turabian in-text references.[1] True APA style is described in their *Publication Manual*, 5th edition.[2] Some seminaries use the APA style, especially for Doctor of Ministry projects, since they often report information from different social sciences.

The APA system has two general formats: the one required for manu-scripts presented for publication by the American Psychological Association, the other for student papers and dissertations (*Publication Manual*, 2001, pp. 331–336). This appendix shows the second use; it employs APA style and uses the same examples that appear in Turabian style in chapter 9.

The APA citation style consists of two parts: in-text citations and a ref-erence list (or bibliography). Without the reference list, the citations make absolutely no sense. Yet, the citations must be clear so a reader can easily find an item in the reference list.

---

1. In chapters 11 and 12, Turabian (6th ed.) compares its two systems: "Parenthetical References and Reference Lists" and "Footnotes and Bibliographical Entries"; neither is APA.

2. The reference list entry would be: American Psychological Association (2001). *Publication Manual of the American Psychological Association*, 5th ed. Washington, DC: Author. See also — among others — the following websites:

http://apastyle.apa.org

http://owl.english.purdue.edu/handouts/research/

http://www.dianahacker.com/resdoc/p04_c09_o.html

Thanks to Bonnie Proctor, Dissertation Secretary at Andrews University, for sharing her exper-tise in APA.

In-Text Citations

In-text citations are enclosed in parentheses within the text. The basic format for this note is the surname of the author (or authors) and the date of publication. If you refer to a specific part of the source named or quoted, you must also add the page(s) where you found the quotation or idea.

If there are two to five authors, use all surnames (Smith, Peters, & Jones, 1999) in the first citation; for items with three to five authors use (Smith et al., 1999) in subsequent citations. For six or more authors, use the first surname plus "et al." in all citations. If the author is a corporate entity, the first note will read (United Nations, 1985); successive notes will say (UN, 1985). The entry in the reference list will have the name spelled out: United Nations. If your paper uses two authors with the same surname, add an initial to distinguish between them: (N. Smith, 1947) and (B. Smith, 1976).

When there is no author, the title (or a shortened form of the title) appears first: (*Education Handbook*, 1987, p. 35); in the reference list this item will be alphabetized under "Education." You may also use the form (Anonymous, 1977), as long as the reference list puts the same item under "Anonymous."

In an in-text citation, as in the text of the paper, you will capitalize the first word and all important nouns in titles as well as the first word after a colon. Titles of articles will be in quotation marks and books or reports in italics or underlined.

The date of publication follows the comma after the author's surname. This date is the year the book or article was published, not the year in which it was written. Thus, you will not need to invent the year Irenaeus wrote *Against Heresies*, but only the year in which it was published in the work you are listing in the reference list.

If you quote, you must provide the exact page at the end of the quotation. The way you introduce the quotation will determine whether author and date are in one set of parentheses and the page in another, or all three are together. For example:

> Speaking of the differences between Acts and Galatians, Johnson (1992) notes that "both sources are partial and tendentious" (p. 270).
> One opinion regarding the differences between Acts and Galatians is that "both sources are partial and tendentious" (Johnson, 1992, p. 270).

A quotation of more than forty words must be treated as a block quotation, which in APA is indented five spaces from the left margin and single spaced. The page number in parentheses follows the final period of the quotation.

Ouro (2000) concludes his discussion of the state of the earth in Gen 1:2 by saying:

> Our study of the OT and ANE literature has found that Gen 1:2 must be interpreted as the description of the earth as it was without vegetation and uninhabited by animals and humans. The concept that appears in Gen 1:2 is an abiotic concept of the earth, with vegetable, animal, and human life appearing in the following verses. (p. 66)

Since APA does not use "ibid.," the author and date are repeated. In this sense, there is no "second note" form.

Letters and other personal communications (such as email and interviews by the author) appear only in the text; they do not appear in the reference list. They are considered unretrievable as sources for other scholars.

APA in-text citations are user-friendly to the writer/researcher. They are, however, often quite unfriendly to a reader who wishes to find a reference. APA style does not require a page number in the in-text citation unless there is a direct quotation. This system works well for citations of a short article; your reader may have to search through only ten pages to certify that the author did indeed say what you said she did. By contrast, if you refer in APA style to an idea on page 270 of Luke Timothy Johnson's 568-page *Acts of the Apostles*, you only need to insert the following: (Johnson, 1992). Finding the page you have in mind may require reading half of the book! To assist your reader, you may insert the number of the page to which you are referring, as if you had used a direct quotation (Johnson, 1992, p. 270). This addition to APA style is permissible, highly desirable, and most useful to the reader. Be sure to follow the instructions of your school, and, more specifically, your advisor, on the use of APA style.

Reference List

Proper APA style for submitting articles requires the reference list to be double-spaced with the first line indented. However, the style for student papers allows for the reference list to look almost like a Turabian bibliography, single spaced and with hanging indentation. The important difference is that the date of publication appears in parentheses immediately after the author statement, which ends with a period or full stop.

The names of all authors are inverted. Initials are used instead of first names: Johnson, L. T. Use the ampersand (&) instead of "and" when there are multiple authors. The list is alphabetized by the (first) author's surname, the corporate author, or the title (if there is no author).

The copyright date is placed in parentheses and followed by a period or full stop. When a particular author has more than one work, the items are ordered chronologically, from oldest to newest. Should there be two or more items published in one year, add a letter to the year: 1993a, 1993b, 1993c. Make sure the in-text notes have the same dates as the reference list.

Titles of books and journals are written in italics or underlined. If a title appears in an in-text citation, capitalize all words except prepositions and articles (after the first one). In the reference list, only the first word and proper nouns of the title are capitalized. Titles of articles have no quotation marks. The italics (formerly underlining) goes beyond the title to the volume number of a journal.

In the facts of publication in the reference list, use postal codes for states. Use the short form of the publisher's name.

Samples

The samples given below for the in-text citation (C) show how to report an allusion or citation. A direct quotation requires a page number, either in the same parentheses with the date or at the end of the quotation. The sample reference list entries (R) are in APA student format.

Books

Authorship

One or two authors

C   (Drummond, 1996)
R   Drummond, L. (1996). *Miss Bertha: Woman of revival*. Nashville: Broadman & Holman.

C   (Aland & Aland, 1989)
R   Aland, K., & Aland, B. (1989). *The text of the New Testament* (Rev. ed.). Leiden: Brill.

Three to five authors

C   (VanGemeren, Bahnsen, Kaiser, Strickland, & Moo, 1993)
Second reference: (VanGemeren et al., 1993)
R   VanGemeren, W. A., Bahnsen, G. L., Kaiser, W. C., Jr., Strickland, W. G., & Moo, D.
        (1993). *The law, the gospel, and the modern Christian*. Grand Rapids: Zondervan.

Corporate author

C   (Southern Baptist Convention, 1975)
R   Southern Baptist Convention. (1975). *Annual of the Southern Baptist Convention*.
        Nashville: Author.

No author, edition other than first, with translator

C   (*Bhagavad-Gita as It Is,* 1972)
R   *Bhagavad-Gita as it is* (Abridged ed.). (1972). (A. C. Bhaktivedanta Swami Prabhupada, Trans.). New York: Bhaktivedanta Book Trust.

Editor instead of author; joint publication

C   (VanderKam & Adler, 1996)
R   VanderKam, J. C., & Adler, W. (Eds.). (1996). *The Jewish apocalyptic heritage in early Christianity.* Assen, Netherlands: Van Gorcum; Minneapolis: Fortress.

Component part by one author in a work edited by another

C   (Davidson, 1998)
R   Davidson, R. M. (1998). Headship, submission, and equality in scripture. In N. J. Vyhmeister (Ed.), *Women in ministry: Biblical and historical perspectives* (pp. 259–295). Berrien Springs, MI: Andrews University Press.

Multivolume Works

One author

C   (González, 1970–1975)

or

(González, 1970–1975, 1:176)

[You may also use vol. 1, p. 176, but use the same format throughout your paper.]

R   González, J. (1970–1975). *A history of Christian thought* (Vols. 1–3). Nashville: Abingdon.

C   (Latourette, 1970)
R   Latourette, K. S. (1970). *Three centuries of advance: Vol. 3. A history of the expansion of Christianity.* Grand Rapids: Zondervan.

Several authors — independent titles for each volume

C   (Rapske, 1994)
R   Rapske, B. (1994). *The Book of Acts and Paul in Roman custody.* In B. W. Winter (Gen. Ed.), *The Book of Acts in its first century setting* (Vol. 4). Carlisle, UK: Paternoster, 1994.

Part of a Series

C   (Booth, Colomb, & Williams, 1995)
R   Booth, W. C., Colomb, G. G., & Williams, J. M. (1995). *The craft of research.* Chicago Guides to Writing, Editing and Publishing. Chicago: University of Chicago Press.

Reprint

C   (Nevius, 1894/1968)
R   Nevius, J. L. (1968). *Demon possession.* Grand Rapids: Kregel. (Original work published 1894)

C   (Reynolds, 1913/1977)
R   Reynolds, H. R. (1977). Introduction to the Gospel of St. John. In H. O. M. Spense & J.
         H. Excell (Eds.), *The pulpit commentary* (Vol. 17, pp. iv-clxi). Grand Rapids: Eerd-
         mans. (Original work published 1913)

Secondary Source

C   In his *Life and Passion of Cyprian,* Pontius the Deacon (as cited in Olson, 1999,
         p. 116) affirmed...
         [Give all the information on the primary source that you want your reader to have, as
         well as the page in the secondary source. The reference list mentions only the secondary
         source.]
R   Olson, R. E. (1999). *The story of Christian theology.* Downers Grove, IL: InterVarsity.

Periodicals

Magazines

C   (Lemonick & Dorfman, 2000)
R   Lemonick, M. D., & Dorfman, A. (2000, May 8). The amazing Vikings. *Time, 155,*
         69–74.

Journals

C   (Shank, 1985)
R   Shank, D. (1985). Mission relations with independent churches in Africa. *Missiology, 13,*
         23–44.

When a journal begins each issue from page 1 (rather than continued paging throughout the volume), specify which issue of the volume you have used.
Thus you will include the number, month, or season in parentheses after the
volume number, though not in italics: *Newsletter,* 4(1), 9.

Specialized Books

Classical Authors and Church Fathers

C   (Irenaeus, *Against Heresies* 2.2.3) or (Irenaeus, *Against Heresies* 2.2.3, ANF 1:421)
R   Irenaeus. (1989–1990). *Against heresies.* In A. Roberts & J. Donaldson (Eds.), *The ante-
         nicene fathers* (Vol. 1:315–567). Grand Rapids: Eerdmans.

C   (Chrysostom, *The Priesthood* 3.17)
R   Chrysostom, J. (1862). *The priesthood.* In J. P. Migne (Ed.), *Patrologia Graeca* (Vol. 48,
         cols. 623–692). Paris: Apud Garnier Fratres.

C   (Josephus, *Jewish Wars* 2.14.5)
R   Josephus, F. (1869). *Jewish wars.* In W. Whiston (Ed.), *The works of Josephus* (Vol. 3,
         p. 317–Vol. 4, p. 352). New York: Oakley, Mason & Co.

Rabbinical Works

C   (Mishnah *Sanhedrin* 10:3)
R   *The Mishnah.* (1933). (H. Danby, Trans.). London: Oxford University Press.

C   (B. T. *Sanhedrin* 97a) or (B. Talmud *Sanhedrin* 97a)
R   *The Babylonian Talmud*. (1935). (I. Epstein, Ed.). London: Soncino.

Bible Commentaries and Concordances
Commentaries — Author given
C   (Polhill, 1975)
R   Polhill, J. B. (1992). *Acts*. New American Commentary. Nashville: Broadman.
C   (Campbell, 1975)
R   Campbell, E. R. (1975). *Ruth*. Anchor Bible, 7. Garden City, NY: Doubleday.
C   (Delitzsch, 1949)
R   Delitzsch, F. (1949). *Biblical commentary on the book of Job* (Vols. 1–2). Biblical Commentary on the Old Testament. Grand Rapids: Eerdmans.
C   (Craddock, 1998)
R   Craddock, F. B. (1998). The letter to the Hebrews: Introduction, commentary, and reflections. In *New interpreter's Bible* (Vol. 12, pp. 3–173). Nashville: Abingdon.
C   (Wright, 1954)
R   Wright, G. E. (1954). Exegesis of the book of Deuteronomy. In G. A. Buttrick (Ed.), *Interpreter's Bible* (Vol. 2, pp. 331–540). New York: Abingdon.

Commentaries — No author given
C   (Hastings, 1971, 17:159)
R   Hastings, E. (Ed.). (1971). *The speaker's Bible* (Vols. 1–18). Grand Rapids: Baker Book House.

Concordances
C   (Young, n.d., 785)
R   Young, R. (n.d.). Analytical concordance to the Bible (22nd American ed.). Grand Rapids: Eerdmans.

Dictionaries and Encyclopedias
Dictionaries and encyclopedias with unsigned articles
C   (Webster, 1976)
C   (*Columbia Encyclopedia*, 1976)

Well-known dictionaries and encyclopedias do not appear in the reference list. Dictionaries and encyclopedias in the area of religion do.

C   (Youngblood, 1995)
R   Youngblood, R. F. (Ed.). (1995). *Nelson's new illustrated Bible dictionary* (Rev. ed.). Nashville: Nelson.
C   (*Seventh-day Adventist Encyclopedia*, 1996)
     [Later references: (*SDA Encyclopedia*, 1996)]
R   *Seventh-day Adventist Encyclopedia*. (1996). (Vols. 1–2). Hagerstown, MD: Review & Herald.

Dictionaries and encyclopedias with signed articles

C   (Lapin, 1992)

R Lapin, H. (1992). Rabbi. In *Anchor Bible dictionary* (Vol. 5. pp. 600–602). New York: Doubleday.

C   (Bultmann, 1964–1976, *Aidōs*)

R Bultmann, R. (1964–1976). *Aidōs*. In *Theological dictionary of the New Testament* (Vol. 1, p. 169). Grand Rapids: Eerdmans.

R Kittel, G., & Friedrich, G. (Eds.). (1964–1976) *Theological dictionary of the New Testament* (Vols. 1–10). Grand Rapids: Eerdmans.

C   (Demsky, 1971–1972, 6:384)

R Demsky, A. (1971–1972). Education: In the biblical period. In *Encyclopaedia Judaica* (Vol. 6, pp. 382–398). Jerusalem: Encyclopaedia Judaica.

Collected Works of Individual Authors

C   (Barth, 1960, III/3, p. 82)

R Barth, K. (1960). *Church dogmatics* (Vol. III/3). Edinburgh: T. & T. Clark.

C   (Luther, 1955–1976, Vol. 51, p. 259)

or

    (Luther, 1955–1976, 51:259)

R Luther, M. (1955–1976). *Sermon on the sum of Christian life*. In *Luther's Works* (American ed., Vol. 51, pp. 259–287). Saint Louis: Concordia.

R Luther, M. (1955–1976). *Luther's works* (American ed., Vols. 1–55). Saint Louis: Concordia.

Book Reviews

C   (Meyers, 1999)

R Meyers, C. (1999). [Review of the book *The Archaeology of Israel: Constructing the past, interpreting the present*.] *Journal of Biblical Literature*, 118, 530–531.

Video and Sound Recordings

C   (Anderson, 1989)

R Anderson, K. (Producer). (1989). *Hudson Taylor* [Videocassette]. (Available from Ken Anderson Films, P.O. Box 618, Winona Lake, IN 46590)

C   (Landriscina, 1985)

R Landriscina, L. (1985). Judío en el Vaticano. In *Mano a mano con el país* (Vol. 5) [Audiocassette No. 64232]. Buenos Aires: Phillips.

Unpublished materials

Academic Sources

Theses and dissertations

C   (Nogueira, 1999)

R Nogueira, P. C. (1999). *Equipping laity for ministry in multi-church districts in Brazil*. Unpublished doctoral dissertation, Andrews University, Berrien Springs, MI.

APA distinguishes between unpublished dissertations (as given above) and dissertations accessed by means of *Dissertation Abstracts International*. The format for the second is:

R   Choi, P. R. (1997). Abraham our father: Paul's voice in the covenantal debate of the second temple period (Doctoral dissertation, Fuller Theological Seminary, School of Theology). *Dissertation Abstracts International, 58* (05A), 1759.

C   (Silitonga, 1988)
R   Silitonga, H. (1988). *Christological implications of Leviticus 16:11–23: A study from an Indonesian perspective.* Unpublished master of theology thesis, Adventist International Institute of Advanced Studies, Silang, Cavite, Philippines.

APA makes no distinction among different kinds of doctoral dissertations. The same goes for master's theses. Your school may allow you to specify the type of dissertation (D.Min., Ed.D., or Ph.D.) or thesis (as in the above example).

Miscellaneous academic papers
C   (Reeve, 1997)
R   Reeve, T. (1997). *The 'Just Man' in the writings of Philo.* Unpublished class paper, THEO 611 Philo Seminar, University of Notre Dame.

C   (Fanwar, 1999)
R   Fanwar, W. M. (1999). *He who created the heavens and the earth: Contributions of Isaiah to Rev 14:7c.* Unpublished seminar paper, GSEM 920 Religious Studies Seminar, Theological Seminary, Andrews University, Berrien Springs, MI.

Syllabi
C   (Vyhmeister, 1999)
R   Vyhmeister, Nancy. (1999). *Course outline for GSEM 854 Ph.D. Proposal Seminar.* Theological Seminary, Andrews University, Berrien Springs, MI.

Class notes
C   (Program in Language Acquisition Techniques, 1980)
R   Program in Language Acquisition Techniques. (1980). [Class notes]. Missionary Internship, Farmington, MI.

Miscellaneous Unpublished Sources
Reports
C   (Seventh-day Adventist Theological Seminary, Far East, 1985)
[In subsequent notes: (SDATSFE, 1985)]
R   Seventh-day Adventist Theological Seminary, Far East. (1985). *Financial statement of graduate apartments, 31 August.* Silang, Cavite, Philippines: Seventh-day Adventist Theological Seminary, Far East.

C   (Association of Theological Institutions in Eastern Africa, 1979)

R   Association of Theological Institutions in Eastern Africa. (1979). *1978/79 Bachelor of Divinity degree syllabus*. Nairobi, Kenya: Association of Theological Institutions in Eastern Africa.

Speeches and presentations

C   (Maxwell, 1976)
R   Maxwell, C. M. (1976). *Which sacrifice, Lord?* [Typescript]. Seminary Chapel sermon. Andrews University, Berrien Springs, 20 October 1976.

C   (Paulien, 1996)
R   Paulien, J. (1996, 24 November). *The lion/lamb king: Reading Revelation from popular culture*. Paper presented at the annual meeting of the Society of Biblical Literature, New Orleans.

Manuscripts

C   (Benoit, 1875)
R   Benoit, P. L. (1875). Photocopy of typewritten transcript of Canon Benoit's diary of a trip to America, 6 January to 8 June 1875, including descriptions of Josephite missions among freed slaves. Archives, University of Notre Dame.

C   (White, 1905)
R   White, E. G. (1905). Letter to Dr. Patience Bourdeau, 8 June 1905. Letter 177, 1905. Ellen White Research Center, Newbold College, Bracknell, England.

Personal communications

In APA style, letters, interviews, and email are considered as personal communications. The name of the source appears in the text; the phrase "personal communication" (or "interview") and the precise date are given in the in-text note. Since information from this communication is not available to the reader, nothing appears in the reference list.

C   Bryan Ball, editor of *The Essential Jesus* (personal communication, 13 March 2000), stated that...
C   Yeow Choo Lak, Executive Director of the Association for Theological Education in Southeast Asia, agrees with this position (interview, Singapore, 15 July 1985).

Electronic Media

CD-ROM

C   (Bunyan, 1998)
R   Bunyan, John. (1998). *Pilgrim's progress, stage 2* [CD-ROM]. Logos Library System 2.1 (Vol. 1). Oak Harbor, WA: Logos Research Systems.

World Wide Web

C   (Hahne, 1997)
R   Hahne, H. (1997). *An annotated bibliography on computer-assisted biblical and theological research.* Retrieved 21 April 1997, from http://www.epas.utoronto.ca:8080/ ~hahne/ scbibann.html.

For further information on the citation of online materials, see *Electronic Reference Formats Recommended by the American Psychological Association,* http://www.apa.org/journals/webref.html.

TRANSLITERATION OF BIBLICAL LANGUAGES

The following is an acceptable academic scheme for transliterating biblical Hebrew and Greek. Students in advanced courses or writing dissertations may be required to use additional diacritical marks for the Hebrew. Each student should consult his or her advisor on this matter.

Hebrew

Consonants

א	= '	ט	= ṭ	פ	= p
ב	= b	י	= y	צ	= ṣ
ג	= g	כ	= k	ק	= q
ד	= d	ל	= l	ר	= r
ה	= h	מ	= m	שׂ	= ś
ו	= w	נ	= n	שׁ	= š
ז	= z	ס	= s	ת	= t
ח	= ḥ	ע	= ʻ		

Masoretic Vowel Pointing

$\_$ = a	$\ddot{}$ = ě	τ = o
τ = ā	' or ' = ê	= ŏ
= ă	. = i	ֹ = ô
.. = e	'. = î	ֹ = û
.. = ē	. = ō	= u

No distinction is made between soft and hard *begadkepat* letters; *dāgēš forte* is indicated by doubling the consonant.

Koine Greek

A α	=	A a	K κ	=	K k	T τ	=	T t
B β	=	B b	Λ λ	=	L l	Υ υ	=	Y y
Γ γ	=	G g	M μ	=	M m	Φ φ	=	Ph ph
Δ δ	=	D d	N ν	=	N n	X χ	=	Ch ch
E ε	=	E e	Ξ ξ	=	X x	Ψ ψ	=	Ps ps
Z ζ	=	Z z	O o	=	O o	Ω ω	=	Ō ō
H η	=	Ē ē	Π π	=	P p			
Θ θ	=	Th th	P ρ	=	R r			
I ι	=	I i	Σ σ, ς	=	S s			

Breathing marks: ' is smooth, no transliteration; ' is rough, transliterate with h.

Before γ, κ, ξ, χ, gamma is transliterated as *n*. In a diphthong, upsilon is transliterated as *u*.

For further details on transliteration of ancient languages, see *SBL Handbook of Style*, 5:1–9.

Appendix C

LIST OF COMMON ABBREVIATIONS

This is a short list of reference works and serials titles in the area of religion.[1] They are alphabetized by abbreviation. Titles of journals and books are italicized (or underlined), but titles of serials are set in roman characters, as are acronyms of authors' names when they are used as sigla. Note that these abbreviations are only illustrative of the hundreds that are used.

These abbreviations are only used in footnotes when a list of abbreviations has been placed before the introduction of the paper or the abbreviation appeared in parentheses the first time it was used. Abbreviations are not used in bibliographies.

AB	Anchor Bible	BAGD	Bauer, Arndt, Gingrich, and Danker, *Lexicon*, 1979
ABD	*Anchor Bible Dictionary*		
AHR	*American Historical Review*	*BAR*	*Biblical Archaeology Review*
AJT	*American Journal of Theology*	*BASOR*	*Bulletin of the American Schools of Oriental Research*
ANEP	*Ancient Near East in Pictures*		
ANET	*Ancient Near Eastern Texts*	BDAG	Bauer, Danker, Arndt, and Gingrich, *Lexicon*, 2000
ANF	The Ante-Nicene Fathers	BDB	Brown, Driver, and Briggs, *Lexicon*, 1907
ASOR	American Schools of Oriental Research		
AUSS	*Andrews University Seminary Studies*	BDF	Blass, Debrunner, and Funk, *Greek Grammar*
BA	*Biblical Archaeologist*	BECNT	Baker Exegetical Commentary on the New Testament

---

1. For a much longer list of abbreviations, especially in biblical and Near Eastern studies, see *SBL Handbook of Style* (Peabody, MA: Hendrickson, 1999), 89–121; the ultimate list of abbreviations appears in *Theologische Realencyklopädie Abkrzungsverzeichnis*, 2nd ed. (Berlin: De Gruyter, 1994).

BHS	Biblia hebraica stuttgartensia	Int	Interpretation
Bib	Biblica	ISBE	International Standard Bible Encyclopedia
BJRL	Bulletin of the John Rylands Library		
		JAAR	Journal of the American Academy of Religion
BR	Biblical Research		
BRev	Bible Review	JBL	Journal of Biblical Literature
BSac	Bibliotheca Sacra	JETS	Journal of the Evangelical Theological Society
BT	The Bible Translator		
BTB	Biblical Theology Bulletin	JEH	Journal of Ecclesiastical History
BZ	Biblische Zeitschrift	JJS	Journal of Jewish Studies
CAD	Chicago Assyrian Dictionary	JMH	Journal of Modern History
CBQ	Catholic Biblical Quarterly	JNES	Journal of Near Eastern Studies
ChrCent	Christian Century	JQR	Jewish Quarterly Review
CH	Church History	JR	Journal of Religion
CJT	Canadian Journal of Theology	JRE	Journal of Religious Ethics
CQ	Church Quarterly	JRT	Journal of Religious Thought
CT	Christianity Today	JSNT	Journal for the Study of the NT
CTJ	Calvin Theological Journal	JSOT	Journal for the Study of the OT
CTM	Concordia Theological Monthly	JSSR	Journal for the Scientific Study of Religion
DJG	Dictionary of Jesus and the Gospels		
		JTC	Journal for Theology and the Church
EDNT	Exegetical Dictionary of the NT	JTS	Journal of Theological Studies
EKL	Evangelisches Kirchenlexikon	KBL	Koehler and Baumgartner, Lexicon, 1958
EncJud	Encyclopedia Judaica		
EvQ	Evangelical Quarterly	L&N	Louw and Nida, Lexicon on Semantic Domains
EvT	Evangelische Theologie		
ExpTim	Expository Times	LCC	Library of Christian Classics
GTJ	Grace Theological Journal	LCL	Loeb Classical Library
HALOT	Koehler, Baumgartner, and Stamm, Hebrew and Aramaic Lexicon, 1999	Neot	Neotestamentica
		NICNT	New International Commentary, NT
HR	History of Religions	NICOT	New International Commentary, OT
HTR	Harvard Theological Review		
HUCA	Hebrew Union College Annual	NIDOTTE	New International Dictionary of OT Theology and Exegesis
IB	Interpreter's Bible		
ICC	International Critical Commentary	NIDNTT	New International Dictionary of NT Theology
IDB	Interpreter's Dictionary of the Bible	NIGTC	New International Greek Testament Commentary
		NIVAC	NIV Application Commentary
IEJ	Israel Exploration Journal	NovT	Novum Testamentum

NPNF	Nicene and Post-Nicene Fathers	TD	*Theology Digest*
NTS	*New Testament Studies*	TDNT	*Theological Dictionary of the NT*
ODCC	*Oxford Dictionary of the Christian Church*	TDOT	*Theological Dictionary of the OT*
PEQ	*Palestine Exploration Quarterly*	TJ	*Trinity Journal*
PG	*Patrologia Graeca,* Migne	TS	*Theological Studies*
PL	*Patrologia Latina,* Migne	TWOT	*Theological Wordbook of the OT*
RelS	*Religious Studies*	UF	*Ugarit-Forschungen*
RevExp	*Review and Expositor*	USQR	*Union Seminary Quarterly Review*
RevQ	*Revue de Qumrân*		
RL	*Religion in Life*	VT	*Vetus Testamentum*
RRelRes	*Review of Religious Research*	VTSup	Vetus Testamentum, Supplements
SBLDS	SBL Dissertation Series	WBC	Word Biblical Commentary
SBLMS	SBL Monograph Series	WTJ	*Westminster Theological Journal*
SBLSBS	SBL Sources for Biblical Study		
SBLTT	SBL Texts and Translations	ZAW	*Zeitschrift für die alttestamentliche Wissenschaft*
SBT	Studies in Biblical Theology		
SCR	*Studies in Comparative Religion*	ZKG	*Zeitschrift für Kirchengeschichte*
Sem	*Semitica*	ZNW	*Zeitschrift für die neutestamentliche Wissenschaft*
SJT	*Scottish Journal of Theology*		
SMRT	*Studies in Medieval and Reformation Thought*		
ST	*Studia Theologica*		

Appendix D

TIPS FOR THE TYPIST

In addition to reading this summary, the typist should refer to chapter 13, especially to the model pages given there. Items are listed here in alphabetical order to facilitate finding.

Corrections

Visible corrections are not allowed in the final draft of a paper. If any correction is made, the page must be reprinted. The nightmare of making corrections on a typed page so that they do not show is over. Computers solve that problem.

Footnotes

Footnotes have three parts: a superscript Arabic number in the text, a two-inch separator space between the text and the footnotes, and the footnote itself. The footnote is indented as much as the paragraph, is usually in the same size as the text of the paper, and begins with a full-size number followed by a period and a space. To achieve this look, use the automated footnote feature, modified as noted on page 82. While the writer of the paper is responsible for the content of footnotes, the typist is responsible for their format. Follow models in chapters 9, 10, and 13.

Headings

Chapter numbers are typed in uppercase letters and Arabic numbers on line 13 (2 inches from the top edge of the paper). The title of the chapter is typed in uppercase letters one triple space below the number (leaving two blank spaces). Other headings are as follows:

First-Level Heading: Centered, Bold

Second-Level Heading: Centered, Not Bold

Third-level Heading: Flush left, Bold

Fourth-level heading: flush left, not bold, only first word capitalized

Fifth-level heading: indented same as paragraph, bold. Only the first word is capitalized. The paragraph follows immediately.

Leave two lines blank before a heading. Leave one blank line after, before the text. For further information see chapter 13.

Indentation

Normal indentation is .5 inches for paragraphs and footnotes. Block quotations are indented .5 inches from each margin. If the quotation starts at the beginning of a paragraph, it is indented another .25 inches. Second lines of bibliographical entries are indented .5 inches, which is the default indent for Word Perfect ™ and Microsoft Word.™

Margins

The left margin should be 1.5 inches. The other three margins should be 1 inch. If 10-point type is used, there will be room for 72 characters on a line. If 12-point type is used, there will be 60 characters. Margins must be observed meticulously.

Page Size

Letter-size paper of good quality must be used. In order to fit within the margins indicated above, there must be no more than 54 single spaces or 27 double spaces of text on a normal letter-size page. In areas where A4 paper is the norm, this size paper can be used. The margins should remain the same, giving a slightly narrower and longer area for the text.

Pagination

Page 1 is the first page of the Introduction. Page numbers are centered at the bottom of the page, on the 61st line of the page. Use the automatic page numbering function of the word processing program.

Pagination of preliminary matter begins on the title page and is typed, centered, at the bottom of the page in small Roman numerals.

Justification

Excepting items that are centered (such as titles, first-level headings, and second-level headings), use left justification throughout. That means that the left margin will be straight but the right margin will be ragged.

Photocopying

Photocopying tends to enlarge the text slightly. This makes it imperative to stay within the margins indicated. Generally, good quality photocopies are accepted as originals.

Punctuation

The spacing required after punctuation marks is one space after period (full stop), comma, colon, or semicolon. For pages of books, there is no space after a colon, 5:66. For pages of journals, there is a space after the colon (1998): 66.

Commas and periods (full stops) go inside quotation marks, unless these enclose only one letter or number: He said "Good-bye." This is Phase "A".

A hyphen goes between two words: even-handed. An en dash is used with inclusive numbers, both pages (158–161) and years (1958–1961). The em dash is made up of two hyphens and signifies a change of thought. There is no space before or after any of these.

In an enumeration, a comma follows each item: He asked for a pen, some paper, an envelope, and a stamp.

Quotations

All materials quoted from another source must be enclosed in double quotation marks. Single quotation marks are to be used only for a quotation within a quotation. The comma and the period (full stop) go within the quotations; the colon and the semicolon go outside. If a quotation is a question, the question mark goes inside the quotation marks.

Block quotations are used for quotations longer than two sentences and eight lines. They must be single spaced and indented from each margin as much as the paragraph. If the beginning of the block quotation coincides with the beginning of a paragraph, the first line has further indentation (another .25 in.).

Spacing

Research papers, theses, and dissertations are double spaced. Block quotations are typed single space. Footnotes and bibliography entries are single spaced, but have a blank line between them. Three lines are left blank above and below a table or figure. Two blank lines precede a heading; one follows it.

Spelling

Either American or British spelling may be used. However, both may not be used in the same paper. The student is responsible for the spelling. The typist is responsible for correct word division.

Table of Contents

Follow the model in chapter 13.

Title Page

Follow the model on page 133. For theses or dissertations add the approval page as illustrated on page 220.

SELECTED BIBLIOGRAPHY

This bibliography is unlike those of a normal research paper, which must include all items referenced in footnotes (except language dictionaries). I have consciously excluded references to illustrations used in the text. Rather, I have included those materials that have shaped my thinking on research and that could be helpful to others pursuing information on research and writing.

Andrews University Standards for Written Work. 10th ed. Berrien Springs, MI: Andrews University Press, 2003. Available at http://www.andrews.edu/GRAD/pdf/sww10.pdf

Badke, William B. *The Survivor's Guide to Library Research: A Simple, Systematic Approach to Using the Library and Writing Research Papers*. Grand Rapids: Zondervan, 1990.

Bissell, Juanita. *A Guide for Research Writing: AIIAS Theological Seminary*. Silang, Cavite, Philippines: AIIAS Publications, 1996.

Booth, Wayne C., Gregor G. Colomb, and Joseph M. Williams. *The Craft of Research*. Chicago Guides to Writing, Editing, and Publishing. Chicago: University of Chicago Press, 1995.

Calabrese, Raymond L. *The Elements of an Effective Dissertation and Thesis: A Step-by-Step Guide to Getting It Right the First Time*. Lanham, MD: Rowman & Littlefield Education, 2006.

Cresswell, John W. *Qualitative Inquiry and Research Design*. Thousand Oaks, CA: Sage, 2000.

Davies, Richard E. *Handbook for Doctor of Ministry Projects*. Lanham, MD: University Press of America, 1984.

Davis, Gordon B., and Clyde A. Parker. *Writing the Doctoral Dissertation: A Systematic Approach*. 2nd ed. New York: Barron's, 1997.

Denzin, Norman, and Yvonna Lincoln. *The SAGE Handbook of Qualitative Research*. Thousand Oaks, CA: Sage, 2005.

Hacker, Diana. *A Writer's Reference*. 3rd ed. Boston: Bedford, 1995.

Hacker, Diana, and Barbara Fister. *Research and Documentation in the Electronic Age*. Boston: Bedford St. Martins, 2006. (See this online: http://www.dianahacker.com/ resdoc.)

Hancock, Dawson R., and Bob Algozzine. *Doing Case Study Research: A Practical Guide for Beginning Researchers*. New York: Columbia University Teachers College, 2006.

Henson, Kenneth T. *The Art of Writing for Publication*. Boston: Allyn & Bacon, 1995.

Hudson, Robert, ed. *A Christian Writer's Manual of Style*. Updated and expanded ed. Grand Rapids: Zondervan, 2004.

Isaac, Stephen, and William Michael. *Handbook in Research and Evaluation*. San Diego: EDITS, 1971.

Kepple, Robert. *Reference Works for Theological Research*. 3rd ed. Lanham, MD: University Press of America, 1992.

Kiernan, Vincento. *Writing Your Dissertation with Microsoft Word: A Step-by-Step Guide*. Alexandria, VA: Mattily, 2005

Lester, James D. *Writing Research Papers: A Complete Guide*. 9th ed. New York: Longman, 1999.

Madsen, David. *Successful Dissertations and Theses: A Guide to Graduate Student Research from Proposal to Completion*. 2nd ed. San Francisco: Jossey-Bass, 1992.

Maggion, Rosalie. *The Nonsexist Word Finder: A Dictionary of Gender-Free Usage*. Boston: Beacon, 1987.

Publication Manual for the American Psychological Association. 5th ed. Washington, D.C.: American Psychological Association, 2001.

Ritchie, Donald A. *Doing Oral History: A Practical Guide*. Oxford: Oxford University Press, 2003.

The SBL Handbook of Style for Ancient Near Eastern, Biblical, and Early Christian Studies. Peabody, MA: Hendrickson, 1999.

Slade, Carole. *Form and Style: Research Papers, Reports, Theses*. 11th ed. Boston: Houghton Mifflin, 2000.

Strunk, William, and E. B. White. *The Elements of Style*. 3rd ed. New York: Macmillan, 1979.

Turabian, Kate L. *A Handbook for Writers of Term Papers, Theses, and Dissertations*. 7th ed. Revised by Wayne C. Booth, Gregory G. Colomb, Joseph M. Williams, and the University of Chicago Press Editorial Staff. Chicago: University of Chicago Press, 2007.

University of Chicago. *The Chicago Manual of Style*. 15th ed. Chicago: University of Chicago Press, 2003.

Walliman, Nicholas. *Your Research Project*. 2nd ed. London: Sage, 2005.

Williams, Joseph M. *Style: Toward Clarity and Grace*. Chicago Guides to Writing, Editing, and Publishing. Chicago: University of Chicago Press, 1990.

Yaghjian, Lucretia B. *Writing Theology Well! A Rhetoric for Theological and Biblical Writers*. New York: Continuum, 2006.

INDEX

We want to hear from you. Please send your comments about this book to us in care of zreview@zondervan.com. Thank you.

ZONDERVAN.com/
AUTHORTRACKER
follow your favorite authors